The Wentworth Prospect

A novel guide to success in B2B sales

John Smibert
Wayne Moloney
Jeff Clulow

This is an IndieMosh book

brought to you by MoshPit Publishing
an imprint of Mosher's Business Support Pty Ltd

PO Box 4363
Penrith NSW 2750

indiemosh.com.au

Copyright © John Smibert, Wayne Moloney and Jeff Clulow. 2021

The moral right of the authors John Smibert, Wayne Moloney and Jeff Clulow to be identified as authors of this work and all accompanying material has been asserted in accordance with the Copyright Amendment (Moral Rights) Act 2000.

All rights reserved. Except as permitted under the Australian Copyright Act 1968 (for example, fair dealing for the purposes of study, research, criticism or review) no part of this publication or its accompanying online reference material at www.edvance.sale may be reproduced, stored in a retrieval system, or transmitted in any form or by any means, electronic, mechanical, photocopying, recording or otherwise, without the written permission of the publisher.

EDVANCE and www.edvance.sale are trademarked properties of John Smibert and Sales Leader Forums.

A catalogue record for this work is available from the National Library of Australia

https://www.nla.gov.au/collections

Title:	The Wentworth Prospect
Subtitle:	A novel guide to success in B2B sales
Authors:	John Smibert, Wayne Moloney and Jeff Clulow
ISBNs:	978-1-922628-52-7 (paperback)
	978-1-922628-53-4 (audiobook)
	978-1-922628-54-1 (ebook – Kindle)
Subjects:	BUSINESS & ECONOMICS: Sales & Selling / Management; Training; Mentoring & Coaching

The authors have made every effort to ensure that the information in this book was correct at the time of publication. However, the authors and publisher accept no liability for any loss, damage or disruption incurred by the reader or any other person arising from any action taken or not taken based on the content of this book. The author recommends seeking third party advice and considering all options prior to making any decision or taking action in regard to the content of this book.

Cover design by Jeff Clulow
Cover layout by Ally Mosher at allymosher.com

Cover images supplied by 123RF, Adobe Stock and Envato Elements
Photographers:
Elnur Amikishiyev & Oleksiy

Proofread by Jess Horton

Praise for The Wentworth Prospect

B2B sales mastery delivered in an ingenious, engaging and hugely entertaining way. Sales experts with decades of experience between them show you how to navigate the complexities of the modern B2B sales experience in a way which will keep you engaged from the first page to the last. A brilliant read!

— Owen Ashby. CEO, Cognisco
Milton Keynes, England, UK

This book is unique. With a very Australian tone, the key player - a female sales professional - takes you on a journey of how a strong, yet empathetic and collaborative, customer-centric sales approach can not only turn a negative opportunity around, but create a strong business relationship moving forward.

— Bernadette McClelland. CEO, 3 Red Folders
International Keynote Speaker,
Author of 'The Art of Commercial Conversations',
B2B Sales Consultant
Melbourne, Australia

The Wentworth Prospect is a delightful narrative that frames a serious and thoughtful methodology for large, complex sales from the point of view of a smaller company sales team trying to land a major deal with a very large company. It's original and entertaining as a novel; deep and powerful as a sales process. Perfect for sales leaders and reps to read and discuss in a book club setting!

— Barbara Weaver Smith, Ph.D.
Founder and CEO, The Whale Hunters
Arizona, USA

The market for sales books is a pretty cluttered one, but every so often a book comes along that breaks the mould. The Wentworth Prospect is that book. Chock full of business lessons and sales insights, it succeeds because of the compelling story it tells and the calibre of business insights crammed into its pages. If you think you've read every sales book worth reading, think again!

> — Cian Mcloughlin. CEO, Trinity Perspectives
> International Keynote Speaker,
> Best-selling author of 'Rebirth of the Salesman'
> Sydney, Australia

Imagine a story about very complex sales with all the elements of a mystery novel.

There are protagonists, a "villain", separate story lines coming together at the end. And of course there is the central character that meets all the challenges put in front of her, ending victorious.

I never imagined complex B2B sales could be so engrossing!

While The Wentworth Prospect is a fun read, the authors manage to keep their focus on helping us better understand how to manage complex buying processes, supporting customers in moving through the buying cycle.

In hindsight, I found the approach really intriguing. There were so many similarities with my own experience in complex B2B sales.

Wayne, John, Jeff managed to entertain me and educate me simultaneously.

I think every sales professional will both enjoy and learn from reading the Wentworth Prospect.

> — David Brock. CEO, Partners In EXCELLENCE
> Author of 'Sales Manager Survival Guide'
> California, USA

The Wentworth Prospect is the antithesis of most B2B sales books. Instead of the typical dry, boring "this is how you do it" instructional manual, The Wentworth Prospect is a wonderful, fascinating story of real people, against great odds, going after the sale and succeeding. It's the B2B sales world told in a memorable novel. It shows the reader how to sell, instead of just telling him/her how to sell. The story will stay with you long after the material from most sales books fades from memory. It's a must read, if you want to know how great B2B selling is actually performed. This fabulous story will truly show you how it's done; don't miss it!

— Robert Terson. CEO, Selling Fearlessly
Illinois, USA

The Wentworth Prospect is a compelling vision for B2B sales. It's a bright future, and if you're a seasoned professional, this book will remind you what the right path to a sale looks like. If you're a newcomer it's a comprehensive, easy-to-digest lesson in best-practise selling. As a story, it will have you hooked and make you smile.

The Wentworth Prospect is a brilliant book that will stand the test of time. Buy it as a gift and share it with all those you care about in the arena of professional sales.

— Tony Hughes. Best-selling author,
Co-founder, Sales IQ Global
Sydney, Australia

An interesting take on a sales education book using a fictitious story to illustrate powerful principles to win more business! As an ex B2B software sales professional turned Sales Advisor/Trainer who's worked with 70+ tech companies and coached 100's of founders/sales professionals I personally resonated with the story, finding it both entertaining and educational - would recommend!

— Alex McNaughten. Chief Revenue Officer, Sales Leaders
Auckland, New Zealand

The Wentworth Prospect was a wonderful read that taught me the secrets of making a sale. The story is so engaging that I didn't even realise how much I learnt from it until the end! I would recommend it to anyone who works in or aspires to work in sales.

> — Aleyna Camlica. Account Business Manager,
> DXC Technology
> Melbourne, Australia

I applaud wrapping a dry theoretical learning exercise with an entertaining novel storyline. It conveys the concept while entertaining in a captivating manner.

> — Derrick Baan. Retired Sales Leader
> and successful novelist
> Brisbane, Australia

If you struggle reading business books but want to get better at complex selling, then this novel is for you. Written like a true-life account of the messy world that is life and business, you'll discover how a real person navigates office politics internally and at the customer while coming to terms with her personal demons, doubts and insecurities to win big at sales. While the story is fun, the sales companion guide the protagonist uses to help her close a large deal, is the true hero in this compelling drama.

> — Edith Crnkovich. Founder, Relatable.IT
> B2B Communications Coach,
> Trainer and Workshop Facilitator
> Sydney, Australia

...easy reading and a useful way to convey important sales messages. It was literally a very "novel" approach and I really enjoyed it.

> — Mark Blum. CEO and Co-founder, Cognian Technologies
> Sydney, Australia

This book will resonate with anyone that either has, or is keen to gain, experience in complex sales. Whilst it is a novel, the situations that the dogged protagonist Sue finds herself confronting on a daily basis are the stuff of reality. From the confusion of influencer personalities and agendas to the politics of both Seller and Buyer organisations, Sue navigates it all thanks to the North Star of the EDVANCE sales process.

— Patrick Boucousis. MD, The Sales Natural
B2B Sales Coach and Trainer
Brisbane, Australia

Breathing life and with it reading enjoyment in this story, whilst demonstrating the execution of sales strategies through the personal encounters, is brilliant.

The Wentworth Prospect should be a must read for any sales programme or tutorial.

Whilst reading Wentworth's story I constantly reflected on my own earlier experience at ANZ.

— Peter Meers. Retired Senior Banker and
Mining Company Executive
Sydney, Australia

The Wentworth Prospect is a great tale of personal growth, overcoming adversity and following a defined strategy despite challenges in order to achieve a goal. There are plenty of lessons and takeaways to be applied by the reader, explained through the lens of a fictional pursuit that has uncanny pain points, both internally and externally, to real life B2B selling.

— Shaun Edsall. Business Development Manager,
DXC Technology
Adelaide, Australia

I've read a lot of sales books and the ones that have taught me the most were those that were not only packed with great ideas but that were also a good read. This book is both. I read it first as a novel and enjoyed it a lot – now I'm going back through it and learning a lot from the EDVANCE framework. There's heaps in there that even an old fuddy duddy silver haired 'Roper-clone' like me can use. Very strongly recommended.

— Steve Hall. MD, Executive Sales Coaching Aust
"C" Level Sales Authority
Sydney, Australia

When John Smibert told me that he and his co-authors were writing a B2B sales guide in the form of a novel I thought it was an extremely ambitious project and one that would be hard to pull off. But they have produced a masterpiece here. It's fast-paced, it's dramatic, it has characters you can relate to and it's page turning. And all through the book best practices around complex enterprise sales are demonstrated exceptionally well. I found the meetings and side conversations between the salespeople and the customer to be very realistic and obviously created from the author's deep real world experience. And there is so much value added material in the form of bonus on-line sales tools and background explanations of the sales principles being followed. I couldn't recommend The Wentworth Prospect enough, I will be buying it for my clients and recommending it for anyone involved in enterprise sales.

— Steven Norman. Founder, Growth Acumen
B2B Sales Consultant,
Author of 'Future Proof Sales Strategy',
Keynote Speaker
Sydney, Australia.

The Wentworth Prospect is an outstanding business book and a great novel. I enjoyed learning and being entertained at the same time particularly about sales and business development. Very on topic for 2021!

— Geoff Olds. MD, Technology 360 Group and Technology FX
Award Winning Entrepreneur and
Author of 'Death of an Entrepreneur'
Sydney, Australia

One of the difficulties sales people have with their sales training, is translating the classroom into the real world.

We learn by stories, by doing – not lectures – which is why I recommend The Wentworth Prospect.

In drawing the readers into a realistic and engaging story about an opportunity – we 'experience' the frustrations of the old way and, become drawn into the logic, and practicality, of a new-way of thinking about and driving forward complex B2B sales.

Shared amongst sales teams, sales leaders could use this terrific tale as a training aid and discussion guide.

I believe this is an all too rare resource for encouraging individual and team sales process improvement. Recommended!

— Jeremy Pollard. Senior Consultant and Director,
Shipley Asia Pacific
Sydney, Australia

Humans tell and consume stories to experience multiple alternative realities, and so make sense of a complex world. That's a hyper-scaled way to learn! Learning from the deep experiences of the authors without needing to commit to their combined 50-year experience in sales. I heartily recommend The Wentworth Project to anyone in sales and anyone that loves a good story.

— Mike Adams.
Author 'Seven Stories Every Salesperson Must Tell'
Melbourne, Australia

I really enjoyed the read. Found it relatable, relevant and a refreshing way to help train the inexperienced through to those more seasoned campaigners. As a sales leader, now in my 37th year managing teams, I continually use real-life examples, anecdotes and case studies to help illustrate points. I find most folk learn better from such an approach, and this book does just that. Does this book work to help salespeople better understand how to develop B2B sales opportunities? Is it a tool sales managers could use to help coach and develop individual salespeople? Will it help turn average into good and good into great... F#@* yeah! I am now looking forward to the sequel...

> — Brett Johnson. Director of Sales, IVE Group -
> Integrated Marketing and Print Communications
> Coach, Mentor, Trainer
> Sydney, Australia

Smibert, Moloney, Clulow have broken the mould with this book. In the past sales books were theoretical and dull and while they may have sold, they sat on the pile of books by the side of your bed that you never read. With The Wentworth Prospect, Smibert, Moloney, Clulow have taken a dry subject and coloured it in. A sales methodology in the form of a novel. If you are just getting into B2B enterprise sales or it's time to update your skills, this book brings sales to life.

> — Timothy Hughes. CEO and Co-Founder, DLA Ignite
> London, England

This is a ripping yarn. It works as a great story AND as a real insight into the latest approaches to complex B2B selling at the highest level. Anyone in sales will enjoy this. A few will appreciate it but the real prize is to implement the lessons it incorporates in the story.

> — Ian Meharg. Head of Business Development,
> Consectus Ltd
> Aberfeldy, Scotland, UK

Acknowledgements

There are many we'd like to thank who have given their time freely to advise, cajole and encourage this book along the road to publication:

Foremost to our wives Joan, Gela and Jo, and to our families for their unlimited patience.

To Tony Hughes for his wonderful foreword and ever-gracious support and experience.

To all our beta readers who found the plot holes, inconsistencies and mistakes we overlooked. You helped make this book better and reminded us that our industry, unlike some of the characters in this story, is actually filled with generous, helpful people.

And to Jenny Mosher and all at IndieMosh for the much-needed inspiration to drag this project over the finishing line.

John, Wayne and Jeff.

Contents

Introduction xv
Foreword xvii
1. She Never Saw it Coming 1
2. Broken 5
3. The Trigger is Pulled 11
4. Rest in Peace 15
5. Return to the Fold 23
6. The Salesperson's Journal 29
ENGAGE 35
7. The Unseen Mentor 37
8. Accomplice 47
9. Hello and Goodbye 53
10. Sketching the Outlines 65
11. A Question of Trust 73
12. Dead in the Water 79
13. The Glass Whiteboard 85
14. Monday Morning Blues 95
15. From the Jaws of Victory 99
16. What Just Happened? 105
17. Don't Screw Up 107
18. A Drowning of Sorrows 115
19. The Boomerang Move 119

DISCOVER AND DISRUPT 127

    20. The Cartographers 129

    21. View From the Inside 137

    22. Divide and Conquer 143

    23. The Usurper 155

    24. At the Bottom of the Hole 161

    25. The Evil Empire 167

    26. Southerly Buster 171

    27. The Door That Melted 177

    28. Running Into Walls 185

    29. Friends in High Places 189

    30. Spitting Chips 197

    31. The Rarefied Air 201

    32. A Bird in a Cage 207

    33. The Soccer Mum 213

    34. The Waiting Game 219

    35. Into the Light 225

    36. In the Back of the Net 229

    37. The Bush Telegraph 233

VALUE PROPOSED 237

    38. The Flying Dutchman 239

    39. A Meeting of Minds 243

    40. A Lot Can Happen in a Lift 251

AUTHENTICATE 265

    41. Show Don't Tell 267

    42. Stacking the Deck 271

43. The Proof of the Pudding 279

44. Bumpy Landing... 289

NEGOTIATE.. 293

45. The Devil in the Details 295

46. A Rock and a Hard Place... 299

47. Defiance... 303

48. The Camel's Back 309

49. Give and Take 317

50. Bolt From the Blue... 323

51. The Back Foot.. 329

COMMIT AND ENACT 335

52. Grab the Sauce 337

53. New Horizons.. 349

Introduction

As partners and sales professionals, Wayne Moloney and I spent many years throwing pebbles into the ocean of B2B selling organisations hoping for positive change.

The impact for the few companies close to us, and their customers, has been gratifying. Many have achieved significant sustainable growth in sales and revenue. Deep partner relationships have developed with customers that are highly valued by both parties.

However, a pebble does not cause a tsunami and that is what is needed to create that positive change.

As buyers have become more empowered, they do not value sellers and their advice like they used too. They do not believe sellers will positively influence their thinking about their business. They do not expect sellers to help explore the current state of their business nor help them peel back the onion skin of their problems to better understand the implications.

That's because their experience has often been that many sellers are focussed on themselves and their product or service – on closing an order, not on genuinely helping the customer achieve a valuable business outcome.

The result of all this is that buyers will only open conversations when they have made their own decision on what they need. And this is far too late in the process for sellers to be of any genuine help.

Wayne and I saw that an earthquake was needed to drive a tsunami of change in the B2B sales world.

In short, we had a vision for a groundbreaking book.

That said, another sales text book was never going to be the answer. There are already thousands of these and more being published every week.

Our friend Mike Adams[1] pointed out that the best way to change people's thinking and behaviour is with stories. So we decided a sales novel was the way to go. We tried for years to write it yet were never satisfied.

And then along came Jeff Clulow, advertising writer and novelist. And our vision came alive.

If you are striving to be a great salesperson, or to transform the way your organisation sells, we think this novel might be a catalyst for your tsunami.

To find out more about this book and how it can transform your business, visit www.edvance.sale

John Smibert
Co-Founder Sales Leader Forums
Founder Sales Masterminds APAC

---

[1] Mike Adams is the author of *Seven Stories Every Salesperson Must Tell*

Foreword

Professional selling is changing faster than at any time in history with the fourth industrial revolution forcing everyone in sales to redefine the way they create value for their employer and customers. Failure to adapt to new expectations and step up with next level thinking and leadership, means a drift toward commoditisation and career extinction.

Although a typical buyer's journey starts within their trusted network or online, it is a misconception to believe that buyers are truly empowered in an age of information overload. Buyers drown in information and have always needed trusted advice. Strategic selling is about early engagement with relevance and context to reframe thinking while co-creating a vision for a brighter future supported by a compelling business case to invest in change. And it all needs to be done while navigating politics, overcoming apathy, dealing with ambiguity, neutralising desperate competitors, and preventing your own team from inadvertently sabotaging sales and customer success.

This book is important because sales leadership is needed like never before. Yet leadership is mercurial stuff and poorly understood. The truth is that sales management often becomes the weak link in the revenue chain for companies; something John and Wayne shine a light on as they explain exactly what it takes to drive sustained sales success.

Together with Jeff, they have masterfully created a book that has the power to transform sales careers. It's a memorable story about sales leadership that contains heart, wisdom, insight and practical advice that can have a huge impact for those seeking to drive improved results and go to the next level in their sales or leadership career.

It is a timeless maxim that value selling demands a deep-seated focus on the needs of customers. The very best sales leaders embrace this and focus on making a positive difference in the lives of others – personally and professionally. But how do we move from price to value, from commodity to consultative, from seller to trusted adviser? John and Wayne explain exactly how to be the person worthy of the sales success you seek whether you are an individual contributor or senior leader.

The EDVANCE process and methodology alone is worth far more then the price of this book or the time you invest in reading how to best apply its magic. Within these pages you will go on a journey of discovery where you meet some familiar characters. You'll see yourself in Sue and you'll relate to the challenge of stepping-up into leadership while managing the chaos and pressure that is the world of sales and commercial leadership. Savour the book as you read and allow the lessons to become part of your own thinking.

Within these pages you will find your true north in selling – that we must always walk in the direction of the customer, beside them and with heart, purpose and integrity. That's why this book is so important. It illustrates how to be authentic and human in the age of the machines by applying timeless principles of trust, insight and value creation. Many of the scenarios within its pages resonated with my own experience and they will for you too.

What John, Wayne and Jeff have delivered with 'The Wentworth Prospect' is a compelling vision for B2B sales. It's a bright future, and if you're a seasoned professional, this book will remind you what the right path to a sale looks like. If you're a newcomer it's a comprehensive, easy-to-digest lesson in best-practise selling. As a story, it will have you hooked and make you smile.

The Wentworth Prospect is a brilliant book that will stand the test of time. Buy it as a gift and share it with all those you care about in the arena of professional sales.

Tony Hughes
Best-selling author
Co-founder, Sales IQ Global
© 2021 All rights reserved

Warning:
This book contains Australianisms.
In case of difficulty, please visit
urbandictionary.com for assistance.

1. She Never Saw it Coming

Sue never saw any of it coming.

Not the success of her first speaking engagement.

Certainly not the deal with WestInvest.

She was watching the lashing rain outside the passenger window of Doug's car as they drove back into Sydney from the Airport. She was dreaming; trying to take in the moment and the changes it meant for her—for her career. In her peripheral vision Sue could make out Doug gripping the wheel, staring into the downpour as he drove. The rain fell like a waterfall and he was concentrating hard to guide them safely through it. He looked tired.

For nearly five long hours on the flight back from Perth, Doug had busied himself writing emails. Sue began work on a new blog post but couldn't concentrate and gave up. She buried her nose in a book for a while and then slept.

The trip to Perth had been a milestone for Sue. People knew her name now. She'd been invited to speak at a national conference hosted by the Australian Cyber Security Centre (the ACSC). Her address centred on the alarming trend that cybercriminals were now leading the cybersecurity industry. Defence systems had become reactive while cybercrime was innovating. Everything was back to front. It was a controversial subject that drew a large audience. Banks, government agencies and the investment sector filled the room, as well as anyone else concerned enough to keep the details of their online dealings safe. Sue fielded a raft of questions and her speech resulted in a wealth of new contacts.

But this wasn't even the high point.

Straight afterwards, Doug asked her in hushed tones to head back to the hotel, book a room in the business centre and wait for him there. Something was up. She made the arrangements and waited. But she didn't have to wait long. Doug soon arrived with a group from WestInvest, a small investment bank based in Perth. Doug had spent the last seven months cultivating WestInvest as a prospect and had invited them to Sue's presentation. Sue watched the meeting unfold. It wasn't really a meeting at all; just a brief, friendly discussion about the future. A look of understanding passed between Doug and the most senior WestInvest executive. There was the slightest of smiles, followed by a handshake that seemed to signify something more than itself. A few of the WestInvest execs complimented Sue on her address and then they were gone. It was the softest close Sue had ever witnessed.

Doug smiled his schoolboy smile at her. 'You helped push that one over the line,' he said.

They celebrated with a few drinks in the bar. Doug was full of praise for Sue, how all her hard work generating content was bearing fruit, how it managed to attract the attention of the ACSC and how well her first speaking engagement had gone.

Now, looking out the passenger window of Doug's car, Sue didn't see the rain. She was replaying the scene, holding on to the feeling; that wonderful, heady feeling of achievement. People had *listened* to her. People wanted to *talk* with her. They wanted her advice and guidance. Best of all, Doug believed in her more than ever.

Sue wanted to tell him all this. She wanted to thank him for the opportunity and how much it meant to have a boss and mentor like him. She was about to turn in his direction when she spotted the intersection ahead on Botany Road. Where were the traffic signals? Were the lights out? Had they malfunctioned? Doug kept driving.

She turned to warn him and saw, over his shoulder, through the driver's side window, the chromed radiator grille emerge from the rain. The container truck hit them at right-angles, at brutal speed, sending the forward momentum of Doug's car violently to one side.

Sue never saw that coming, either.

2. Broken

Sue's eyelids were already half open when she woke. The light flooded in, bringing pain.

Her ears rang like church bells but she could still make out the sounds of muffled conversation, a TV or radio somewhere. Something inside told her to lay still. She'd lost track of time, of place, and now she felt a growing sense that something serious, something monstrous had just happened.

Panicked, Sue opened her mouth to call out but no sound came. She tried lifting an arm but it was held by something: something thin and flexible buried in her flesh. She tried to move her head, to look around but her vision swam and she was dragged down, down, spinning into a black pit of nausea.

***

When Sue next surfaced into the light she couldn't tell if it was minutes later, or days.

Moving only her eyes, she surveyed the scene around her.

Above her a TV hung from the ceiling. It was on. A cooking show. Mercifully the volume was so low as to be almost inaudible. Looking to one side she saw a closed door. Sue's eyes moved to the other side of the room. Flowers. Flowers in vases, flowers in cellophane, flowers in small arrangements and flowers tied in ornate bouquets.

Who the hell were they for?

It was then Sue saw the bag of clear liquid hanging from a stand. She traced the line of tubing that ran from it down to the needle in her forearm. It was held in place with surgical tape. An intravenous drip. She knew where she was now.

And she knew that the flowers were for her.

* * *

Sue's returns to consciousness were brief and disorienting. Each time she had to struggle to remember where she was. But as the answer became more fixed in her understanding, another question surfaced.

How did she get here?

She tried to remember. She closed her eyes and saw a roomful of people. They clapped their hands, smiling. They were applauding her. She remembered speaking to them. A presentation? A conference? Nearby, Doug stood applauding her too. He was beaming with pride. People asked questions. Lots of questions. Everyone wanted her opinion. After the questions they clamoured around her with even more questions. She remembered one man in particular. He was lean and darkly handsome with thick waves of charcoal hair. Was he Indian? His accent was cultured, educated. Oxbridge perhaps? He held out his business card with a pleasant smile but there was an urgency in his expression. Sue took the card, studied it for a moment and slipped it into the hip pocket of her business suit.

Perth.

Sue remembered Perth.

* * *

In the darkness Sue heard a voice.

'...with the arrival of the new moon in Virgo, this month will bring its fair share of mixed blessings...'

Sue knew the voice well. It was a woman's voice. A friendly voice with an accent nearly as broad as the land it came from. Sue swam towards it through her lethargy.

'...your love-life might take a dive, but your career is definitely in the ascendant.'

Sue's eyelids peeled open. 'Coops?' she said, with a cracked voice, 'that you?'

The reading stopped. A face loomed into Sue's immediate vision. It was a young face, round and pretty, with a faint splash of freckles across the bridge of the nose that told of a childhood spent outdoors.

'It's me alright.'

Sue tried speaking but her mouth was too dry.

'Oh, you must be parched. Here you go,' said Coops, offering Sue a plastic cup of water with a drinking straw.

Sue took a careful sip. 'You've been reading to me?'

'Thought it might help,' said Coops, holding up a magazine.

Sue held out her hand. Coops took it.

'Welcome back,' said Coops. 'We missed you.'

Sue squeezed Coops's hand.

'How you feeling?' asked Coops. 'They've been pumping you full of drugs—for the pain.'

'Not too bad,' lied Sue. She was all pain. She couldn't pinpoint any one particular source. It was a throbbing ache that crept down into her bones.

'Good news is you'll heal Sue. The worst of it is that your leg's broke. Other than that, concussion, a couple of cracked ribs and some bruises.'

Sue let out a sigh. 'My leg is broken?'

'Yep, tib and fib snapped clean above the ankle. The doc says it's a *spiral fracture*. They whacked a bit of steel in there so you'll be up and about in no time. Oh,' added Coops, 'and you've got a broken cheekbone.'

Sue let out another sigh. 'Do you have a mirror, a compact or something?'

'Yep,' said Coops, 'but you can take it from me, you look like shit.'

Sue smiled. She could always trust Coops to tell it like it was. She came without a filter, but you always knew where you stood with Coops. That's why Sue loved working with her so much.

'Do you remember much?' asked Coops.

'I remember being in Perth. I remember the ACSC conference,' said Sue, 'I was speaking to a large crowd. They were all clapping.' In her mind's eye Sue saw the lean, dark stranger in front of her. She took his business card and pocketed it. 'And there was this guy, Indian, well-dressed, good-looking...'

'Oh yeah?' interjected Coops.

'I can't remember his name or what he said but I know it's important.'

'Nothing else?' asked Coops.

Sue was suddenly back in the meeting room at the hotel, watching a handshake.

WestInvest.

Suddenly animated, Sue tried to sit up. She let out a cry, feeling the consequence in her rib-cage. 'Coops, there was a deal—we've got a new client—we've got to tell the office...'

'Calm your farm, you'll do yourself a mischief,' said Coops, easing Sue back onto her pillow. 'We know all about it. WestInvest. It's all being taken care of. Doug sent out all the emails shortly before...'

Sue gasped. The memory struck her with all the force of a container truck. She was in the car again. She saw Doug staring into the sheets of rain. Ahead, she saw no lights where the traffic signals should have been. Then she saw the chromed radiator grille.

'Doug!' cried Sue. 'Where's Doug?'

Coops's expression saddened. Her eyes showed the first sheen of tears.

'Doug's gone Sue. Doug's gone.'

3. The Trigger is Pulled

Sue was comfortable enough to raise her bed to a sitting position. She thought to read but watching TV seemed less physical. A movie was playing, a romantic comedy. She liked these kinds of films, perhaps because romance was such a novelty; something that simply didn't fit into her working schedule. It was on her to-do list. Right down the bottom. Below *exercise*.

'You just love those crappy rom-coms, don't you?' said Coops, arriving with a basket of fruit. She placed it on a table within Sue's reach and read the enclosed card. 'Wishing you a speedy recovery, with warm regards from all the staff at WestInvest.'

Coops sat on the edge of Sue's bed. 'They seem like a good client.'

Sue forgot the movie and turned to Coops. 'So how's it going? With WestInvest?'

'Oh, pretty good. They're right into the concept of cloud and the systems architecture is being built.' Coops turned to Sue with a smile. 'And they're a *bank* Sue, they've got the budget and they're willing to spend to get it right. They're a great win for us, for Tesico.'

Sue nodded. WestInvest certainly was the kind of client Tesico Australia needed. They weren't huge, but as a company they were large enough to influence Tesico's bottom line substantially.

'So tell me, how'd you land them?' asked Coops.

Sue took a deep breath. 'Well, it was all Doug,' she said.

'But you worked on that deal for over seven months. You were with Doug every step of the way,' said Coops. 'So how'd he push the product?'

'Funny thing is, he didn't really,' said Sue. 'In the beginning he just asked questions about their online security. Lots of questions. We listened to a lot of people and, it's funny...'

'What is?'

'He didn't mention the product or the Tesico name once.'

'But he must have at some point.'

'Oh sure, but that was much later,' said Sue. 'By then they were already sold on the promise of what we could do. They were sold on Doug.'

Sue thought back to the meeting in their Perth hotel. She saw the handshake again. Doug and the WestInvest client. It was such a simple, everyday gesture but somehow this handshake was different. It was more than just business etiquette; something in the two men's eyes confirmed this. It was the handshake worth millions.

'So, he must've had a plan? Did he have some kind of *method*? Come on Sue, I want to understand.'

'Well, he was teaching me. It was a new way of doing things, something he said he'd been working on for years. He explained some of it, as we went along mostly. He even had a name for it, he called it EDVANCE.'

Coops nodded thoughtfully.

'He told me it was important to find a champion—someone with the power to drive change. And he mentioned the word *disruption* a lot.'

Coops's brow furrowed. 'What does that mean?'

'Not sure. He was trying to teach me.'

'Shame he didn't write it all down.'

'I think he was beginning to,' said Sue.

'Mind if I change the channel?' asked Coops, nodding at the TV. 'This shit is doing my head in.'

As Coops picked up the TV remote Sue tried to remember what Doug had told her about EDVANCE. It was just fragments of advice that made no real coherent sense. Doug had said he'd train her properly one day. He just needed a little more time to refine the process. Now that day would never come.

'Holy crap,' exclaimed Coops, 'Wentworth's been hit!'

Sue broke from her introspection and looked to the TV. Coops had changed to a news channel. A caption ran across the bottom of the screen: *cyberattack on Wentworth. Bank admits losses.* A young spokesman stood on the steps of the Wentworth Bank tower with an array of microphones thrust in his face. He smiled with calm reassurance while explaining that no serious damage had been done. Sue recognised the thick waves of charcoal hair and the Oxbridge accent.

'Oh my God, Coops. It's him—that's the guy I met in Perth!'

'Blimey Sue, you could've told me he was a Wentworth bloke,' said Coops, raising the volume of the TV. 'What's his name?'

Sue tried to visualise the business card in her hand and shook her head. Wentworth—Australia's largest investment bank. What was his name? Why hadn't she paid more attention?

'Missed it,' said Coops, throwing the remote onto the bed as the smiling spokesman disappeared. The story switched to a team of reporters and financial analysts in a studio. 'That's gonna hit them where it hurts, smack in the old share price.' Coops wasn't wrong. The next image showed a graph of Wentworth's tumbling stock. 'Look, they're dragging the whole market with them,' she said.

Sue and Coops listened to the commentary, engrossed, as they learned a malware attack had gained access to employee computers inside the bank's networks. The bank confirmed there had been losses from central accounts but insisted that individual customer accounts were not affected. Wentworth had issued a bland statement about *how important cybersecurity was to them and that they had systems and measures in place to monitor and protect customers*. It was a weak attempt to calm the shareholders. They had not disclosed the amount of the losses but a spokesperson from the ACSC revealed that Wentworth may have been targeted by a multinational hacking group responsible for the theft of over one billion dollars from banks in over thirty countries.

Coops was already checking a newsfeed on her phone. 'Listen to this Sue,' she said. 'Some industry commentators believe the bank's losses could have run to as much as one hundred million dollars.' She turned to Sue. 'That's no small hack.'

'There's an opportunity here,' said Sue as the station went to a commercial break.

'Too right,' agreed Coops. 'This is one of those trigger events you keep telling me about. Shame you can't remember the name of that fellah.'

Sue saw the handsome Indian man again, smiling but anxious, holding out his business card. She remembered taking the card and placing it in her hip pocket.

'Coops,' began Sue. 'Do you know what happened to the clothes I was wearing—when they brought me in?'

Coops shrugged. 'I'd guess they'd be somewhere. Admissions might know.'

'Can you find out?'

'Okay,' said Coops. 'But you sure that's a good idea? You were pretty messed up.'

'It's important Coops.'

Coops nodded.

'And I'll need my laptop, and my phone. We've got a lead to follow.'

Coops smiled. 'Bloody oath.'

4. Rest in Peace

'You shouldn't be doing this y'know,' said Coops as she manoeuvred Sue's wheelchair towards the hightop cab outside the hospital. 'You're not well enough.'

Coops had just spent the last hour or more dressing Sue and moving her from the bed into the wheelchair. Then she'd tried to hide the bruising on Sue's face with a thick render of makeup. Sue had seen herself in the mirror for the first time. Her cheek was swollen and black, the eye above it bloodshot. Rather than hiding the swelling, the makeup seemed to draw attention to it.

'How do I look?' asked Sue.

'Like plastic surgery gone wrong,' replied Coops.

Sue laughed a little. She could afford to. The painkillers were kicking in.

It wasn't the right kind of day for a funeral thought Sue as they loaded her into the cab. It was bright and cloudless. It was one of those days when Sydney shone; when surfers headed for the beach suburbs, carrying their boards on public transport, mingling with well-heeled businesspeople. It was a day for sunglasses. Perhaps that made it the right kind of day after all. Sunglasses would hide the tears.

'So who's coming?' asked Sue as the taxi left the hospital.

'Dunno,' replied Coops.

'You okay?'

Coops pulled a face, sighing. 'Not really.'

'Doug?'

'Yes. And no.'

Both women studied the warm day outside. The world seemed without a care.

Coops turned to Sue. 'I've been thinking how good it would be if they promoted you—you know, to Doug's role.'

'National Sales Manager?'

'Exactly. Makes sense, doesn't it? Then maybe I could move into sales and work with you.'

'That's never going to happen,' said Sue. 'I could never fill Doug's shoes...'

'Why not?' insisted Coops.

'Because I simply don't have the experience, or the ability. There's still so much I don't know about complex B2B sales. I need a mentor.'

Coops turned back to the view outside. 'You've got ten times more ability than the dickhead they've chosen,' she mumbled.

'Who?' asked Sue. 'Who have they chosen?'

'Tony bloody Roper.'

Sue knew the name. He was one of the regional salespeople from Tesico's global head office in Singapore. He was a South African national who'd worked in Asia for many years, selling whatever he could for whoever would let him. He'd joined Tesico Singapore late in his career when it was only a startup. The company had quickly broadened its business base across Asia Pacific. It added offices in Amsterdam, Sydney and eventually New York. It was a youthful company, filled with youthful people and youthful ideas. Yet Tony Roper was in the twilight of his career, close to retirement. He was a square peg.

'I've heard of him,' said Sue.

'You don't know the half of it,' said Coops. 'He's been in the office for five minutes and he's got everyone offside with his targets, his KPIs and the shithouse leads he's been asking everyone to follow up. He wants hard selling, and *fast*. His view is the Sydney office is up shit creek and he's here to save us.'

'But he can't be a permanent replacement for Doug?' offered Sue.

'He's not,' said Coops. 'But try telling *him* that.'

* * *

As the cab pulled up on the gravel outside the crematorium, Sue turned to Coops.

'It'll happen Coops, you'll get that job in sales. You're a natural.'

Coops placed her hand over Sue's. 'I want a mentor too Sue. I want to learn from you. I'm fed up with this mishmash of a support role. My career's going nowhere.'

Sue understood. Coops's role was Sales Enablement and Marketing Coordinator, a complex title with an even more complex job description. On the one hand Coops had to provide tools, sales content and training for the Australian-based sales team and, on the other, she had to answer to the Singapore-based marketing department, fulfilling a marketing role in the absence of a dedicated Australian team. People tried to make her feel better about her job by telling her it was progressive, that it was hybrid, cross-disciplinary. Coops understood this to mean she just had lots of bosses, who all wanted a piece of her at precisely the same time.

Outside the crematorium chapel was a sizeable crowd of mourners. Doug was loved and admired, not just by his colleagues at Tesico, but by his customers and the wider industry. It looked as if the whole of Tesico Australia was in attendance. They crowded around, expressing concern for Sue's injuries but overjoyed to see she was on the mend. No-one offered their condolences. They didn't need to. Their grief was shared. Everyone was mourning

Doug Churchill. Everyone, that is, except the new National Sales Manager. Tony Roper was conspicuous by his absence.

'Now what are you doing here?' An Asian woman in her mid-forties stepped from the crowd. She was stylish, fashionable even, in her mourning attire. A short bob of hair framed a kindly face. 'You should be in the hospital, concentrating on getting better,' she continued in a matronly tone.

'That's what I told her,' said Coops.

'Michelle, what a surprise,' said Sue. 'I didn't know you were in Sydney.'

'I had to come, Doug was a great friend.' Michelle Yim was the Singapore-based Global Sales Director for Tesico. She had been with the company since its inception eight years before and was instrumental in expanding their client base across Asia-Pacific. A shrewd businesswoman with the highest of profiles in the region, Michelle also had tremendous empathy for her people. She was very fond of Doug and turned to him for advice on many occasions.

'Then you'll understand why I had to attend too,' said Sue.

Michelle nodded, accepting Sue's reason. 'Also, I'm here to help out with the transition. We'll be looking for a new National Sales Manager but in the meantime, I've appointed Tony Roper to look after things.'

'A caretaker role?'

'As far as everyone at Tesico is concerned, yes,' said Michelle. 'His role is temporary but, as far as our customers are concerned, he's the National Sales Manager, period. I want us to look in control. Even in the face of this tragedy.'

'I understand,' said Sue.

'And I need you all to support and help him in his role. The same way you all helped Doug.'

'Of course,' said Sue. 'I'll be back to work next week hopefully.'

Michelle shook her head. 'No, right now your only responsibility is to get well Sue.'

'But what about WestInvest?' protested Sue. 'I know them, I know their business and they need continuity from us. This is a tricky stage of the deal for them.' Sue also thought about the lead on Wentworth that she wanted to follow up.

'Don't concern yourself with WestInvest. I've met them and explained the way forward as I see it. Tony will take point. He'll handle their business from now on.'

Coops coughed involuntarily.

Michelle's voice softened. 'Sue, your health's more important. When you come back to work, I want you fully recovered, fit and healthy.' She made to leave. 'So take as much sick leave as you need.'

The service was long. Not because of the celebrant's address but due to the queue of people who read eulogies. One by one they shuffled quietly up to the lectern, pieces of paper in hand, and recounted a kindness, a story or a debt they personally owed Doug. He had touched so many hearts over his career. Sue tried to shift her weight in her wheelchair. The painkillers were wearing off.

Sue was grateful when the service ended. She was slumped in her wheelchair, folded in on her pain; pain both physical and emotional. A wake was to be held at a city hotel near the Tesico office but Sue asked Coops to put her into a cab and send her back to the hospital. She needed to be on her own.

As Coops wheeled Sue away, someone laid a hand on Sue's shoulder.

'Sue, can we talk?'

Sue looked up to see Fiona Churchill, Doug's wife. Sue had met Fiona only a handful of times before.

'May I?' Fiona asked Coops, indicating the handles of the wheelchair.

Coops relinquished her grip on the wheelchair. 'Be my guest,' she said.

Fiona gently wheeled Sue into a rounded alcove where niches

lined the wall. The light of a single, circular aperture lit them from above. Fiona halted and walked to face Sue. She was tall, elegant, and maintained a kind of courageous composure. She would have been a good match for Doug, Sue thought.

'Doug often spoke of you,' said Fiona. 'You were his favourite. He said of all his proteges, you had the most potential.' Fiona bent down and took Sue's hand. 'I'm so glad you were spared, Sue. Thank-you for coming today. You must be in pain.' Sue could now see the red-rimmed eyes close up. Fiona looked tired, all cried out. Sue understood that her own grief would be nothing compared to Fiona's. Sue had lost her boss and friend. Fiona had lost far more. 'Did you know he was writing something?'

'A book?'

Fiona attempted a smile. 'Perhaps. More like a record of his dealings, his thoughts and ideas.'

Sue tried sitting up. 'Did you come across the word EDVANCE?'

Fiona shrugged. 'Not that I remember. I only glanced through it. It's all just sales-speak to me.'

Sue nodded, deep in thought.

'But it's no use to me and I'd hate to throw it out in case it might be of value. I thought if anyone could benefit from it, it'd be you. I wondered if you'd like to have it?'

Sue cleared her throat. 'Very much, yes...'

'And if it's not worth anything, then it'll be a memento. Something to remember him by.'

Sue was too choked with emotion to offer thanks.

'I'll have it sent to the office for you,' said Fiona.

***

By the time the orderly had wheeled Sue to her room in the private ward, she was in a world of pain. All she wanted was to lie down but found her bed littered with objects in plastic bags. As the orderly began moving them for her, she realised what they were: her belongings, taken from her at the time of her admission. Coops had been good to her word.

Sue told the orderly to leave them nearby and help her onto the bed. The orderly obliged and left Sue lying in her dark jacket and skirt, rifling through the contents of the bags.

In one bag Sue found her mobile phone, laptop and charger. In another she found her clothes. Coops was right: Sue's shirt and business jacket were torn and bloody. She clutched them for a moment and her eyes began to sting.

Reaching into the pocket of the torn jacket, Sue found what she was looking for: a business card. It read *Raf Singh. IT Security Manager, Wentworth Banking Corporation.* Sue sighed in relief. There was an email address and a mobile number too.

Sue was consumed with tiredness and pain but there would never be a right moment for this. She picked up her phone and turned it on, praying it still had power. It buzzed into life and the screen showed she still had fifteen percent charge. Enough.

She also saw a new text message.

Without thinking, she opened it.

It was from Doug. It read—*so proud of you.*

Sue covered her eyes with her forearm and lay back on the bed.

Then the tears came.

5. Return to the Fold

In the days that followed, Sue called Raf Singh several times. He didn't answer. She texted him her details, reminding him of the ACSC conference.

By the following week she still hadn't heard anything. Did he not want to talk? If not, why had he given her his card?

Sue tried to remember what he'd said, to recall the subject of their brief conversation, but she drew a blank. All she remembered was the look of anxiety in his eyes.

Thinking ahead, Sue asked Coops to help out, quietly. Coops loved this kind of work: research, digging up dirt. She had a nose for it. Coops started putting together everything she could find out about Wentworth: their current security arrangements, who their suppliers were and who their top execs were. She found their LinkedIn feeds and saw what they were reading, and what they were posting. She found articles they'd published in the industry press, and everything written about the bank in the media for the last six years. Coops had also investigated the cyberattack itself and its implications for the bank. She'd even spoken to a contact at the ACSC who revealed what they had all guessed at: the attack was far larger than Wentworth was admitting.

Perhaps this was why Raf hadn't returned her calls? The bank was in a tailspin.

The following Monday morning, and despite Michelle Yim's directive, Sue hobbled into the Tesico Sydney office on elbow crutches. Her leg was in a plastic boot, a soft, move-able cast held in place with adjustable straps. Her ribs still gave her pain but, so long as she stayed on painkillers and didn't overdo it, she could sit, use a phone, use her laptop and function to a degree.

'Jeez girl,' said Coops, meeting her in the reception area. 'You're tough as baling wire.'

There was a buzz in the office. People were moving about in a frenzy of activity. 'What's going on?' asked Sue.

'Morning prayers,' said Coops. 'It's a new thing.'

'What are we praying to?'

Coops took Sue by the elbow and led her into the conference room. She whispered into Sue's ear: 'Tony Roper and his godlike wisdom.'

Tony Roper was a broad-shouldered, square-shaped man in his late fifties. He looked as if he'd been strong once and carried himself like he still was. To Sue, he looked like a retired boxer who'd let himself go. He caught sight of Sue and walked over, pointing at her while speaking to everyone else.

'See this? This is what I'm talking about. Commitment! Fresh from a car crash and she's back at work. This is what I call a girl with a *can-do* attitude.'

Several people in the room smarted at the word *girl*. Tony Roper began to applaud and the room followed suit. 'Welcome back Sue.' He smiled.

What followed was a work-in-progress, a rundown of active projects on the Tesico customer relationship management database. Roper interrogated the room on each project and Sue could see that people were falling over themselves to demonstrate progress. When Roper deemed progress too slow the result was a string of underhand remarks. Sue could see the meeting for what it was: a public humiliation of the Tesico salesforce to drive productivity.

'Cindy Cooper?' asked Roper, glancing at some notes in his hand.

Sue shot a look at Coops. Coops's jaw was already jutting.

'Cindy Cooper, what have you been working on?' said Roper, scanning the room.

'Nobody calls me that,' muttered Coops, between clenched teeth.

'Cindy Cooper?' repeated Roper.

'Nobody calls me that,' said Coops plainly. Roper turned his gaze on her.

'She prefers the name Coops,' said Sue as intermediary. 'That's what everybody calls her.'

'Really?' asked Roper with a smile, delighted he'd touched a nerve. 'So tell me, *Coops*, what leads have you been working on?'

'I don't think that's fair,' began Sue, 'she's only in a support role, in sales enablement and...'

'Was I talking to you, Novak?' Roper shot the question directly at Sue. He turned and addressed the wider room, 'What is our job people? Each and every one of us? We're all here to *sell the product*. There's nothing else. Every single last one of you is here to contribute to the sale of Tesico product. That's what puts our meals on the table, that's what pays our mortgages and that's what puts our kids through school.' He turned his attention back to Coops. 'Now, what have you been working on—*Coops*?'

Coops was lost. Sue came to the rescue.

'We've been working on Wentworth together,' said Sue.

'Wentworth?' asked Roper with sudden interest. 'Tell me, what have you got?'

'We're trying to get to them, following up after the cyberattack,' said Sue.

'Yeah,' scoffed Roper, 'you and everyone else!'

Sue paused, remaining calm. 'Coops has been running a lot of the background and—and we may have a contact on the inside.'

Roper nodded, considering. 'Good. See me straight after. Everyone else, back to your desks.'

* * *

'They might be one of Australia's biggest banks but their security provisions are up shit creek,' explained Coops. 'They're still relying on a software-based firewall approach, they've got this rabbit-proof fence mentality. *Keep the little buggers out,* that's what they're thinking. But that just causes a shed-load of maintenance headaches. The hackers would be having a go, then they'd fix the hole, then the hackers would have another go, they'd fix the hole and so on and so on. I reckon that whole system's held together with patches. The media knows it, the punters know it and that's why the Wentworth share price is heading south.'

Roper regarded Coops in silence for a while. His eyes narrowed. 'Where are you *from* Coops?'

'Coota,' said Coops with pride. 'Coops from Coota, that's me.' She thumbed the brim of an imaginary hat.

Roper was nonplussed.

'Cootamundra, you know, in the Riverina. Best grazing country in New South Wales,' explained Coops.

Roper shook his head and turned to Sue. 'So we think they would be open to a cloud-based security solution like ours?'

'Hard to say,' said Sue. 'They're probably considering it but, as we all know, the switch from a firewall solution to a cloud-based security system is always difficult at the best of times. It's difficult from a technology point-of-view but it's even more difficult from a cultural point-of-view. Many institutions still don't trust cloud-based security like ours, mainly because they don't understand it.'

'Like trying to get Nan to bin her passbook and bank online,' offered Coops.

'And, given Wentworth's size as an institution, their arrangements would be firmly embedded,' said Sue. 'The scope of the transition would scare them into indecision.'

'Who's their current provider?' asked Roper.

'CBIS,' said Coops. 'They have offices and network centres within Wentworth. The two companies are joined at the hip.'

'Makes sense,' said Roper. 'CBIS are the market leader. So we're in the same old fight we're always in: change a company's mindset from a firewall solution to a solution in the cloud.'

'And demonstrate that we do cloud better than anyone else,' said Sue. She realised this was an immense undertaking. Wentworth was a colossal prospect, CBIS was a colossal competitor and Tesico was still a small player in cybersecurity.

'What does your contact at Wentworth say?' asked Roper.

'We haven't spoken yet. I've put in a call,' said Sue.

'So you're nowhere?' said Roper, exasperated.

'I don't think so,' replied Sue. 'He approached me at the ACSC conference in Perth, right after I'd spoken about exactly these issues. He seemed *interested*.'

'Then call him. Call him again, and again and again, until you get hold of him,' said Roper. 'I want this. I want this office on the map. And Wentworth will do just that. I need you to give this everything Novak.'

'You realise I'm technically still on sick leave?' said Sue, holding up one of her elbow crutches. 'And I begin physio in a week.'

Roper frowned. 'Then you'll just have to figure out your priorities. Opportunities like Wentworth don't grow on trees.'

Sue was taken aback. 'Well, the best option would be if Coops assists me then. She's already done a lot of the research...'

'But as you pointed out,' began Roper, 'she's no salesperson, she's in a support role, in enablement and marketing.'

'And as *you* pointed out,' replied Coops with a touch of bravado, 'everyone here is in the job of selling the product.'

Roper sat back in his chair, smiling. 'Very well,' he said.

* * *

The Tesico sales office was a humble affair on a single floor of a building on Kent Street. The majority of the salesforce worked at desks in the partitioned, open-plan interior. The only office belonged to the National Sales Manager—now Roper—but there was a breakout room for discussions or important calls, and there was a larger meeting room for presentations and for use as a war-room.

Sue hobbled on crutches towards her desk, stopping to chat on her way. Many of her co-workers were delighted to see her back.

Her desk was piled with mail. She leafed through the envelopes, opening some and promptly discarding others straight into the wastebasket. She soon came across a package delivered by courier. It was heavy, not paperwork but something else. Curious, Sue ripped the package open. Inside she found a deck of what looked like oversized playing cards, except these were playing cards unlike any she'd ever seen. She saw illustrations of champions, messengers and mercenaries. Each had a description on the back.

There was something else inside the package: a black, oblong box. An external hard-drive.

Then she flipped the packaging over to check the sender's name and address.

It was from Fiona Churchill.

6. The Salesperson's Journal

Sue made it home while it was still light. The pain was creeping back and she needed to be alone. She also wanted to take a closer look at the hard-drive she knew came from Doug via Fiona.

Sue's rented apartment was on the second floor of a building in Potts Point. It didn't have harbour views as such, but you could glimpse the water as far as Cremorne between the buildings opposite. During the day you could sometimes see a flash of green and gold as the Manly Ferry sailed past. The apartment was small but the building was quiet. Best of all, a sliding glass door opened onto a sun-drenched, north-facing balcony. It was here that Sue would while away her Sunday mornings with the *Weekend Financial Review* and a pot of coffee.

Sue removed her makeup and took a shower. In her bathroom mirror she studied the palette of dark colours that formed the bruise on her cheek. Mercifully the swelling had subsided and the white of her eye was no longer crimson. She struggled into a bathrobe, poured herself a glass of Yarra Valley Prosecco and seated herself at her modest dining table. Then she turned on her laptop.

Opening her bag, Sue pulled out the strange playing cards and the external hard-drive. She placed them both on the table. She wondered what the purpose of the cards might be but guessed the answer lay somewhere on the hard-drive. She plugged the drive into her laptop and navigated to its contents. Inside she found a single file titled *EDVANCE*. Sue let out a long breath. She double-clicked and a lengthy document opened before her.

> *For many years now, I've struggled with a doubt. Our profession seems to have taken a wrong turn somewhere. A wrong turn that I worry may lead us to obsolescence. Bit-by-bit our usefulness as salespeople is being eroded. Our customers have access to more information than ever before. They have their own procurement teams and purchasing consultants. They arrive at their own solutions without our help. Our ability to advise, to help them to the right answers is in jeopardy. More and more, we enter their decision-making process too late, and it's our own fault. We rely on outdated tactics and strategies to coerce them into a solution that serves us, not them as customers. We've lost sight of their needs and it angers them. So we are invited, late to the table, as mere providers; as negotiators to be bargained and haggled with. Our conversations are less about business solutions and more about fulfilment.*
>
> *Perhaps the image of our past, of hawkers, tub-thumpers and door-knockers, haunts us still. Business-to-business selling has evolved. We offer increasingly complex solutions for increasingly complex applications, yet I still see a degree of distrust among prospects. They prefer to do without us, convinced that no-one knows what they need better than themselves. They fear our intervention will only shake this conviction and trick them into a solution they don't want. We've done this to ourselves.*

> *I am proud to call myself a salesperson. I always have, because I've seen the positive change I can bring about. I've seen the interests and fortunes of my customers soar, and they've seen it too. I've always thought that my career, my profession, stood on safe ground. But there are tremors in this industry. And now, I see the cracks appearing underfoot.*
>
> *It's taken me years but I can now see a way forward. This vision has coalesced into a theory that I've now proved to work. This book, this journal (call it what you want) outlines a new methodology, a new approach to this business we call sales. It's a way we can gain early involvement and exert positive influence right from the start of the Buyer's Journey. It will also help us drive consensus towards a sale.*
>
> *But method and theory are nothing without a plan, a map, a guide to follow. So I have placed this methodology within a framework, a structure, a simple step-by-step process for the salesperson to follow.*
>
> *I call this process EDVANCE.*

Sue gave a long sigh. So this was Doug's new approach to sales, to business-to-business selling? This was what helped him win WestInvest. Sue took a sip of Prosecco and continued reading.

> *As salespeople we are taught to focus and rely on the Sales Process. This, we have come to believe, is the correct path to a sale. Yet it ignores the simple truth that buyers have their own process too: the Buyer's Journey. The reason we come so late into the process is that the Buyer's Journey and the Sales Process do not align. This is why so many of us are forced into transactional sales roles, while others react by falling back on outmoded sales tactics, creating discord and distrust. And so the cycle becomes self-perpetuating.*

The key to breaking this cycle is to align the Sales Process with the Buyer's Journey. To do this, we must understand our customers. We must focus on their process, not our own.

The solution is to ENGAGE early. As early as possible. And that's the first step in the EDVANCE process:

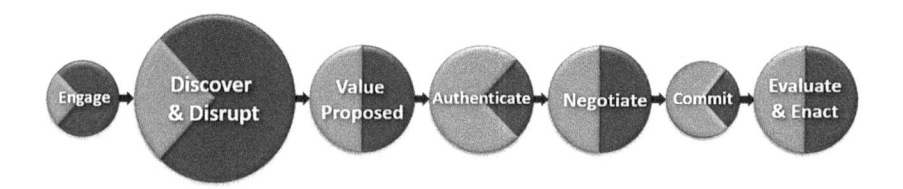

E - ENGAGE
D - DISCOVER AND DISRUPT
V - VALUE PROPOSED
A - AUTHENTICATE
N - NEGOTIATE
C - COMMIT
E - EVALUATE AND ENACT

Sue sat back. What followed in Doug's book was a whole section dedicated to the first part of the EDVANCE process, the ENGAGE part. She wasn't ready to read on, not yet. There was so much to take in already. The introduction to Doug's book rang true for her. She'd seen the problems in many of the situations she'd faced herself. But Doug had figured a way around them.

Sue jumped as her phone buzzed on the table beside her. She picked it up to discover a new text message. As she opened it her heart started to pound. It was from Raf Singh. It read: *Call me tomorrow. Lunchtime.*

A dull ache had worked its way into the back of her eye-sockets. The sky was now dark outside and she was tired and sore. But this,

this text from Raf Singh, and the discovery of Doug's book made her buoyant. Sue transferred the contents of Doug's hard-drive onto her laptop, then closed it down. She was determined to end the day on a positive note.

Her phone rang on the table, loudly. It was Coops.

'Hi Coops, everything okay?'

'Not really,' said Coops. 'You won't want to hear this but—WestInvest are looking iffy.'

'Iffy? Why, what's happened?'

'Dunno. They're just talking about pulling out. They want to talk to you in person—tomorrow.'

'Sure,' said Sue. As she hung up, her headache went up a notch.

This book comes with free access to an
online reference companion.

By scanning the QR Code or by navigating to
edvance.sale/recap/intro/ now, you will gain a deeper
understanding of the EDVANCE process and the methodology
applied by the characters in the story, including:

- An introduction to EDVANCE
- Aligning the Buyer's Journey and Sales Process
- Applying these methods in your own business

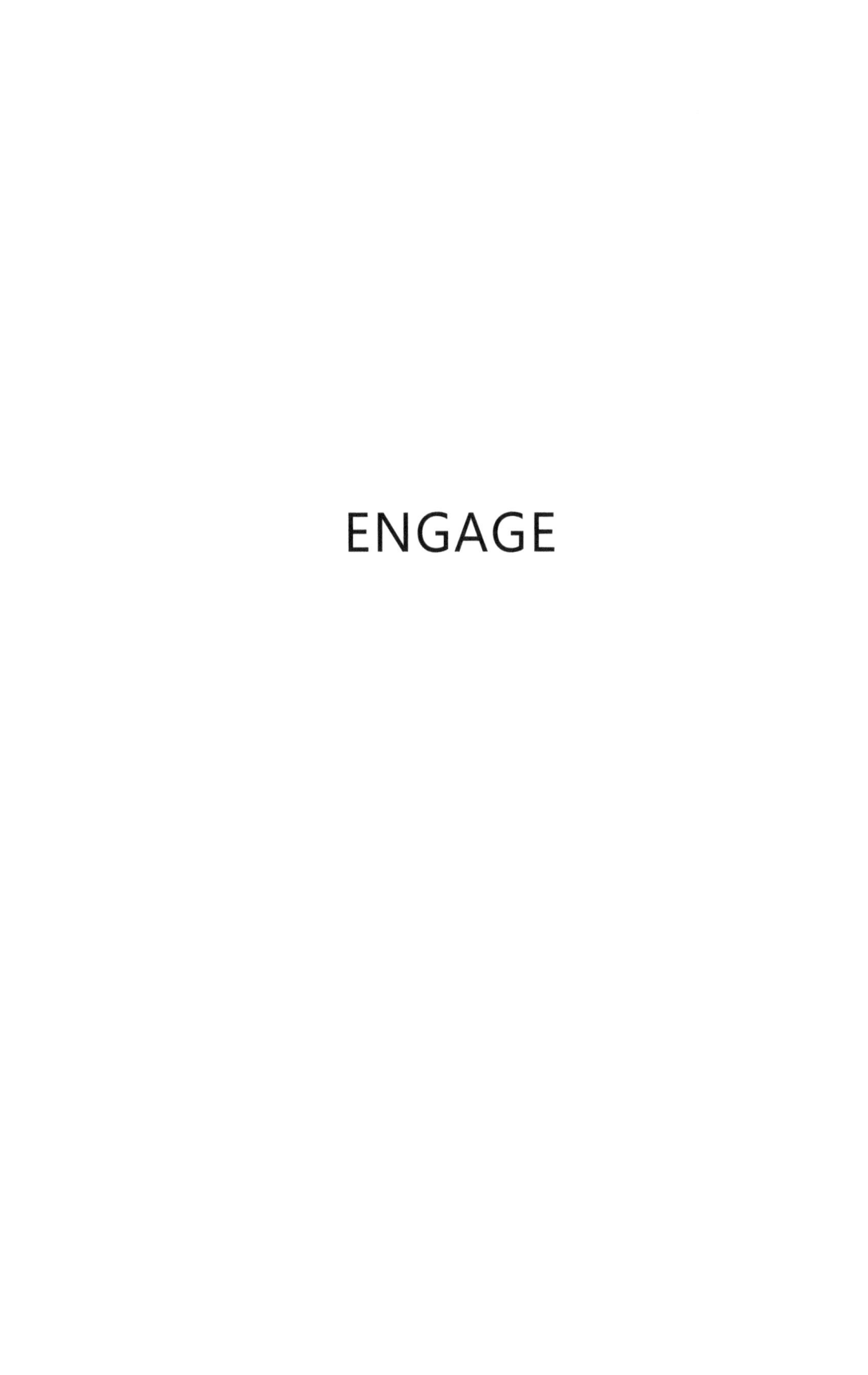

ENGAGE

ENGAGE

7. The Unseen Mentor

Sue got to the office as early as she could. She'd been for a routine check-up and X-rays for her leg and ankle.

It still wasn't early enough for Roper.

'Glad you could put in an appearance,' said Roper through the open door of his office as Sue swung past on her elbow crutches. He didn't look up from his laptop. Doug had chosen that office because it had a view. Sue guessed Roper liked it because it let him keep an eye on everyone. He was a timekeeper, a human punch-clock. Sue thought to remind him once again that she was still on sick leave but sensed it wouldn't appeal to his compassion.

Coops heard the comment and rolled her eyes. She followed Sue to her own desk and the two women hid behind the partition.

'Does he know anything about WestInvest?' asked Sue.

'Maybe, probably. It's his sale now, so I guess they would have told him,' said Coops.

'Then why do they want to talk to me?'

Coops shrugged and handed Sue a sheet of paper with a name and contact for WestInvest. Sue knew the name and thought back to the hotel in Perth. It was the same man who had shaken hands with Doug. Sue put her landline on speaker for Coops's benefit and

37

reduced the volume so that no-one else could eavesdrop. Coops sat down to listen.

'Good morning, this is Sue Novak from Tesico,' said Sue as the call went through.

'Hi Sue, thanks for calling.'

Sue remembered the fruit basket back in the hospital. 'Thanks for the card and the fruit,' she said.

'Glad you got it. We heard you were back at work. How's the recovery going?'

'Slowly,' admitted Sue. 'But I can get about. I can work at least.'

'That's good,' came the reply. 'We were all so sad to hear about Doug. Such a terrible loss.'

'Thanks,' said Sue. Her voice quavered slightly. 'We miss him too.'

'But we're all so happy to know you're going to pull through.'

'Thanks,' said Sue. She wiped the corner of her eye with the back of her hand. 'How can I help?'

There was a pause. 'It's delicate. I wanted to talk to you because—well, you were involved when Doug was advising us.'

'Yes?'

'It's no secret to say that we trusted him, Sue. Immensely. You too. We felt you understood our issues, the direction in which we want our business to move and you were working to that end. And when we heard your address at the ACSC, we knew Tesico was the right fit for us.'

Sue listened. She sensed there was a *but* coming.

'It's just that, there seems to be a change of heart at Tesico.'

'In what way?' asked Sue.

'Doug was very clear with us about every stage in which the Tesico solution was to be deployed. He set out objectives and timeframes right the way through. And he promised us that once the Tesico security system was in place, there would be help, that there would be full change management support. He even had a name for this support phase. He called it *enactment...*'

ENGAGE

Sue thought for a moment. The term was familiar. Then she remembered, it was in Doug's journal. It was the last step in the EDVANCE process: *enact*.

'You see Sue, the installation of the technology and functional training is only part of the process for us. Our people need to know how to apply it and how we need to change. We need to understand what it can do, how the data it provides can improve our business, how we should redesign our processes. We need to know how it will affect our customers and what experiences you can share to help us in this. The human side of this change is more important to us than the mere technical aspects. We're in the service industry, Sue. We need training for all our people, we need product fine-tuning and marketing material to educate our customers...'

'And what, this support is no longer being offered?' guessed Sue.

'No, other than basic training it's been withdrawn by Tesico. Change management was agreed to upfront. Doug saw this as an important step, as we do. It was on the Heads of Agreement and now it's been retracted. We feel cheated and we feel our time has been wasted.'

Sue thought for a moment. This all sounded like Roper's doing. 'And what if I can get change management support back for you? Are you still happy to proceed with Tesico?'

'Yes,' came the reply. 'Yes we are, but if not, then we'll have to begin again. There are other suppliers out there who can provide a cloud-based security system and support it properly. We don't want to go through the whole procurement process again, but we'll be forced to if Tesico doesn't meet us on this and honour the original agreement.'

Sue shot a concerned glance at Coops. 'I'm sorry to hear this. I promise to do everything I can to get the change management you need...'

'Thanks Sue. I knew you'd help us.'

The phone rang off.

Sue sat back in her chair.

'Holy shit,' said Coops.

Sue rummaged in her bag and pulled out her laptop. She fired it up, intending to check the customer relationship management database on the Tesico network. 'Is there anything in the CRM about this? About change management support being dropped?'

Coops shook her head. 'Not a skerrick.'

Sue looked at Coops in disbelief. 'This is Roper, isn't it? Why would he deliberately scuttle the WestInvest deal?'

'Buggered if I know,' said Coops. 'You gonna have a word with him? Tell him to pull his head in?'

'I guess I'll have to,' said Sue.

'About time someone did,' said Coops.

* * *

'You spoke to WestInvest?' exclaimed Roper. 'Behind my back?'

'Not behind your back,' explained Sue. She was standing in Roper's office, leaning on her elbow crutches. Roper had not invited her to sit and she didn't particularly want to. 'They asked to speak with me. I know them from when I was working with Doug. They just wanted a sympathetic ear...'

'They are *not* your prospect Novak. What part of this don't you understand? This was made very clear. Your only job is to concentrate on Wentworth.'

'But is it true?'

Roper glared at Sue.

'Is it true that the change management support that was promised to WestInvest is now off the table? Did you tell them that?' pressed Sue.

'Yes, I did!' Roper began. 'But that's none of your business.' He began to thump his chest. 'My client, my call, my decision.' He aimed a blunt finger at Sue. 'Not yours!'

'But why for heaven's...'

'You're going to have to understand some things Novak,'

interrupted Roper. 'I have a job to do here and you're interfering. I do not want you speaking with WestInvest again.'

Sue felt lost.

'Are we clear?' asked Roper.

Sue nodded, reluctantly.

'This is a small office, in a small market, making small returns. Change management is not our area of expertise. I've gone through the figures and we can't make a good margin from it. We're not bloody wet-nurses. We can't afford the time or the resource.' Roper pointed to the office outside his door. 'Take a look, how many people do we have? We're struggling to turn a profit as it is, we're struggling to make software sales, and that's our job. And guess what happens when I stop salespeople from *selling*, and commit them to unnecessary, time-consuming, wild goose chases like change management?'

Sue remained silent.

'We don't sell anything! That's what happens,' said Roper. 'There's only one path to success for this office and it's all about efficiency. From now on, everyone will stick to their job descriptions. Nothing extra-curricular. No bundling, no *all-in-one* solutions that lump software and change management together. You will flog the product and move on. The faster, the better.'

'But they need our help,' said Sue, quietly.

'I don't *care* about WestInvest!' said Roper. 'I care about *us*, this office, *Tesico*. I care about our bottom line. That's all I care about.'

Sue was suddenly reminded of one of the passages she'd read in Doug's journal: *We rely on outdated tactics and strategies to coerce them into a solution that serves us, not them as customers. We've lost sight of their needs...*

'I'll set things straight with WestInvest,' said Roper 'I'll explain we don't have the resource. I'll give them some names of intermediaries and consultants who can help.'

Sue considered this. Sure, there were independent operators who specialised in change management, but they didn't know their way around the Tesico product or WestInvest's infrastructure. And they certainly didn't have the kind of relationship Doug had taken so long to build.

Roper stared Sue straight in the eye while speaking. 'If that makes them happy, fine. If it doesn't, then good riddance.'

Sue manoeuvred her crutches to leave.

'And Novak...' said Roper, returning his attention to his laptop screen.

Sue turned, with difficulty, to face him again. 'Yes?'

'Make sure you're here Friday afternoon,' said Roper, his eyes not leaving his screen. 'And every Friday until further notice. I have a weekly conference call with Michelle in Singapore and I want you in it. I want progress on Wentworth.'

Sue nodded and left.

* * *

'Will he change his mind?' asked Coops over the top of Sue's partition.

Sue shook her head.

'WestInvest will spit chips...' said Coops.

Sue fumed. 'He's going to give them some names of change management specialists who could help.'

'So we won't be partnering with anyone?'

'No. It'll be a separate arrangement.'

'So bang goes any kind of team approach?'

'Yes.'

'And WestInvest will have to stump up more cash?'

'I guess they will.'

Coops whistled. 'Then they'll walk.'

Sue gave a grim nod. Then she glanced at her wristwatch. 'Do you want to hear some good news though?'

'Sure.'

Sue reached for her phone and dialled a number. She motioned to Coops to remain quiet by placing a forefinger to her lips. Sue frowned as the call went to voicemail. She left a message: 'Hi Raf, this is Sue Novak. I got your text. It's lunchtime—I'll try you later.'

Coops cocked an eyebrow.

'That was the Wentworth guy I met in Perth, the one we saw on TV, remember?'

'Fair dinkum?' exclaimed Coops. 'Can he open the door to Wentworth?'

'Too early to tell. I haven't spoken with him yet. We're still playing phone tag.'

Coops rounded the partition to sit beside Sue.

'And take a look at this,' said Sue, pointing to her laptop screen.

'What am I looking at?'

'Remember how I said Doug was writing something, a record of his methods?' said Sue.

'Yeah?'

'Well, this is it.'

'So,' asked Coops, 'any good?'

'It's great,' said Sue. 'Doug developed a whole new way of looking at sales. He called it a new methodology. And to put this method into action he also created a process to follow, a way to make sense of it all. He called this process EDVANCE. I've only just begun reading about it.'

Coops wheeled her chair closer. 'C'mon then, show us.' She nodded in the direction of Roper's office. 'If the boss chucks a hissy, we can tell him we're working on Wentworth.'

Sue clicked open the EDVANCE file.

> *E is for ENGAGE.*
>
> *Our profession has changed over the years from the image of the snake-oil salesperson to a career chosen by highly educated individuals who deliver sustainable solutions to their customers. The way buyers buy has changed too. Today they have more and more access to*

information about products and services that may suit their needs—and the people who supply them. That's why being known, trusted and respected as a salesperson is more critical than ever. And there are a multitude of new tools to help you do this. Becoming adept with these tools can be your greatest strength.

Broadly, the engagement step is about building your personal brand. It's about building a level of trust among the target customers you hope to convert to buyers and then engaging with them successfully. Building a strong personal brand establishes credibility and showcases your expertise. It gives you the opportunity to become a thought leader and helps set you apart from your competitors. Most of all, it helps connect you with your ideal customer.

The engagement step begins early in the buying process. The earlier the better. As far as the buyer is concerned, they are in the 'Business as Usual' stage and are unlikely to be aware of a problem at all. This is where you begin to build your personal brand.

When external forces (such as a trigger event) cause a buyer to become aware of a problem, they will enter the 'Status Quo Challenged' stage of the Buyer's Journey. If you've built your profile correctly and have nurtured a degree of trust, then the buyer will understand you already have a viewpoint on their issue and will be receptive to meeting you.

This is the process step I call 'engagement'.

But how do you build trust? How do you build your profile? There are many ways, and social media is one of the best places to begin.

Used correctly as a platform, social media can set you apart. Differentiation is the key here. Research other salespeople, your competitors, on social media and see how they're positioning themselves. Then try to find a different approach. Think 'what do I want to stand for?' And 'what is my unique promise of value?' Then develop a series of viewpoints around this approach supported by unique insight. Take a position and be consistent. This is how you'll be seen by your potential customers.

Once you've decided on a stance, everything you say, do or write should re-affirm this stance. Use your viewpoints as starting points for articles. Get known for them. Don't be frightened of being controversial. Challenge the status quo. That way, when the status quo changes for your potential customers, you'll be there to help them.

If you decide to post articles you've written, go for quality over quantity. Everyone hates a 'blaster'. Be more of a thoughtful curator. If you've built your profile well and your viewpoint is both clear and meaningful you will be seen as a voice of reason, a 'sense-maker', able to decipher and decode the tsunami of information that drowns potential buyers.

Make sure you monitor trends and be quick to comment if the situation presents an opportunity. This is known as 'trigger event monitoring'.

Social media can also help you find customers because it can be used to identify industry and market trends that impact specific business sectors and the companies that work in these sectors. It pays to build a list of these players and to understand how changes may help them move along the Buyer's Journey.

Once you've built a profile on social media, this will be your 'home turf'. From here you can connect with prospects. A strong profile here will open up other avenues too. You will be a sought-after commentator. Speaking opportunities, industry publications and the general media may follow.

Coops stared at the screen. 'So, it's all about us, the salespeople, not the company, not Tesico?'

'It's about building your own personal brand,' said Sue.

Coops looked at Sue. 'So, relying on the marketing people to do all the blogging, the articles and the outreach programs isn't the way to go?'

'They'll help position the company, they help position Tesico. But the customer doesn't buy from a marketing department, that's what Doug is saying here—customers buy from us. People buy from people.'

Coops was thinking. 'So, if I want a sales job, I should start building my personal brand?'

Sue nodded. 'Now I see what Doug was doing when he encouraged me to write all those posts about cybercriminals leading the cybersecurity industry.'

'He was getting you to challenge the status quo...'

'And,' said Sue, 'it led to that speaking gig at the ACSC.'

'And that led to WestInvest...'

'And it might help us engage with Wentworth,' said Sue.

Sue's phone suddenly buzzed. She picked it up and swiped the screen. 'It's a text... from Raf Singh. Nine-thirty tonight, Cordelia's, Surry Hills.'

'Congratulations,' Coops smiled. 'You know that mentor you said you wanted?'

'Yes?' said Sue.

Coops nodded towards the laptop screen. 'I reckon he's still here,' she said.

ENGAGE

8. Accomplice

Cordelia's was housed in a sandstone terrace on Bay Street in Surry Hills. It was intimate, favoured by young, inner-city couples at the end of their day as an easy alternative to their apartment kitchens. The cuisine was simple, bordering on rustic, with a good dash of Mediterranean inspiration. It was also a good place to talk business if you didn't want to be recognised. Sue scanned the terrace at the back of the restaurant and the main seating area indoors. There was also a quieter room upstairs where Cordelia's channelled their overflow of patrons on busy nights. This is where Sue found Raf Singh.

Raf leapt to his feet with a look of horror when he saw Sue hobble to the top of the stairs on her crutches. 'I'm so sorry...' he apologised as he rushed to help her. 'I had no idea you were injured.' He helped Sue into a chair. 'If I'd known...'

'It's fine, it's fine,' said Sue.

Raf sat. 'I heard about Mister Churchill,' he said. 'My sympathies.'

'Thank you.'

'Were you involved in the same accident?' asked Raf.

'Yes.'

'I didn't realise, I'm sorry...'

'Please, don't apologise.'

'Are you okay to continue with this?'

'Sure,' said Sue. She wasn't being entirely truthful. The day had been long and even the painkillers didn't cut it at this late hour. She settled into her seat and studied the man opposite. He was slim, neat and well-dressed but there was a creased, worn-out look to him. He looked gaunt, paler than she remembered.

'I apologise for not getting back to you sooner Miss Novak, and—and for meeting so late, I hope I haven't inconvenienced you.'

Sue smiled. Again she heard the genteel chime of his Oxbridge accent. He'd been educated in the UK for sure. Perhaps that's why he apologised so much.

'Please, it's Sue.'

Raf smiled. He summoned a waiter. 'Something to drink Sue?' he asked her.

'Prosecco, please.'

Raf ordered for both of them and the waiter swept quietly away.

'I enjoyed your speech at the ACSC,' he began, 'very much.'

'Thanks.'

'I've also read some of your articles and posts.'

'I'm flattered, but there's only a few out there at the moment,' Sue confessed.

'I believe you understand the current situation more clearly than most,' said Raf.

'Thanks.'

'I also admire the fact you're always so—impartial.' He smiled. 'You focus on the trends, on the landscape—not your own product.'

'That's important to you?' asked Sue.

'It makes me feel I can talk to you...'

Sue waited, as Doug had taught her. This was leading somewhere and she didn't want to interrupt.

Raf continued. 'Your view is that cybercrime, in terms of

innovation, is way ahead of cybersecurity. I agree with that. Companies sit inside their fortresses, believing themselves to be safe while the criminals are tunnelling under the walls, picking the locks, and chipping holes in the defences. By the time anyone learns of an attack, the defences have already failed, the data is looted and the damage is done. It's a never-ending siege. And the only recourse is to rebuild the walls or fit a bigger lock. Then wait for the next attack—while the hackers figure out which vulnerability to exploit next.'

Sue knew he was describing the situation at Wentworth. He just wasn't admitting it.

The waiter arrived with the drinks. Raf took a sip and waited until they were alone again. 'What do you know of the cyberattack on Wentworth?'

'I know that your customers' data is safe for now and that no core systems were compromised, I know it was malware…' said Sue, repeating what she, and everyone, already knew from the media coverage. 'I'm guessing,' she now began to theorise, 'the malware was delivered behind your firewall by an employee's infected laptop. I'm guessing you've been working around the clock to patch the system and assess the damage, that's why we're meeting so late, isn't it?' Sue remembered the advice of Coops's contact at the ACSC: 'I also think the attack cost Wentworth far more than you're publicly admitting. I think you're going to get attacked again. And I think you know it.'

Raf blinked. Sue looked at his haggard face and knew she was right.

There was a long silence before Raf responded. 'As I said Miss Novak—I mean, Sue—you understand the situation more clearly than most.' He leaned towards her. 'So, if you were in my shoes, tell me—what would you do?'

Sue knew she had to be careful. Although Raf had probably researched the Tesico product thoroughly, she knew the last thing he'd want was a sales pitch. He respected her impartiality, he'd said that.

We've lost sight of their needs...

Sue remembered the words from Doug's journal. She remembered Doug never mentioned the Tesico name up front, that it began with the customer, not the product. He had also mentioned the importance of finding *a champion*, someone who had the power to drive real change.

Sue studied Raf. He was an IT manager, not Chief Information Officer. He was a few levels below the real power within Wentworth and so, by definition, no champion. So why were they talking? What did he really want?

'What would I do?' she began, 'I'd find someone outside Wentworth, an industry commentator who could help take you on a *Journey of Discovery.*' She was pulling out terms she'd heard Doug use. She understood them in principle, but not fully. Not yet. She needed more time with Doug's journal. 'Someone who can take you deep down the hole, and uncover all those things about your business that you never, ever considered. Then, when you have a single, clear idea of what you *need*, not what you *want*, that same someone can lead you out into the daylight and up the hill towards a solution.'

'It would have to be someone who understood the cybersecurity landscape...' mused Raf. 'Someone with credentials in the industry.'

'Exactly,' said Sue. 'Someone say, who'd spoken at the ACSC—someone *impartial.*' Sue loaded the last word with emphasis.

Raf smiled. 'Are you suggesting you're the right person for the job?'

'Absolutely,' said Sue.

Raf nodded. 'I believe you might be. So where do we start?'

'Well,' said Sue. 'It all begins with me sending you a discussion document tomorrow—an outline for the way forward.'

'Very good,' said Raf, 'but please let's keep this between ourselves for now. We never had this meeting, did we?'

'Of course not.' Sue reached for her glass of Prosecco. 'But tell me, what do you hope to gain by all this? What is it Raf Singh really wants?'

Raf's eyes met Sue's but he looked away as he spoke. 'Change,' he said.

Sue reflected, watching him from the rim of her glass. She thought: *but that's not all, is it?*

This book comes with free access to an
online reference companion.

By scanning the QR code or by navigating to
edvance.sale/recap/engage1/ now, you will gain a deeper
understanding of the EDVANCE process and the methodology
applied by the characters in the preceding two chapters, including:

- Challenging the Status Quo
- Trigger Event Monitoring
- Domain Expertise
- Applying these methods in your own business

9. Hello and Goodbye

After a short and fitful sleep, Sue awoke with a throbbing in her leg. Although her ribs didn't hurt too much when she was up and about, they hurt like hell when she was lying down. She looked at the alarm clock on her bedside table and groaned. It was just after 4 am.

Sue reached for a glass of water and her painkillers. Swallowing a few, she lay back on the pillow.

She had dreamt of Doug. That they were driving along Botany Road through the grey sheets of rain. Sue was asking Doug about Wentworth. How should she begin the next phase of EDVANCE? Was Raf really on her side? What does *Discover and Disrupt* mean? How would she recognise her champion? She pleaded for help but Doug just stared at the rain ahead.

Waking to the memory of his loss all over again was more painful than her ribs or her throbbing leg.

How *would* she begin with Raf? She had no idea what her discussion document should look like. In her mind she'd already written it twenty different ways. What would Doug have done? What would he have told her to do?

Sue decided to find out. She wouldn't sleep now anyway.

She rolled onto her side with a moan and swung her legs to the floor. With the help of her arm she pushed herself to a sitting position. She'd discovered it was far less painful to get up this way than attempt sitting up using only the muscles in her abdomen.

Her laptop was already on the dining table. She turned it on and began the next section in Doug's journal.

> *D is for DISCOVER and DISRUPT.*
>
> *Of all the process steps in EDVANCE, this is perhaps the most important. It's also where you'll spend most of your time. It's the step which marries with 'Investigate' in the Buyer's Journey.*
>
> *The purpose of discovery is to help the customer see their own challenges and associated implications; to define their deep-seated and often unidentified needs. This takes their focus away from the solution they think they want to the solution they never knew they needed.*
>
> *The disruption component of this step is not negative. It refers to the process of shaking the customer's predisposed thinking in order to help them see other solutions. In this light, the disruption is positive.*
>
> *Through the discover and disrupt components of this step you will help expose the current paradigm of thinking of each stakeholder in your customer's organisation. By taking each of them on a Journey of Discovery, you can help them to a new paradigm. The reasons for this change in paradigm must be presented in a way to help the customer see the positive side of the risk/reward equation as it relates to them. Simply put, your buyer has developed a fixed train of thought. We must derail this train to get them on the right track.*
>
> *To begin this phase, you will need the help of a Change Agent. Please study the Stakeholder Archetype cards.*

ENGAGE

The cards. Sue reached for the deck of mysterious cards she'd left on the table and spread them out. There were six cards in total. On each of the cards a different character was depicted.

Sue returned to Doug's journal.

> *These cards will help you identify the roles of the stakeholders you will meet inside your customer's organisation. The cards will guide you in determining where you should concentrate your efforts, who has influence and who doesn't. They will help you in formulating the questions you need to ask and how you should approach each stakeholder.*
>
> *The three Change Agent archetypes are the CHAMPION, the SAGE and the INQUISITOR. These are the most influential of the archetypes as they have the power to drive consensus for your proposal within their organisation. They may hold this influence through position, authority or strength of personality.*
>
> *The CHAMPION is of particular significance as the only Change Agent with the practical know-how and resource to fully implement a proposal in the physical sense. They are often hands-on and project-oriented. This makes them especially valuable.*

Sue looked from her screen to the archetype cards. She picked up the Champion card and flipped it over. On the reverse, her eyes rested on the words: *Focuses on: getting the job done.*

Her eyes returned to the laptop screen. She continued to read.

> *Without the allegiance of at least one Change Agent, you are best to walk away. Your battle can never be won.*
>
> *Find a Change Agent. Better still, find your Champion.*

Sue sat back in her chair. Staring at the Champion card, she was coming to the conclusion that Raf was no Champion. He just didn't have the power. So which card was Raf? Where was he in Doug's deck of cards? She read on.

> The remaining three archetypes are ACCOMPLICE, MESSENGER and MERCENARY. These are classed as the Advocate archetypes. When positively disposed, the Advocate archetypes may seem extremely helpful and sympathetic. But you must exercise care and judgement. The inexperienced salesperson is often drawn to concentrate on these relationships. Advocates, however, lack the influence of the Change Agents to drive consensus. They can only assist you on a personal, rather than organisational, level.
>
> It must always be remembered that your relationship with any of the six stakeholders can be positive, negative, or neutral. And their disposition may change considerably throughout your relationship. For instance, a Champion who supports you will advance your cause, a negatively-disposed Champion will actively fight against you. Equally, never underestimate the power of an Advocate's negative influence. When positive, they may be powerless to drive consensus to your proposal, but when negatively disposed they are adept at sowing the seeds of discord and distrust within their organisation. In this way, their negative influence is more powerful than their positive influence. So take heed.
>
> As part of the EDVANCE process we will plot these archetypes on a 'Stakeholder Map' to monitor the shifts in relationship between yourself and each stakeholder. This map will provide useful insight on how consensus is being driven among the stakeholders.
>
> If your engagement strategy is successful, your first contact may come from any of the six Stakeholder Archetypes.

ENGAGE

> *Your first contact will likely have read your articles, visited your social media feeds and have found an affinity with something in your portfolio of viewpoints. You may have initiated this or they may have found your content through other means. This will lead them to remember you and develop a respect for your domain expertise and your personal brand. In many cases, it takes the external force of a Trigger Event to provoke contact.*

Sue thought of Raf; how her articles and her address at the ACSC had prompted him to make contact. So, if he wasn't powerful enough to be among the Change Agents, that meant he had to be an Advocate.

Sue studied the illustrations on the three Advocate cards. But which was Raf?

Sue picked up a notepad and pencil. Her mind began to spin with ideas for the discussion document she needed to write for Raf. She jotted down each one before returning to Doug's journal. She was focused now, alive with concentration.

> *If your first contact turns out to be a Change Agent, then congratulations, you may have a powerful ally. If, however, they are an Advocate, then you must encourage them to introduce you to a Change Agent, preferably a Champion.*
>
> *The Change Agent you find with the help of an Advocate may need convincing. Your Advocate can assist you in this. Supply your Advocates with the information and ideas they need to bring about an introduction to a Change Agent. Then be prepared to win the Change Agent over with your stories and viewpoints.*
>
> *You will recognise a Change Agent because, unlike Advocates, they will have the authority to introduce you to key decision makers. Their willingness to do this will*

indicate their acceptance of your cause. Change Agents are also tough customers, they will question your proposal rigorously. This is because the final decision (and responsibility) often lies with them.

Before your first meeting with a Change Agent, you must be well prepared. Put yourself in their shoes. What are they likely to be frightened by? What values do they protect? What could be their unspoken needs?

Don't forget the power of Storytelling throughout the Journey of Discovery. In these initial meetings, use stories that strengthen your connection to all parties. Connection stories include:

Your Personal Story. Tell your customer who you are, why you do what you do and what you believe. Don't paint yourself as a success story but tell them of your failures too, and what you learned from them. This will strengthen trust and understanding between you. It will also give you the opportunity to end with 'what about you?' Your prospect will likely tell you their own personal story. This will provide useful information for pinpointing their archetype and their disposition towards you.

Your Company Story. Tell them about the organisation you work for; how it came to be; how it grew and the difficulties it faced. Then turn the question to your customer's company. You'll learn much.

The Story of Key People in Your Organisation. This will help the prospect understand and relate to other members of your team they haven't met yet. It fosters their positive reception and helps your customer understand the size and scope of your company. It also prepares the way for your eventual handing-over of the project to other members of your team.

ENGAGE

Later, as your relationship with your prospect grows, you may introduce other stories. These should include Stories That Influence Change and Stories That Drive Consensus to Commit. Telling such stories during the Value Proposed, Authenticate and Negotiate steps of EDVANCE will help your prospect understand the value of your proposal. Of particular importance during this phase is the Success Story. This is a story that recounts the success of another of your customers. It is a way to prove your concept in action and is particularly useful during the Discover And Disrupt and Authenticate steps. Further, a well-told success story allows the buyer to experience being your client even before a final agreement is struck.

Begin Stakeholder-Mapping as early as you can. Plot each against two simple axes: their Influence and Strength of Relationship with you.

Begin a Competitive Analysis. Take a long, hard look at who you'll be up against. What's the best way to deal with them: offensively, defensively, or do you flank them?

Begin a Gap Discovery. Look at the customer's current state and try to uncover the gaps that prevent them from being where they want to be, or should be.

Through your interviews, help each stakeholder discover and clarify their unique situation: their challenges, problems and associated implications. Get them to verbalise their wants and needs. To do this, you must display all the inquisitiveness of a child who continually asks 'why?' Asking 'why' will disrupt the paradigm of their current view. It will peel back the superficial wants and beliefs to reveal the deep-seated needs and realisations. Strive to dig deeper and deeper to reveal the bedrock of these problems. Take your

59

customer down into the darkest labyrinths. Lead them deep into this hole.

When these deepest needs and realisations are evident, this will be their Discovery.

This Discovery is shared. In many ways, it will be your Discovery too.

Armed with this Discovery, you can now lead them back up into the light. Help each stakeholder see a new way of addressing the challenge or opportunity, and the value in doing so. Help them paint a picture of what the future could look like.

Now you will be leading them up the hill towards a solution. A solution of their own devising, yet a solution to which you can uniquely deliver. And to your next task: help the customer realise the value of implementing this new way of thinking.

Sue looked down at the sheet of paper underneath the point of her pencil. The paper was covered in a scrawl of notes. She closed Doug's journal on her laptop and looked up for the first time in hours. It was daylight outside.

From somewhere came a ringing noise. Lost in her thoughts, Sue was slow to react. It wasn't her phone. It was coming from her laptop. She hit the *accept* icon on her video chat app and a screen popped up. It took her a while to recognise that the face on the screen belonged to the WestInvest client she'd spoken to days before.

'Hi Sue,' he said. 'Sorry to call so early, but I wanted to catch you before you got to the office.'

'That's okay,' said Sue. 'I was working anyway.' Sue was mortified. She'd accepted his call as a video chat and realised she was still in her pyjamas and bathrobe. Without the camouflage of make-up her face would look a mess.

'Yes, I saw you were online and thought I'd take the opportunity,' he said, then paused for a while. He looked uncomfortable, unsure how to proceed. 'I wanted to call you because, well, I think we owe it to you personally. You've been a tremendous help and we don't want you to think that our decision reflects on you in any way.'

'Oh,' said Sue. This didn't sound good.

'We've decided to end our relationship with Tesico. We don't consider this a breach of contract because Tesico hasn't honoured the Heads of Agreement.'

'I see,' said Sue.

'You're the only one that knows this. I'll be calling Mister Roper shortly.'

'But didn't he share some suppliers with you—some change management specialists who could help?'

'Yes, he did.'

'And, was that not an option?' asked Sue.

'Not the way we see it.' There was a long pause. 'Sue, for a single contract price you agreed Tesico would take full responsibility for delivery. One approach, one contract, one team. Now Tesico is absolving itself of a great part of that responsibility and WestInvest needs to hire a separate supplier...'

'Then, did Mister Roper suggest any adjustment to our contract price?'

'No.'

'Well, if that's the issue, then I'm sure I can...'

'Please don't bother,' came the reply. 'It's gone beyond that.'

'How?'

'We were always wedded to the idea of a team approach. That's what Doug promised and that's what we still want. There's pressure from within the DMU and the wider C-Suite to go with CBIS. Have you heard of Brenda Huffington?'

'Yes,' said Sue, 'she's quite famous in our industry.'

'So I believe. Anyway, she's met directly with our CEO and that pretty much sealed the deal. Sue, this isn't the way I wanted to go. I honestly believe that your cloud-based solution would benefit us in the long run. But we have an urgent need and the CBIS solution is a tried-and-true product. They assure us it'll be future-proof too. They're already talking about next-gen firewall software. And CBIS has agreed to full change management, with support, training, everything.'

'I understand,' said Sue. 'I'm very sorry I couldn't solve this for you.'

'Thanks for trying, Sue. Goodbye.'

Sue hit the disconnect button and sat back in her chair.

Nearly eight months' worth of hard work down the toilet.

'Thanks Tony,' said Sue.

ENGAGE

You may now wish to download the Archetype Cards mentioned in the story for your phone, tablet or mobile device. Scan the QR Code or visit edvance.sale/archetypes/ now.

Having the cards on-hand will help you follow the story as the characters plot the stakeholders towards consensus. The cards and map are a valuable reference and an essential part of stakeholder mapping within the EDVANCE process.

ENGAGE

10. Sketching the Outlines

Once, Sue had loved sitting in this office. When it was Doug's office. It had been a place of discussion, respect, and shared ideas. She had learned so much in this room.

Now it was another man's office and Sue no longer recognised it.

'I don't understand,' said Sue. 'The WestInvest deal was worth a lot of money to us.'

'You're just not getting it, are you Novak?' returned Roper.

Sue sat in one of the small, hard chairs that faced Roper. She was uncomfortable, not because of her tiredness or pain, or even the chair itself. She was uncomfortable with the tone of the meeting.

'But you want to put Tesico Australia on the map, don't you? Wouldn't WestInvest have done that?'

'Not with change management as part of the bundle!' declared Roper. 'It would have offset any profit we'd make from the original deal.' He sighed, lolling in his chair, tilting the back of it at a precarious angle. 'Take it from me, I've been around far longer than you and I've seen what happens with customers like these. The after-sales part of the process becomes never-ending. What looks like a good deal for us up front just becomes a drawn-out loss.'

'But we just fobbed them off with a list of unknown suppliers—without changing our original fee,' pointed out Sue.

'They are *not* unknowns,' stated Roper, 'they're all perfectly capable outfits. And the fee was open for re-negotiation. The ball was in their court. Who knows, we *might* even have turned a profit. But they went elsewhere.'

'Because they wanted a team approach, a single deal, like the one Doug struck.'

'And it was a bad deal!' said Roper, a little too loudly. 'Yes, it all looked wonderful to start with, but they're a needy customer and you and Churchill were happy to go on some hand-holding exercise with them, skipping off through the flowers together, wasting time and money.'

'Show some respect,' said Sue, her ire rising.

He studied Sue through narrowed eyes. 'You need to move on, Novak.'

Sue wasn't sure whether he was referring to Doug or WestInvest. Perhaps he meant both.

'So tell me, where are we with Wentworth?' asked Roper after a time.

Sue was reticent. 'Okay I guess, I still haven't got a meeting with any of the decision-makers,' she said, 'but I'm working on it.'

'Then work on it, *quickly*,' said Roper. 'I have a meeting with Michelle this Friday and I want progress.'

'What if Wentworth want change management as part of our offer too?' asked Sue.

Roper's chair was now vertical. 'They must agree to change management from a separate supplier under a separate contract—not ours!' he growled. 'Don't you see? I'm trying to reduce Tesico's risk, our level of exposure. Any mistakes by a third-party supplier become our responsibility when it's our names on the contract!'

Sue thought to ask him whether he'd risk a deal the size of Wentworth on this basis but decided she'd gone far enough.

Roper began jabbing a thick forefinger into his desk. 'Wentworth must use their own consultants and this must be made clear upfront. I'm trusting you to explain that.'

* * *

'A document, what kind of document?' asked Coops, excited.

'A discussion document that will get us in front of Wentworth. Something that can start a dialogue.'

Sue was back at her own desk, debriefing Coops on her meeting with Raf Singh.

'Like an introduction to Tesico? Our history and success stories?' asked Coops.

Sue shook her head. 'No, it has to be about them—and their issues.'

'Do we know enough about the situation?' asked Coops.

'Perhaps not,' admitted Sue. 'But we can take a guess for now. We know that Wentworth's current system is a firewall that runs across their entire network. We know it's a CBIS installation and that CBIS has support staff embedded in Wentworth. We also know that it's been compromised and is likely to be hit again.'

'So there's panic?' asked Coops.

'Perhaps. But there's certainly dissatisfaction. That much was clear from Raf, and it's likely to be felt by other employees too.' Sue's brow creased. 'But we need to tread carefully with this Coops...'

'Oh?' said Coops. 'How come?'

'Well, for starters, my meeting with Raf was very hush-hush. I'm sure he's keen to look for alternative security arrangements but I bet there's a lot of support for CBIS inside Wentworth's walls.'

'So he's a bit of a rebel?'

'Not sure. There may be others in the company who think the same way. I'm just worried that we don't know who'll end up reading this document of ours,' said Sue.

'So we shouldn't take shots at CBIS?'

'Not at all,' said Sue, 'or at firewall systems in general. We have to be unbiased. As I said, we have to keep it about Wentworth, about their issues. The best next step would be to understand them more fully. That's what this discussion document has to work towards.'

'If we're going to get a handle on their problems, we're going to need to ask them a heap of questions, right?'

'That's what this initial document needs to outline,' said Sue, 'the questions we have for them.'

'Well,' said Coops, 'first we need to ask them to come clean on the attack. We're going to need to know all about it, how big a hit they took...'

'...and which parts of their business were affected,' said Sue.

'Yeah,' agreed Coops, 'which departments in particular.'

'That's right,' said Sue. 'Each department, each manager might have an entirely different take on the attack. It'd be good to know if everyone views the threat in the same way.'

Coops flipped open a notebook and began writing. 'So, we can start by asking to meet with the heads of the departments most affected.' She looked up. 'But will they be the real decision-makers, the people we really need to talk to about cybersecurity?'

'Not necessarily, we need to identify the real stakeholders too. I think the first thing to understand is how the bank handles big decisions like security. How do they decide? What's their formal decision-making criteria and their buying process? Who gets involved? Is the whole thing handled inside the C-Suite or beyond? Only then can we decide who we really need to talk to.'

Coops stopped scribbling and looked up. 'All good, and if your hunch is correct, there's going to be a bunch of different agendas.'

Sue smiled. 'You can bank on it. Once we know who the real stakeholders are, we need to figure out what their motivations might be.' Sue thought back to the section of Doug's journal she'd read earlier that day. 'You know, Doug was developing a really neat way to do this...' She dived into her laptop bag and surfaced with Doug's deck of cards. She spread them out on the desk.

ENGAGE

'What are *they*?' asked Coops. 'Tarot cards for salespeople?'

'No, Doug calls them *Stakeholder Archetypes*. They're for mapping, *people mapping*. They can help us understand the role of each stakeholder, the amount of power they hold and their relation to each other and to us. And we can monitor how those relationships change over time.' Sue placed a finger on the cards. 'Three of these archetypes are Change Agents. They're powerful, they can drive a project over the line. And the other three cards are Advocates. They don't have the power but they're a great source of information. And they can introduce us to a Change Agent if we get them onside.'

Coops picked up one of the cards and turned it over, studying the back.

Sue took a sheet of paper and began drawing a graph. She labelled the vertical axis *relationship* and the horizontal one *influence*. 'This is how Doug suggests we plot them.' Next, Sue drew a horizontal and vertical line through the centre of the graph, separating it into quadrants. She pointed to the uppermost quadrant on the right. 'This is where we want to move the most influential stakeholders—where they have the best relationship with us and have the influence to take our proposal on board.'

'Sure, but to have that amount of clout, they'd need to be Change Agents, right?'

'Correct,' said Sue, 'they're the ones with the most power to drive consensus. The Sage can inspire others with the potential of an idea, the Inquisitor will pull it to pieces to see if it really works, and the Champion...'

Find your Champion...

'The Champion,' continued Sue, remembering Doug's words, 'is the most powerful Change Agent of all, because they're more than just ideas people and drivers of consensus. The Champion also has the operational know-how to make an idea reality.'

Coops nodded, trying to take it all in. 'So, this Raf Singh fellah. What's he?'

'Well,' sighed Sue, 'he's only a second level IT Manager, so doesn't wield much in the way of influence...'

'So he's here,' said Coops, pointing to the bottom left quadrant of the stakeholder map, 'no relationship, no influence...'

'Yes, but I think we can foster that relationship, he's certainly open to it. He might not have the decision-making power of a Change Agent, but he may have the ear of one.'

'So you think he's an Advocate?'

'Exactly,' said Sue. She picked up the Accomplice card and placed it slightly below the centre of the map. 'I think this is him.'

'Accomplice?' queried Coops.

'Yes, I think he values relationships; he's a people-person, a networker. He's also social and probably well-liked. That's why Wentworth chose him as a spokesperson.'

'What if he's this guy?' asked Coops, pointing to the Mercenary card.

Sue shook her head. 'I don't think so. The Mercenary acts only in their own interests. I think Raf is bigger than that. He didn't talk about himself. He's deeply worried about Wentworth. He wants a solution, not for himself, but the bank.'

'And this discussion document we're going to prepare for him,' said Coops. 'You're hoping he'll share this with the right people inside Wentworth?'

'I'm hoping he'll share it with a Change Agent,' said Sue.

'Was there anything else in Doug's book that could help us?' asked Coops.

'Not specifically,' Sue admitted. 'But there are things we need to get started on. He mentions the need to run a *Gap Discovery* when we're clear on the issues. Doug explains it as a snapshot of where the customer is now, and where they could potentially be. The gap in the middle shows us the steps needed to get them there. The steps we need to help them make. He also mentions the need for a detailed Competitive Analysis.'

'*Our* competitors?'

'Yes,' said Sue. 'The other organisations we'll be up against and the comparative value of their offerings.'

'Like CBIS?' offered Coops.

'Not just CBIS but any other vendors they're likely to consider. It'll also help us decide on how we tackle each one. Whether we go for the jugular, put up a strong defence or try to outflank.'

'So this could be bigger than a simple two-horse race?'

'We have to assume so,' said Sue. 'If you were Wentworth, would you only look at one alternative?'

Coops nodded. 'Right, so we have to figure out who else they're talking to. We could take a punt, and a little digging might give us some clues. Leave that to me.' Coops flipped over to a fresh page in her notebook and continued scribbling. Then she faced Sue with a frown. 'Realistically Sue, will they ever walk away from CBIS? It's a huge ask.'

'Well, put it down as another question we need to ask,' said Sue. 'Whose decision is it to change the current security arrangement? Would they really make that call? What's the risk of *not* making that call?'

Coops wrote as Sue fired the questions they needed answering. One by one, the list of questions grew. Sue began writing them into a discussion document. She included an offer to sign non-disclosure agreements and, so the whole thing didn't seem like a long list of questions, she gave an overview of the *Journey of Discovery* and what it would do for Wentworth. It was late in the day by the time the document was ready. Sue was careful to send it to Raf Singh's personal email address, as he'd asked.

Sue and Coops were among the last to leave the Tesico Sydney office. Roper was long gone when Sue stopped beside Coops's desk on the way to the door.

'Fancy a drink at the Stockman?' offered Sue.

Coop's eyes were wide with delight. 'Too right!' she said. 'I'm dry as a chip.'

This book comes with free access to an
online reference companion.

By scanning the QR code or by navigating to
edvance.sale/recap/engage2/ now, you will gain a deeper
understanding of the EDVANCE process and the methodology
applied by the characters in the preceding chapter.

You'll also see the Stakeholder Map in action and how Sue and
Coops have plotted their single stakeholder so far.

11. A Question of Trust

Coops ran an idle finger around the rim of her glass of Bundaberg rum and Coke. Sue knew what it meant: Coops was thinking.

Sue surveyed the busy bar in the Stockman Hotel. The building was old with high, echoing ceilings that seemed to amplify the chatter. It was one of the first pubs to be built on the outskirts of the Haymarket area, close to the long-gone cattle-yards. Coops liked it because it owed its history to the cattlemen, graziers and grain merchants who'd drank there. It was a link to her own past, to her childhood on the farm in Cootamundra. But the stock-whips that had hung from its walls and the oil paintings of bullock-carts had long since disappeared. Now it was a slick city pub with mood lighting and a cocktail menu. Like Coops, it was something born of the country that had found its home in a modern city.

'It's got me stumped Sue,' said Coops at length.

'What has?'

Coops looked up. 'Doug's book. I mean, there's some great advice in it, and you're getting a lot out of it...'

Sue put down her glass of Prosecco. 'Yes?'

'It just seems to be taking us home the long way,' said Coops.

Sue was surprised. 'How's that?'

'We know a bit about the attack at Wentworth, right?' whispered Coops.

'Right,' confided Sue.

'And we've got a good idea the Tesico product can solve their problems, yeah?'

'Completely.'

'And we've got a good idea that Raf knows this, right?'

'Right,' said Sue, unsure where this was heading.

'Then why can't we just ask Raf to get us in front of one of these change agents and pitch the product straight to them?' said Coops. 'If Raf's behind us there's a good chance we can land this without going through all this discover and disrupt stuff. I mean, why bother with a *Journey of Discovery* at all? Why can't we just cut to the chase and close the deal fast?' Coops took a drink. 'And just think, that'd keep Roper off our backs too.'

Sue took a deep breath. 'This new process Doug was working on might take more time, but I've seen it in action. It works Coops. Pitching too hard and too fast can create distrust. It can ruin the relationship with the customer right from the start. And, in any case, one stakeholder's approval won't seal the deal. There might be many more. And there's probably a complicated political landscape inside Wentworth too—we'll need to spend time learning how to navigate it.' Sue took a drink before continuing. 'As Doug explains it, there's a huge difference between closing a deal and helping the customer realise the value for themselves. The best path to success is to help the customer discover the real issues, and the value of a new way, on their own. Then they'll lead themselves to Tesico. There won't even be a need to close. It's not a salesperson-customer relationship any more. Instead, it's a partnership.'

Coops nodded. 'But at the end of the day, we know the product we want them to buy, right? How do we stop them leading themselves someplace else?'

'Well that's always possible, but that's how trust works, right?'

said Sue. 'It's better to trust them to come to the same conclusion as us, rather than trying to force them. Can you see that?'

'Sure,' said Coops. 'And I guess the solution architecture might need to change anyhow?'

'That's right,' said Sue. 'We're not selling fruit and veg here. This isn't transactional selling, it's complex B2B and the way the product is applied will need to be adapted to Wentworth's needs. At this stage, no-one knows what that might look like. It's only through discovery that we'll find all that out.'

Coops appeared to understand now. She grinned, then hopped from her stool and stood, hands raised to theatrical effect.

'And now,' said Coops, 'here's an idea I've been cooking up.'

'Okay...' said Sue, intrigued.

'Now, if I'm going to be a great salesperson, like you and Doug...'

'Well I'm not...' began Sue.

'Hear me out,' interrupted Coops. 'If I'm going to be a great salesperson some day, then I need to get started on my *engagement strategy* quick smart...'

'Agreed!' said Sue, raising her glass in salute.

'Then what about this...' said Coops, excited. 'I begin a podcast, or a slot on the radio, in the Sunday morning business program—and I call it...' she made a big reveal in the air with her hands. 'Cybersecurity Round-Up with Coops Cooper!'

Sue nodded, processing.

'Get it? Round-up, you know, like a muster, a cattle drive—with yours truly.' Coops thumbed the brim of her imaginary hat once again and shifted her weight from foot to foot. If she'd been wearing jeans, her thumbs would have found the belt-loops. 'It'll be a regular rundown of all the news in cybersecurity country, all the innovations, the latest trends and threats, I can interview IT people and company owners and stuff!'

'I love it,' said Sue. 'It's very—*you*...' She studied Coops's beaming smile, the faint splash of freckles and her country-music-star good looks. 'You know, I reckon you may even be aiming a little low. A face like yours should be on TV.'

Coops was agog. 'You reckon?'

'Why not?'

'Oh, oh, what about...' Coops was practically hopping with excitement, '...a YouTube Channel?'

'Even better,' admitted Sue. 'I can picture it now.'

Coops was on a roll. She sat sideways on her bar-stool, then swivelled to face an imaginary camera, flicking her hair to dramatic effect. 'G'day, Coops Cooper here with the latest Cybersecurity Round-Up.'

Sue laughed.

Coops continued in her best anchorwoman style. 'This just in: eighty-three percent of companies cite firewall software as a principal hindrance to digital innovation.' She pointed to the imaginary camera. 'Is your company one of them?'

Sue was impressed. 'Is that true?'

'Sure is,' said Coops. 'Marketing has subscriptions to Nielsen, Roy Morgan and a bunch of others. So I get to trawl through them for all the latest research.'

'That's a great insight,' said Sue, 'we can use that with Wentworth.'

'There's plenty more where that came from,' said Coops. 'I figure on starting each podcast with a *disruptive* insight, something that'll get people talking...'

'You mean get people to comment, on the video-blog? Online?' asked Sue.

'Yep.'

'Coops, you're a bloody genius,' laughed Sue, clapping her hands.

'That's what me old dad always said!' Coops tucked her jaw into her chest, giving herself a double chin, and mimicked her father's gruff tones: 'Coops, you're a bloody genius, get yourself off to university, you're too bloody smart for the faaarm!'

Sue laughed again.

Sue's phone rang. She placed it to her ear. 'Hello... hello?' she said, unable to hear clearly above the reverberant noise of the bar. Sue reached for one of her crutches and signalled to Coops that she was fine. Alone, she hobbled into the street outside.

'Sue it's Raf.'

'Oh hi Raf.'

'Sounds like you're having fun.'

'Oh, just winding down after a long day,' said Sue.

'Thanks for the doco you sent over.'

'You're welcome. Hope everything makes sense?'

'Sure, it's great. I've even shared it with some colleagues—they're interested too.'

'Great.'

'How are you placed next Monday?'

'What time?'

'Say, ten am?'

'Should be fine,' said Sue.

'Good. There's someone I'd like you to meet.'

12. Dead in the Water

Shortly before 11 am on Friday morning Sue scrambled into a cab outside the Prince of Wales Private Hospital. The physiotherapy session had taken more out of her than she'd anticipated.

Switching on her phone, she saw a text from Coops: *Where the hell are you?*

As the cab joined the dense traffic heading for the city, Sue put in a call to Coops. 'What's up?' she asked.

'Oh Sue, it's Roper. He's—well, ropeable!'

'What about?'

'Said you need to be here for a call with Michelle Yim in Singapore. I tried calling but your phone must've been off.'

Sue looked at her watch. 'But Michelle isn't until this afternoon…'

'Michelle can't do this arvo. It's been brought forward.'

'How could I possibly know that? Did you tell him I was at physio?' asked Sue.

'Sure, but it didn't stop him from cracking the shits—just get here quick as you can. I think Michelle's standing by.'

Sue hung up and directed the driver through some short-cuts.

By the time Sue struggled into the Tesico office on her crutches, Roper was waiting to ambush her from the open door of his office.

'People have been waiting for you,' Roper remarked.

'Tony, I had physio this morning—I thought you knew.'

He beckoned her in with a dismissive look and pointed to a chair. 'Sit.'

Roper swung the large monitor on his desk so that Sue could see. 'Next time,' he warned, 'be here first thing. I don't want Singapore thinking I run a sloppy office.' He hit the call icon on his video chat app and straightened his tie. Sue did her best to appear relaxed. Seconds later, Michelle Yim's face appeared on-screen.

'Sue,' exclaimed Michelle. 'Wonderful to see you. How's the recovery going?'

'Oh, it's going well thanks...'

'Good, good.' A concerned look crossed Michelle's face. 'I didn't expect you to be back at work so soon. You're not here against doctor's orders are you?'

'Well, not really, I...'

'And Tony's not driving you too hard?' asked Michelle with a conspiratorial grin.

'Oh, nothing I can't handle,' said Sue. 'I'm sorry about the mess-up with the appointment time. It's my fault. I was at a physio session.'

'Oh, don't worry,' Michelle brushed the apology away with a smile. 'Your health's more important.' Sue suddenly wished she was working in Singapore.

'So Tony, I saw your email about the WestInvest business. That is most upsetting,' said Michelle. 'I guess the situation is beyond recovery?'

'Yes,' said Roper. 'It's dead in the water.'

'You say it was over expectations on change management?' asked Michelle.

'That's right.'

'What expectations?'

Roper shot an accusing glance at Sue. 'Ask *her*...' he said.

Sue was taken by surprise. It took her a while to defend herself. 'WestInvest had been promised change management services as a part of our delivery and it was later withdrawn—but not by me.'

'Is this true?' Michelle asked Roper. 'Did we drop change management at the last minute?'

'Michelle,' began Roper. 'WestInvest were a selfish, needy client who wanted an all-in-one solution without paying for it. Churchill was duped and so was Sue here. They promised WestInvest the earth to sweeten the deal, and WestInvest would have sucked up our resources beyond any reasonable level of commitment. It was a dumb deal.'

'Tony, we're not going to talk about Doug in that way…' Michelle was showing some of the iron she was famous for. 'Change management is more and more a part of our business. We're partnering closely with Onicas throughout the region and together we're providing this service for our largest customers.'

'Onicas?' Roper looked as if he'd stepped in something unpleasant.

'Yes,' said Michelle. 'You remember. You've worked with them before.'

'I most certainly *have*…' replied Roper. 'But we don't work with them down here.'

'Well,' said Michelle, 'we have to change that. I'll put you in touch with Jamie DeSouza. He heads Onicas in Sydney. He's worked with us on projects across APAC and we have a good working relationship.'

'That's all very well,' Roper went on, 'but in Asia, their contracts, *your* contracts—are huge. This is Australia, if we start bundling our proposals with Onicas, we'll never be competitive. Our margins will narrow to zero. And as a team, we'll have to accept *their risk*. That's no way for a small outfit like Tesico Australia to function. We should be targeting prospects who can provide their own change management. It's the fastest and safest way to growth. And we *need* growth Michelle. We're way behind targets.'

Sue bit her lip. She wanted to tell Michelle that WestInvest would have put them ahead of target if they'd only listened and worked with them, but the comment would have been incendiary.

Roper sat forward in his chair, close to the webcam. 'Michelle, you've given me a job to do here. All I ask is that you go with me on this.'

Michelle stared back. 'Very well,' she said. 'Let's just say WestInvest's interests and our own didn't mesh. That's what we'll tell the press.'

Tony sat back with a smug smile. 'But it's not all doom and gloom down here Michelle...'

'Oh, how so?'

'You heard about Wentworth getting hacked?'

'Yes?' said Michelle, her interest piqued.

'Well, I've been trying to leverage that, they're still using a firewall, so I've been working to get our product on the consideration set. I've briefed Sue here to help me.'

'That's excellent news,' said Michelle. 'So where are we with that?'

Roper swung his chair to face Sue. She felt herself under the microscope again.

'Well, uh, we've started on an opportunity analysis, a SWOT, some competitive analysis and...' blurted Sue.

'I mean in terms of who we've met...' said Michelle. 'Who have we been talking to?'

'Well,' said Sue, feeling bamboozled. 'We've been talking to Raf Singh, their IT Security Manager...'

'And?' smiled Michelle.

'And he's managed to get us a meeting with someone on Monday...' said Sue.

'Who?'

'I don't really know but we think it could be someone—important.'

'Oh,' said Michelle, her smile fading.

'Michelle,' interjected Roper, 'it's still very early in the game, but I'm developing a strategy. It looks hopeful, that's all we know as yet.'

'Well done Tony,' said Michelle. 'Let me know how it goes.'

'Of course,' smiled Roper. He looked at Sue and inclined his head towards the door. It was a dismissal. Sue stood and limped out, closing the door behind her as Roper launched into the remaining items on the meeting agenda.

Sue stood stock-still in the open-plan area outside. Her head was a scramble. *What the hell just happened?*

She understood now why Roper had wanted her in the meeting; why he'd delayed Michelle until Sue was available: he wanted someone to blame for WestInvest.

He was also planning to take credit for Wentworth. But there was something else. He was setting Sue up—in case they failed with Wentworth too.

ENGAGE

13. The Glass Whiteboard

'That's who we're up against,' said Coops, depositing a copy of *Corporation Magazine* on the coffee table.

Sue picked up the magazine and studied the cover. It displayed a middle-aged woman, standing sideways with arms folded. Her hairstyle was engineered to add height and it looked like she'd borrowed it from a soap-star several decades before but forgot to give it back. Her expression was the perfect blend of authority and benevolence: like a mother listening to a four-year old's excuses for bad behaviour. The headline on the magazine's cover read: *Brenda Huffington, Empress of Influence.*

'Brenda will come at us with everything,' said Sue, still looking at the magazine. 'She needs to keep Wentworth...'

'For the revenue?' asked Coops.

'Partly,' said Sue, 'but Wentworth is Australia's biggest investment bank. CBIS needs the credential more.'

'So it all comes down to pride,' observed Coops.

It was Saturday morning and the two women were in Sue's apartment, preparing for the Monday meeting with their mysterious new contact at Wentworth. Part of their preparation was to look at the competitive landscape and here both women knew they had a fight on their hands.

'I've heard she's a ball-breaker,' said Coops.

'She certainly has a reputation for being ruthless,' said Sue, dropping the magazine onto the coffee table. 'With her competition *and* her own staff. There are a few people out there who'll never work in sales again, thanks to Brenda Huffington.'

Sue was right, Brenda Huffington had been National Sales Manager for CBIS for over fifteen years and was a force to be reckoned with. As an industry commentator, both in Australia and the world beyond, she was a celebrity. Her network extended to the highest echelons of the top corporations and she had placed CBIS product with nearly every single one of them. She'd personally mentored some of the brightest stars in the field of complex business-to-business selling. Brenda Huffington could make your career. Or she could break it.

'Reckon she's plotting a way to deal with us right now?' asked Coops.

Sue was tempted to reassure Coops that she doubted it; that CBIS would consider Tesico too small to be a threat. But she knew Brenda Huffington was smarter than that.

'Maybe,' replied Sue.

'Really? You reckon she's onto us?'

'She's not stupid. CBIS is a giant in cybersecurity but their in-house approach is beginning to show its age. Network-installed firewalls have become harder and harder to maintain and CBIS's customers are beginning to voice their frustrations. That's what's happening at Wentworth.'

'She's stuck with the CBIS firewall product?' offered Coops.

'That's right. CBIS aren't innovating fast enough. There's talk of next-gen firewall but no details of when CBIS will bring it to market. My guess is, that's what Brenda will be selling. She'll be trying her damnedest to keep Wentworth in the CBIS stable by promising a migration to next-gen down the track. In the meantime, she'll be discrediting cloud-based security solutions like ours.'

'Right,' said Coops, 'she'll be white-anting us for sure, working on all those fears people have about the cloud, stirring the pot with stories of the Dark Web and such...'

'And she'll be highlighting the strength and dependability of CBIS's service to industry over the years,' said Sue.

'And the flakiness of all these new little tech startups like ours?'

'She'll stress we're untried, an unknown. She'll appeal to Wentworth with flattery. She'll tell them they're a big bank that needs the support of the biggest provider in the sector. I think she'll also paint a dangerous and complicated picture of what'll happen if the bank decides to switch vendors.'

Coops sighed, 'They certainly *are* a big-arse bank and CBIS have departments of people sitting inside Wentworth Tower right now. The two companies are stitched together like a pair of old knickers. It'll be a bugger of a job to unpick them.'

'She may not need to make that point directly,' said Sue, 'a lot of people in Wentworth will be frightened to part company with CBIS. Brenda will work on that. I think fear will be a big part of her strategy. And, let's not forget that CBIS is the incumbent, Brenda already has the ear of all the decision makers she needs. Probably even the CEO.'

'So,' said Coops, 'we've got Buckley's, is that what you're saying?'

Sue didn't answer directly. 'We just need to find sympathetic ears of our own to whisper into.'

'Well, let's figure out who that might be.' Coops unfolded a large sheet of paper across Sue's coffee table. It detailed the structure of Wentworth's senior management in an organisational tree. 'I got this from their annual report. It's still current.'

Sue leaned forward.

'So where is this Champion we're looking for?' said Coops. 'Do you think that's who you're going to meet on Monday?'

Sue shrugged. 'No idea.' She took in Wentworth's senior

structure. 'Well, Raf's not senior enough to be included here, but he does work under this guy...' She placed a finger on the management tree.

Coops leaned over. 'Peter Ludick, Chief Information Officer? Well, he's certainly got the authority, but...' Coops drew in a long breath, shaking her head. 'I don't know Sue. I'm not sure he's our Champ.'

'Why not?'

'Well, for starters, he seems to be a Huffington fanboy. They go to trade events together, appear in interviews together and seem to speak the same lingo. Ludick talks about the CBIS next-gen firewall system as *best practice*. He's even written recommendations on LinkedIn for Huffington and very positive reviews for CBIS on their website.'

'So he and Huffington are *simpatico*?'

'Yeah, whatever that means,' said Coops. 'Also, he's the one who brought in CBIS in the first place. That was five years ago when Ludick joined Wentworth. That's why they hired him: to update the bank's security from the get-go, amongst other things.'

'Interesting,' said Sue. 'Then he'd know the upheaval caused by a security makeover. He wouldn't want to go through that again.'

'Probably not,' agreed Coops, 'and he's probably scared of being proved wrong too, to be seen as making a crappy decision in the first place.'

'So ego might be a factor?'

Coops nodded. 'But there's another reason I don't think you'll be meeting Ludick on Monday, why he may not be our Champion...'

'Oh?'

'Raf doesn't report to him directly,' said Coops. 'I ran a LinkedIn Sales Navigator search—Raf is way down the pecking order.'

Sue looked back at the bank's structure tree. 'Then what about this guy, the GM of Data Security?' she said, pointing.

ENGAGE

'Sure, Raf reports directly to him, but he's in the same boat: no power to make change. At best he'd just be another Advocate. If your meeting is with him, you'll have to figure out how he or Raf can get you in front of a Change Agent.'

Sue smiled. Coops was picking this up quickly. She ran a finger over the name of the CEO and followed it down to the Chief Operating Officer. 'What about the COO? Maria Kutcik?'

Coops shook her head. 'Heaps of influence but she and Raf are levels apart so it's unlikely you'll be meeting her either. They might know each other enough to say *hi* in the corridor, but that's about it.'

Sue studied the map for a while. This time it was Coops who placed a finger on the structure tree. It was a senior position at the furthest edge of the bank's structure. It seemed to be all alone, unconnected to any kind of hierarchy.

'What about this bloke?' asked Coops.

Sue bent close to read. 'Robert Meade, Chief Information Security Officer.' Sue sat slowly back. 'The CISO, of course...' she said.

* * *

Saturday morning became Saturday afternoon. Over lunch, Sue and Coops completed as much of the competitive analysis as they could, then switched tracks to the SWOT and the *Gap Discovery*. They made little headway. There were still some very large holes in their knowledge.

'Why don't we take a stab at Doug's stakeholder map?' offered Sue, once it was clear they were running out of steam.

'Right you are,' said Coops, picking up the stakeholder archetype cards.

'Shame we don't have a whiteboard or something,' observed Sue.

Coops shot a smile at Sue, then produced a pack of whiteboard markers from her bag. She got to her feet. 'Way ahead of you girl,' she said, and pointed to the glass sliding door which opened onto Sue's balcony. 'May I?'

Before Sue could answer, Coops had uncapped a marker and begun drawing the axes of a stakeholder map on the glass door.

'Be my guest,' said Sue in astonishment. 'Hope they're not permanent?'

Coops licked a finger and rubbed out a section in one of the lines to prove it wasn't. She grinned at Sue before continuing work. Within a few minutes Coops had labelled the axes in terms of influence and relationship. She drew the cross-hair that separated the map into quadrants then, lastly, she plotted Raf on the map, exactly where Sue had placed him: near the centre and to the left— neutral relationship, low influence.

'Meade and Ludick would be bottom right,' said Sue.

Coops nodded and added the CISO and CIO into the bottom right quadrant. 'Low to bugger-all in terms of relationship but probably a ton of influence.' She turned to Sue. 'So do we want to take a punt at what archetype these blokes might be?'

'Well, we know a little about Ludick,' began Sue. 'We think he'll remain negative because of his attachment to CBIS and he has the authority to be a Change Agent, which makes him a negative Champion, Sage or Inquisitor.'

'Either way, he could be trouble, right?'

'I think we have to assume so,' said Sue. 'What do we know about the CISO, Robert Meade?'

Coops smiled. 'Now he's interesting...' She walked back to the coffee table and picked up her notes. 'He wasn't always the Chief of Information Security. In fact, that's a very new position for Wentworth. He was originally brought in to oversee the development of the bank's mobile apps a few years back. At that time, he reported directly to the CIO.'

'Ludick was his boss?' asked Sue.

'Yep, and now the two of them are on an equal footing.'

Sue looked back to the Wentworth structure tree on the coffee table. Coops was right, the CISO, Robert Meade and the CIO, Peter Ludick were now peers. Both answered directly to the CEO. 'Do we think they're like-minded when it comes to data security?' asked Sue.

'Dunno,' said Coops. 'But as the CISO, Robert Meade can stick his fingers in a lot of pies. He has no department as such but his responsibilities are wide-ranging. He's responsible not just for protecting customer data, but the bank's infrastructure too.'

'So he could be treading on Peter Ludick's toes, in the area of cybersecurity?'

'Could be. And if the two of them don't see eye-to-eye, well, that's another whole can of worms,' said Coops.

'Potentially,' mused Sue, 'they could be presenting two entirely different stories to the CEO.'

'And imagine how that'd make the CIO, Peter Ludick feel, to have his ex-lacky now on the same level and ratting on him to the CEO?' continued Coops.

Sue nodded. 'It'd make for a highly-charged political situation.'

Coops smiled. 'Yep, there could be some real biff between these two if they're not on the same team.'

'So how did Robert Meade get to be the CISO?'

'The position was created by the CEO, Craig Martin,' said Coops, pointing to the apex of the structure tree. 'Both Martin and Meade have been with the company for three years, so neither of them were around when the bank brought in CBIS.'

'So neither of them saw the upheaval that caused?'

'No,' said Coops. 'So they're more likely to be neutral on the issue of cybersecurity. Ludick, on the other hand, well, we know he's best mates with Huffington.'

'The creation of this CISO role and the appointment of Robert Meade,' asked Sue. 'What does that say about the CEO, Craig Martin?'

'Yeah,' agreed Coops. 'That got me thinking too. I reckon Craig Martin must have a lot of trust in Meade to put him in the role.'

Sue picked up her notebook and made an entry.

Coops continued. 'The CISO role is commonplace these days but it must've been a progressive move for a straight-laced outfit like Wentworth. Says a lot about the CEO, Craig Martin, and the direction he wants for the bank.'

'I've heard of Martin,' said Sue as she wrote. 'He's in the press a lot, he *is* quite progressive, isn't he?'

'Sure is, he's a real character. Always on the TV or blogging, or being interviewed. Great presenter, very convincing. He's a celebrity CEO, very new-age, full of big ideas, concerned about sustainability and corporate ethics and whatnot. And his real big thing is digital innovation.'

Sue scribbled another note. 'If he's that progressive, he might be open to cloud-based security.'

'That's what I'm thinking,' agreed Coops.

Sue sat back, considering. 'But if Martin is such a celeb, why didn't he face the press when Wentworth was hacked? Why was Raf the spokesperson?'

It was a good question. One that had both women quietly stumped for some time.

'Perhaps he decided to distance himself from the whole shitstorm?' offered Coops.

'Or, perhaps he was *advised* to...' countered Sue.

Coops stared at the Wentworth structure tree again. 'Who would've wanted him to keep his head down?'

Sue waved a hand over the structure tree. 'It could be anyone in the C-Suite, most likely the COO or the CISO. Who knows? Either way, Martin is lucky, someone has got his back.'

The afternoon drew on and the two women fell into a friendly chat about their lives outside the Tesico office. Coops gathered her pens and notes together, took a photo of Sue's sliding glass door with her phone, then wiped the door clean.

'Thanks Coops.' Sue stood near the door of her apartment,

propping herself on her elbow crutches. 'You're such a big help with all this...'

'No worries,' said Coops.

'I think you should come with me on Monday—to Wentworth.'

'For real?'

'Why not? I'll clear it with Raf. Just come to work prepared.'

Coops's eyes sparkled. 'Great. I'll see you in the office Monday then...'

'See you Monday,' said Sue.

This book comes with free access to an
online reference companion.

By scanning the QR code or by navigating to edvance.sale/recap/engage3/ now, you will gain a deeper understanding of the EDVANCE process and the methodology applied by the characters in the preceding three chapters, including:

- The Journey of Discovery
- Updated Stakeholder Mapping
- Storytelling
- Applying these methods in your own business

14. Monday Morning Blues

It was just after dawn when Sue rose on Monday morning. The dull ache in her leg and ribs was more effective at getting her out of bed than any alarm clock. Her mind had been alive most of the night too, with thoughts of the meeting, the questions she needed answering and what she needed to accomplish. She climbed into an Uber just as the sky glowed with its first pinks and mauves, promising another cloudless Sydney day.

The taxi ride into town was brisk, the streets empty of traffic. Sue hobbled into Tesico's offices on her elbow crutches and was the first to turn on the lights for the day.

It was still hours before the meeting but there was much to do. Sue had re-read the opening chapters to Doug's journal on Sunday morning while she sat on her sunny balcony. Doug had emphasised the need to have some stories to tell in these important initial meetings. She'd worked long and hard at her own personal story; felt frustrated when it sounded boring and embarrassed when it didn't. Sue opened her laptop and set about adding some final polish. Writing about yourself was hard, she decided.

Shortly before nine, Coops swept into Sue's cubicle, her laptop bag under her arm. 'Alright girl, grab your lappy and your lippy—we've got some minds to disrupt!'

Sue looked up. 'Wow, someone's been shopping.'

Coops posed in her new business suit. 'Whaddya think? I was aiming for *not too serious, not too sexy.*'

'Perfect,' smiled Sue. She packed her shoulder bag and the two women headed for Tesico's main doors.

'You two, in here,' called Roper from inside his office.

Sue and Coops filed inside, standing just inside the doorway.

Roper closed the lid of his laptop and looked up. 'This meeting with Wentworth, do you know who it's with yet?'

'Raf and one other,' returned Sue.

'Who?'

'We don't know yet.'

'It's your job to find out Novak. If you don't know who you're talking to, how can you possibly prepare?'

Sue didn't reply. She wanted to demonstrate a level of trust to Raf. But she didn't want to reveal this to Roper. Trust didn't seem to be something he understood.

Roper's eyes bored into her. 'You have *prepared*, haven't you?'

'Of course, we've prepared a list of questions for Raf and...' stumbled Sue, 'the other person.'

Roper shook his head. Then he was on his feet, collecting his jacket from the back of his chair. 'We won't be asking any questions. You'll be keeping quiet and watching and learning how a real salesperson closes a deal.'

'You're coming with us?' asked Sue.

'Did you think you were going without me?'

Sue was alarmed. 'But Tony, Raf is my contact. This is delicate, I'm trying to respect his confidentiality. And we've already sent him a discussion document—it's how we plan to proceed.'

'*I* will decide how we proceed,' Roper returned. 'I'm the most senior salesperson in this office. Wentworth is a large prospect and best not handled by a couple of juniors.' He levelled a forefinger at Sue. 'Your job will be to keep quiet and observe.' The forefinger swung to aim at Coops. 'And you, you're not going anywhere.'

Sue could read the hurt in her friend's eyes. Coops glowered for an instant, her lower lip sticking out like the bottom drawer of a filing cabinet. Then she swung around on her heel and headed for the door.

'And Cooper,' commanded Roper. Coops halted in the doorway without turning around. Sue could feel the enmity radiating from her. 'Get us some brochures and collateral for the meeting, there's a good girl.'

Roper turned to Sue. 'Well, what are you waiting for? Go get us a cab.'

ENGAGE

15. From the Jaws of Victory

Raf Singh wore a look of puzzlement as he greeted Tony Roper. Sue had called Raf early that morning, asking if she could bring Coops. Raf wasn't expecting to meet the Tesico National Sales Manager instead.

Raf signed his two visitors in and hurried them through security. Sue sensed he was uptight; maybe he was anxious to keep his two charges unnoticed, or maybe there was more riding on this meeting than Sue had anticipated. The party entered a crowded lift which didn't thin out until they reached the upper floors of Wentworth Tower. Once alone in the lift, Raf broke the silence. 'Today you'll be meeting with Robert Meade, our Chief Information Security Officer.'

The CISO thought Sue. Butterflies took flight in her stomach. This was better than she'd hoped.

Raf turned to Sue. 'He's seen the discussion paper and he's particularly interested in your idea of a *Journey of Discovery*. He knows you'll have questions, and he's prepared to help as much as he can. I think, given that time is short, let's deal with the big questions first.'

Sue nodded. Roper gave an irritated sigh.

Robert Meade turned out to be a tall man in his early fifties. His expression was a mix of intelligence and warmth. When he spoke, he spoke slowly. Sue saw the burned-out look in his eyes and realised he was just exhausted, like Raf. Wentworth was still working night and day to repair and test the CBIS firewall.

Sue introduced Tony and herself to Meade. Then she gave some background on herself: her degree in cybersecurity and how she'd first worked at a bank herself; how she'd become disillusioned, how she'd seen the shortcomings of their systems and looked for a way to be involved in security design and development. That's when she jumped ship and retrained. Meade listened, attentive, smiling. He smiled with his eyes, Sue decided. She liked that. In her peripheral vision Sue glimpsed Roper scowling.

'Enough about you,' interrupted Roper trying to make the reproach sound good-humoured. He turned to Meade. 'Let's talk about solving Wentworth's problem.'

Robert Meade's smile faded. 'That would be great Mister Roper—except we don't know what it is yet.'

Roper forced a conciliatory smile. 'Well, believe me, we've got a pretty good idea.'

'Oh?'

'You were hacked.'

Meade looked suddenly tired. 'Yes. We were hacked. You're right. But the hack was the consequence, not the problem. The problem lies somewhere in our digital exposure. Ours is not one network Mister Roper. It's a combination of many; it's large and it's complicated. Ask anyone here where the fault lies and they'd all give you a different answer. Is it in our employees' laptops or the servers? Is it a weakness somewhere among our core accounts or our customers' accounts? Is it a problem with our security provisions or the operational side of our business? We simply don't know.'

Roper's face was screwed into a ball of non-understanding. 'Look,' he said, 'the problem is this—you're relying on a firewall to keep your business safe. And your business is complex, advanced, cutting-edge, I get that, but firewall software is outdated. It was developed when the internet was in its infancy. Even next-gen firewall technology won't solve your problem. It's time to move on.'

Meade threw a disappointed look at Raf.

'I think, perhaps, we should return to the discussion document?' suggested Raf. He looked at Sue. 'You wanted to help us pinpoint the problem? You have some questions?'

Sue stirred into action. 'Ah, yes. We wanted to start by understanding the precise nature of the attack.'

Roper let out a quiet sigh.

The smile returned to Meade's eyes and he asked Raf to brief the Tesico team. Raf explained that the malware had indeed found its way behind the Wentworth firewall through an employee's laptop as Sue had correctly guessed. The employee hadn't been doing anything unauthorised, but had simply opened an email with a PDF attachment. Although seemingly harmless, the PDF contained a string targeted to compromise Wentworth's email client. The malware was activated via a firewall back-door, alerting its source in North Korea. From there, the hackers, believed to be a global network, gained a foothold inside Wentworth and attempted to move laterally across their systems into customer accounts. It was during the transition between two infrastructures that a security anomaly was flagged and the breach discovered.

'By the firewall?' asked Sue.

'No,' admitted Meade, 'by our account monitoring systems.'

Sue wrote into her notebook, then fired a fresh question at Meade. 'There's a lot of noise in the press that banks like Wentworth aren't taking cybercrime seriously, especially for their customers. Cybercrime is the biggest-growing threat in finance today, but the feeling is, there's a real knowledge gap between the IT professionals and the C-suite execs. Is that what's happening at Wentworth?'

Meade gave a slight nod. 'It's true, we're no different from many big institutions. Our C-suite officers are chosen for their ability to lead, to build, to govern. Not to watch our backs for a digital attack. We rely on our technical experts to do that.' He smiled at Raf. 'But their hands are tied because the systems we employ to prevent these attacks are often decided upon by the C-suite.'

'So there's a gap in understanding?' asked Sue.

'You could say so,' said Meade. 'Which is why we're interested in having someone with authority and experience in your industry help us close that gap.' Again Sue saw the smile form at the edge of his eyes. 'We've become reactive, we've become followers Miss Novak. The cybercriminals are the innovative ones now, always one step ahead of us.'

'Well, your days of being followers are over,' interrupted Roper with a broad smile. 'Tesico has exactly the solution you need. Our technology is the next generation in cyber-protection. Because it's cloud-based, it can learn, so you'll never be reactive to cyberattacks, you'll be proactive. In a way, it's more of an offensive system than a defensive one. No-one else in the world offers this kind of technology...'

Raf shot a look of alarm at Sue.

'As Raf said,' Meade began, 'I thought we were here to begin pinpointing *the problem*, to find a way forward?' said Meade.

Roper smiled. 'This is the way forward. Believe me. Artificial Intelligence has progressed in leaps and bounds over the last decade. Particularly in its application to security...'

Raf was wide-eyed. He stared at Sue, imploring her to do something.

'Of course AI can be embedded in software,' continued Roper, 'but that's not making the most of its capability...'

'I think we still have some questions for Mister Meade...' tried Sue.

'And, with respect,' Roper turned on Sue, '*I'm talking* Miss

Novak.' He looked back at Meade. 'Now the reason our AI, the Tesico product, is placed in the cloud, is because that's where you can take full advantage of its ability to monitor all your interactions for malicious code. In the cloud it's scale-able too...'

'Forgive me Mister Roper,' said Meade, cutting Roper short, 'I do know a little of the Tesico product and I admit that I find it interesting. But the change to a new security system is a massive undertaking and can't be decided on a whim. Nor can it be decided upon by one person, such as myself. No-one at Wentworth really understands the full problem, and so we have no idea of the solution we genuinely need.' Meade threw a fatigued look at Raf. 'I must admit, I'm a little disappointed. I'd been led to believe this meeting would be a preliminary exchange of information, that Tesico would be happy to help investigate the problem more fully before recommending a course of action.'

'There's no need, your course of action is clear,' smiled Roper. 'Our product is being used by some of the biggest banks in Asia-Pacific. It's tried and trusted. And we can prove it.'

'Banks are as different as cybersecurity companies,' countered Meade. 'I don't care about other banks. I only care about Wentworth.'

'But the solution we offer is world-leading. And it's entirely proprietary. You can't get the same level of security anywhere else,' said Roper.

'I don't care about your solution,' said Meade politely. 'I care about our problem, about the problem inside this bank.'

'Perhaps we should allow Miss Novak to continue with her questions?' asked Raf, attempting to defuse the situation.

'I agree,' said Meade, under his breath.

'The longer you hang on to CBIS and their firewall software approach, the greater the risk of another attack,' pressed Roper. 'The Tesico solution is your only real option.'

Meade smiled politely.

'And, seeing as there's a need for urgency here,' offered Roper, 'I'd be prepared to discuss a deal to help an early decision.'

Meade studied Roper in silence for a moment, then said, 'You've given us a lot to think about Mister Roper. Thank-you for your time today.' The comment was cordial enough but it signalled the end of the meeting. Roper smiled and rose. The two men exchanged business cards while Sue looked at Raf. He was shaking his head, eyes closed.

Raf led Sue and Tony Roper down to the lobby in silence. He bade the Tesico team a businesslike good-bye. It wasn't until Sue was seated in the back of a taxi that Roper spoke. 'What the hell was that with all the damn questions?'

Sue didn't answer.

'Questions like that only demonstrate you don't know the prospect; that you haven't done your homework.' Roper turned to gaze at the world outside the passenger window. 'You'd better start shaping up Novak. Wentworth is a big career opportunity. Don't screw this up for me.'

ENGAGE

16. What Just Happened?

Sue passed the rest of the day in a daze. She tried catching up on some mundane housekeeping: expense claims and CRM reporting; anything to stay out of Tony Roper's way.

Coops was busy on a long call with the Singapore marketing team, so Sue stayed at her own desk.

It wasn't until late in the day that she got the call from Raf.

Sue was leaning on her crutches outside the front door of her apartment, searching in her bag for her keys. It was a complicated balancing act.

Her phone rang and she somehow fumbled it to her ear.

'Raf?'

'What happened today? Who was that Roper guy?' he asked. The Oxbridge accent was still courteous but Sue could hear the frustration just below its surface.

'Raf, I'm so sorry...'

'What happened to the questions you wanted to ask?'

'I know, I know, I was meaning to—but...'

'Robert was looking forward to meeting you, I sent him some of your articles and I told him about your address at the ACSC. He was really on-board Sue.'

105

'I know...'

'He wanted a frank, open discussion about the problem and to set some goals for the way forward. Instead he got a sales pitch.'

'It's my fault Raf, I should've briefed Tony more thoroughly. I didn't know he was planning on attending,' explained Sue.

'The meeting was supposed to have been with *you*. That's what I'd set up with Robert.'

The fact stung Sue like a barb. She knew she'd let Raf down. 'Look, since Doug Churchill died, things have changed at Tesico,' she began, attempting to explain in a way that didn't cast blame. 'There's been a change in management, and with that, there's been a change in strategy.'

'Sue, are you willing to help us or not?'

'Of course,' said Sue. She felt she was losing any last measure of trust he had in her.

The phone remained silent. 'I believe you,' Raf said.

Sue warmed to his words. Perhaps she hadn't lost him yet.

'But this change in management,' said Raf. 'It could be Tesico's undoing.'

ENGAGE

17. Don't Screw Up

'He's been calling for you,' said Coops, sticking her head around Sue's partition and nodding in the direction of Roper's office.

Sue had been trying to piece together a plan of action for Wentworth; a way to recover Tesico's reputation. It was beneath Roper to walk over to her desk or pick up the phone and call her. He sat at his desk with his door open and called instructions or names. This was the way things were done now.

Sue limped into Roper's office and saw Michelle Yim's face on his desktop screen. They were in teleconference. Sue sat, confused. It wasn't Friday. This wasn't one of their scheduled meetings.

'I am very sorry to hear things have ended with Wentworth,' said Michelle.

'Ended?' Sue replied. 'I know the meeting didn't go smoothly but I don't think anything's *ended*.'

'Oh yes it has,' said Roper. He thrust a printout of an email in front of Sue. It was addressed to Roper from Robert Meade; short and to the point.

After careful consideration, we don't think Tesico is the right cultural fit for us at this time.

'What happened?' asked Michelle. 'What went wrong?'

107

Sue was silent. Roper drew a long breath. 'I know exactly what went wrong,' he said, angling himself towards Sue. 'Cooper and Novak here didn't do their homework. To start with, they didn't even know we were meeting with the CISO and we weren't prepared for that. I had to tap-dance like crazy to keep the meeting on-track. It was a shambles.' He faced Michelle. 'They've wasted too much time chasing down a prospect that's just too big for us. I have to say, I suspected this from the start. And Novak here has placed too much emphasis on this Raf Singh character. He's got no power to make any decisions. As a contact, he's next to useless.'

Michelle's eyes narrowed. 'But Tony, I thought Wentworth was *your* lead?'

Roper stared at his desk for a while, Sue could tell he was searching for a way to change the subject. 'Look, Michelle,' he said. 'This office is so way behind target. Novak and Cooper are more behind than anyone, because they've wasted their time on leads like WestInvest and Wentworth. I didn't want to do this but I'm going to have to bring in some tough measures. I'm assigning them some leads I've been working on; practical, achievable leads; leads I expect them to convert; leads they *will* convert. Otherwise, I'll be holding them accountable.'

Sue began speaking in her defence but Roper shot her a look of warning.

The gesture didn't go unnoticed by Michelle. 'Sue, you want to say something?' Sue felt Roper's continued glare. She knew she was on dangerous ground.

'No, not just now...' muttered Sue.

Michelle seemed to think for a while, then she spoke to Roper. 'Very well Tony, your call.' Then she hung up.

Roper rifled through a pile of paper on his desk and produced a single sheet. He placed it in front of Sue and jabbed at it with an emphatic finger. 'These are your leads. These are the companies I want to buy a Tesico product.'

Sue ran her eyes over the long list of small investment companies, insurance providers and FinTech start-ups. 'But Tony, these aren't leads, they're just targets.'

'Then turn them into leads,' said Roper.

Sue opened her mouth to protest.

'Or you and your friend Cooper will get your marching orders,' he said.

'What?'

'You heard. I'm placing you both on notice until you hit target.'

Sue was speechless.

'Don't worry, I'm not singling you out. The whole office is on notice until I say so. Until we make some kind of return. Melbourne is exempt. They've got a promising lead down there and they're making good progress.'

Sue still didn't know how to react.

Roper leaned forward. 'And make no mistake Novak, this is no idle threat. If this office doesn't shape up, I'll have no option but make a clean sweep and bring in salespeople who understand how to get the job done.'

'You can't do this,' said Sue under her breath.

'Can't I? Just watch,' said Roper. 'If you want to keep your job, then it's simple: don't screw up. I suggest you take these leads, get back to your desk and start making some calls.'

Sue stood and headed for the door. She was on auto-pilot.

'And send your little cowgirl friend in.'

Sue walked to Coops's desk and passed on the instruction.

'Sue, is everything okay?' asked Coops. All Sue could do was shake her head.

From her own desk, Sue watched. The door to Roper's office was closed now. All she could see was the back of Coops's head as Roper stabbed the air in front of her face with a forefinger. A minute later Coops stood and opened the door. She was holding back tears. Coops walked to her desk, picked up her bag and coat, then turned and hurried from the building.

Sue's phone rang.

'Hello?'

'Sue, it's Michelle.'

'Michelle?'

'Sue, you were going to tell me something just now, in the meeting...' said Michelle. 'But didn't get a chance.'

'No.'

'Will you tell me your side of the story, what happened at Wentworth?'

Sue thought. She'd always considered herself a team player; she'd always protected her colleagues and accepted the glory of success or the blame of defeat as a member of the team. But Roper's attack was personal and she wanted to respond. Besides, wasn't she on notice now? She had nothing left to lose.

'Wentworth need help,' began Sue. 'They need to understand the problems they're faced with before they can work their way to a solution.'

'Sounds reasonable, they're a big bank.'

'Yes,' said Sue. 'And I get the sense there's a lot of stakeholders and none of them are aligned.'

'That's fairly typical,' agreed Michelle.

'The original contact came through me. Raf Singh had read some of my blog posts and heard my presentation at the ACSC. Coops and I prepared a discussion outline. We weren't expecting him to share it with the CISO, Robert Meade, or to set up a meeting with him.' Sue paused to collect her thoughts. 'When we met Meade he seemed, well, reasonable. What he was looking for was outside help, an honest broker who could help close the gaps between the stakeholders and guide them to a solution.'

'Great, that's a rare opportunity. So what went wrong?'

'Tony didn't see it that way. He tried to give them a solution, he tried to close quickly.'

Michelle remained silent for a while. 'Look, Sue, in time we'll find a replacement for Doug, someone bright and wonderful you can all look up to. Tony's role is temporary, he's close to retirement. But, until we find a replacement I need someone who can get the Sydney office back on track. Tony's a taskmaster, I know that, but he's got his work cut out and he's doing the best he can.'

'But it wasn't the right way to handle Wentworth Michelle. Hard-selling them wasn't the way to go.'

Michelle considered this. 'Sue, I'm interested in your opinion, what about Robert Meade's email? What do you think he means by *not the right cultural fit at this time*?'

In all the recent turmoil Sue hadn't considered this. It was a shrewd observation. 'Well, I guess *cultural fit* could point to a personality issue. And *at this time* could mean they didn't have a problem with Tesico before.'

'Before Sydney's change in management?'

'Yes, Raf told me as much,' said Sue.

'So you're still in touch with him?'

'Yes.'

'Then I think you should call Raf and see if there's any way you can get back in front of them.'

'I was going to try...' said Sue.

'On your own,' added Michelle.

'Okay...'

'Do you think they've left a back door open?' asked Michelle.

'Perhaps.'

Michelle took a deep breath. 'You might be right about the correct approach with Wentworth. Perhaps Tony's not the right person, not the right *fit* for them. Perhaps *you* should follow up.'

'Without Tony?'

'I'll get him to concentrate on the Melbourne deal. It's more suited to his *unique talents* anyway. You can report directly to me on Wentworth. I'll talk to Tony about it.'

'Okay, then I might need your help with some other things Michelle...'

'Go on.'

'I need Coops to assist.'

'Very well,' said Michelle, 'but I don't want her to ignore any of her responsibilities in enablement.'

'And did you know Tony has put the entire Sydney office on notice?'

'Yes.'

'Can you get him to lift it?'

Sue heard Michelle sigh. 'I'm not going to. I've placed him in charge down there and I have to trust him to manage the way he sees fit. Listen Sue...'

'Yes?'

'If you really want to dig the Sydney office out of this hole, make Wentworth your priority. Right now it's your best answer.'

'Great,' thought Sue as Michelle hung up. 'In other words, *don't screw up.*'

* * *

Sue began at once. She called Raf and tried to make it all sound like good news: that she could act independently from now on. That there would be no further interference from Tesico's local management.

'That's good to hear,' said Raf.

'Can you pass this onto Robert Meade?' asked Sue.

'Sure.'

'Is there any way I can get to see him, to begin again?' Sue pleaded.

'I'll try, but no promises, okay?'

'Okay.'

'Sue, I might be a small cog in a big machine but I still have a reputation here.'

'I know.'

'Just understand I'm risking that.'

'I know, thanks Raf.'

'There can't be any more meetings like the last one, or it's over.'

'I understand.'

After the call Sue felt a little more hopeful. Raf hadn't deserted her and there was even a slim chance to meet with Robert Meade again. From there she'd begin the long process of recovery and the re-building of trust for both Tesico and herself. Then loomed the even larger task: leading Wentworth to Tesico. The small bubble of Sue's hope popped as she considered the realities. Who was she kidding? Landing Wentworth was an impossible task. Her job with Tesico was as good as over. Sue's gaze swept across the office, at her colleagues on their phones and on their laptops. Without Wentworth their jobs were as good as over too.

Doug—help me. You'd know what to do.

Sue's eyes came to rest on the empty chair at Coops's desk.

She checked her wristwatch. Sue knew exactly where to find her at this time of day.

18. A Drowning of Sorrows

Coops had hemmed herself in behind a high table in one corner of the Stockman Hotel. Her eyes appeared to be working independently and it looked to Sue as if she'd got through half a bottle of Bundaberg rum on her own.

Sue leaned her crutches against the wall and eased herself onto a stool.

'Well this is a shit sandwich and no mistake,' said Coops.

'It's not all bad,' offered Sue. She was about to tell Coops her news, but Coops wasn't listening, she was consumed with hurt.

'You know what he said?' Coops went on. 'He said I'd never make it in sales, that I didn't have the aptitude, the smarts for it...'

'Coops, that's not true.'

'Anyhow, it doesn't matter, does it? I'll be out of a job in a month. I'll never get to work in sales...'

'Yes you will.'

'I miss Doug,' said Coops.

Both women studied the table in silence for a time.

'So do I Coops,' said Sue. 'But remember what you said, it's like he's still here, mentoring and guiding us.'

Coops sniffed loudly.

'I haven't read the rest of his journal yet, but I'm sure he can still help us with Wentworth.'

Coops took a gulp of her rum and Coke. 'That train's already left the station darl...'

'No it hasn't,' said Sue with a smile.

Coops brought her glass down heavily on the table. The ice inside it rattled. Coops stared in disbelief. 'Whaddyamean?' she said.

Sue's voice fell to a whisper. 'Raf's going to try to get us back in front of Robert Meade. There's still a chance. And I've spoken with Michelle Yim, she'll keep Roper out of our way.'

'Fair dinkum?' Coops sat upright with a wobble. 'Do we keep our jobs?'

'Only if we land Wentworth,' said Sue.

'Bugger!' said Coops, loudly enough to turn the heads of one or two patrons. 'Then I guess we'll just have to land Wentworth.'

'I guess.'

Sue bought herself a glass of Prosecco and another rum and Coke for Coops. As the evening became night, they ordered more. Sue hadn't planned on a night out but somehow it just happened. The Prosecco was almost as effective as the painkillers, except it made her laugh more. She wanted to throw off the worries of the office and not have Wentworth or Tony Roper on her mind for a while. She wanted to be with Coops, she wanted to share their troubles and their support for each other.

As the Stockman Hotel closed, Sue and Coops found a taxi and fell into the back seat. Sue was always amazed how much Coops could actually drink and still manage to walk or speak.

They drove to Sue's apartment first. As Sue clambered out Coops leaned across the seat to say goodbye through the open window.

'Sue?'

'Yeah?'

'Don't worry, alright?'

'Worry?' replied Sue.

'I mean about me,' said Coops. 'If we don't land Wentworth and I'm out of a job, don't worry, I'll be alright—and I won't blame you. You've always looked after me.'

The door closed and the taxi took off with Coops singing. Badly. Sue stood alone on the lamp-lit street for a while. She didn't know whether it was the alcohol or the stress, but she felt like crying.

Sue's phone buzzed in her bag. She retrieved it and focused with difficulty on the screen. She had a new text message, from Raf. It read: *tomorrow 7.30 am.*

19. The Boomerang Move

Sue set her alarm clock for 5.30 am but woke before it sounded. She hauled herself from the bed, the ache in her head now adding itself to the more general aches of her injuries.

She swallowed her painkillers, took a shower and made a pot of coffee.

Within two hours, she was sitting in Robert Meade's office with Raf once more. She thanked Meade for agreeing to see her again and apologised for the tone of the previous meeting.

'It certainly wasn't helpful,' said Meade. 'But I'm happy to start afresh. And I'm sorry we have to meet so early. Raf and I are fully committed today.'

'That's fine,' said Sue, guessing there were still hard at work patching and testing the CBIS firewall.

'Raf has shared some of your articles and blog posts. They're um...' he searched for the right words, 'thought-provoking.'

'Glad you thought so.'

'It's good to see someone looking at the entire landscape rather than just opportunities to push their product,' said Meade. Sue guessed he was talking about Roper. 'Raf also showed me your discussion document Miss Novak. Would you like to recap?'

'Sure,' said Sue. 'The first step is to uncover all the issues and problems Wentworth faces. It's not just about cybersecurity but all the parts of your business that were affected. Some of them may even seem unrelated but we need to take them all into consideration, to understand the full extent of the problem.'

'And that's what you mean when you talk about this *Journey of Discovery*?' asked Meade.

'Exactly.'

'So how does that work?'

'Well, I'll need to interview each and every department head, to discover how the attacks affected their operation. If needs be, we'll dig deeper, interviewing everyone in the management chains most impacted.'

'I can tell you now, each one has a different idea of the solution we need,' said Raf.

'That's why it can't be about the solution, not just yet,' said Sue. 'If you leap straight to solutions, then it's only natural people are going to be entrenched in their thinking. They'll be thinking about themselves, their departments and the best solution for *them*. Everyone will have a different opinion, a different agenda. That's why it's impossible to get people to agree on a solution up front.' Sue let that thought remain with them for a bit. 'But it's far easier to get people to concentrate on the *problem* and agree on that first.'

Meade and Raf exchanged a brief glance. Sue could see the smile form at the edges of Meade's eyes.

Sue remembered a passage from Doug's journal.

They've developed a fixed train of thought. We must derail this train to get them on the right track.

'Interesting,' said Meade. 'So you don't set yourself the hard task of trying to gain consensus on the solution, you gain consensus on the problem to begin with?'

Sue nodded. Another passage from Doug's journal surfaced in

ENGAGE

her mind: *Strive to dig deeper and deeper to reveal the bedrock of these problems. Take your customer down into the darkest labyrinths.*

'It's a lot like going down into a deep, dark hole,' said Sue, 'to discover those deep-seated challenges.'

'So this is the discovery part of the journey, right?' said Raf. 'Understanding the problem is the first step of discovery?'

'Correct,' said Sue.

'So, once we've got this discovery, then what?' asked Meade.

'Then we climb up out of the hole, into the light and we head up the hill towards a solution.'

Meade smiled. 'Sounds all very metaphoric.'

'I'm sorry.' Sue smiled in return. 'The practical way to get there is through *Gap Discovery*.'

Meade raised an eyebrow in question.

'The *Journey of Discovery* will help you understand where you are *right now*—your *current state*. It'll bring to light all the problems your business faces at this point in time and their implications, no matter how seemingly unrelated they are, as a result of your security arrangements. This will be your *discovery*.'

Meade nodded.

'Then we visualise where you could be, where you need to be, if all these issues were solved. This will be your *desired state*. It's the future Wentworth needs to move towards.'

Meade nodded again, thinking.

'The gap, the bit in the middle, is the way you get there.'

Meade leaned forward, his eyes narrowed. Sue sensed she'd piqued his interest with this. 'So this can help detail the steps we need to make? The operational and process steps needed?'

Ah, process, thought Sue. *That's important to you Robert Meade, isn't it?*

'Sure,' said Sue. 'The *Gap Discovery* is the beginning of a very formal change process. The practical steps you'll need to take will

121

become very clear. It's a map for your entire journey of change, from beginning to end.'

Robert Meade was silent for a very long time. He turned and stared through his window at the sky outside. Raf shot a faint smile at Sue, this was obviously a good thing.

Sue studied Robert Meade. He was interested in process, in the practicalities of change, the very real steps needed. In her mind, Sue saw Doug's stakeholder cards. A phrase from one of the cards struck her. *Focuses on: getting the job done.* It was the Champion archetype.

Robert Meade, are you my Champion?

Meade swung his attention back to Sue. 'This will be a lot of work for you Miss Novak,' he said with a degree of finality. The fact he spoke as if he'd already made up his mind wasn't lost on Sue. 'But what if this *Gap Discovery* points to a solution not offered by Tesico?' he asked.

'That's the risk we'll always have to take,' said Sue. 'I'd be naive to think Wentworth won't look at a long list of cybersecurity vendors. For me, the most critical task is to identify your need and find the correct solution for Wentworth.'

Meade stared at Sue for a while, lost in thought. Then the smile reappeared in his eyes. He retrieved some documents from his desk and handed one copy to Raf, another to Sue. 'I've put together a project team to address this issue,' he said. 'The team's job is to assess the impact of the cyberattack and make recommendations.'

Sue looked over the list of names. An org-chart showed their places in Wentworth's management structure. Raf's name was among the project team members, as was Robert Meade's.

'Miss Novak,' said Meade, 'I'd like to see your approach in action—before we make any formal decision. I'm also thinking this project team might be a good place to start. But perhaps instead of asking for their recommendations, which we know will be contradictory, perhaps we need to ask them to dig for the problems first, as you suggest. Do you think we can align thinking in this way?'

ENGAGE

'Perhaps,' said Sue. 'Will the final decision on which vendor you appoint rest with this team?' asked Sue.

'No,' said Meade. 'That will be decided upon by a Decision Making Unit, a DMU, pursuant to us issuing a Request For Proposal.'

Sue considered this. She knew that, if the final decision rested with the members of the Decision Making Unit, then that's where she ultimately needed to drive consensus. The project team contained a few unfamiliar names, and their positions, like Raf's were a few levels removed from the real influence at Wentworth. Sue thought of the stakeholder cards. Although the project team didn't have the final say, there might still be useful advocates among them who could pave the way to the change agents in the Decision Making Unit.

'So who's in the DMU?' asked Sue.

'That hasn't been decided upon as yet. Usually it's made up of C-suite execs.'

'Then I think the best course of action is for me to interview each member of the project team first and meet with each member of the DMU once we know who they are.'

Meade turned to Raf. 'I'm thinking we should circulate links to some of Miss Novak's written articles as an introduction for the project team. We should position her as an industry commentator as well as a Tesico employee.'

Raf nodded.

'Miss Novak is to have full cooperation and disclosure from each member of the team. If anyone is proving difficult to pin down, let me know, will you Raf?' Meade turned back to Sue. 'And once the DMU is announced, I'll try getting you in front of them too.'

'I'm guessing you'd certainly be on the DMU Mister Meade, and the CIO, Peter Ludick?' asked Sue.

'Highly likely but we can't confirm yet.'

'And what about your CEO, Mister Martin, he'd definitely have to be part of the DMU, surely?'

'Craig is often part of the DMU in name only. He tends not to get too deeply involved and will rubber-stamp the DMU's decision on most issues,' said Meade.

Sue nodded. 'You know, I can't help wondering...'

'Wondering what?' asked Meade.

'Why Mister Martin didn't play his usual role as spokesperson for the bank when news of the cyberattack broke?' asked Sue. 'He's such a larger-than-life character, and he's very persuasive. I thought he would have been the obvious choice to calm the shareholders. But you chose Raf instead?'

Meade's expression was unreadable. Raf shifted uncomfortably in his chair.

'Raf is well respected here,' began Meade. 'I value his judgement and input. He's also a very capable presenter. That decision was mine.'

'It just looked as if your CEO, Mister Martin, was being—*protected*,' said Sue.

'He was,' admitted Meade. 'By me.'

Sue thought this over. 'You know, I usually start by asking two important questions Mister Meade.'

'Then by all means go ahead.'

'What is it you fear?'

Meade stared at Sue. 'I fear another attack,' he said. 'I fear these digital criminals will do far more than simply steal from us. I fear they'll undermine us as an institution. I fear they'll ruin careers, that they'll bring us down.'

'Could they really bring down Wentworth?' asked Sue.

'Wentworth is a very big ship Miss Novak. But we're sailing a dangerous stretch of sea, and it's foolish to think that big ships never sink.'

'Thanks for being so open,' said Sue.

'Your second question?'

'What is it you want out of this process?' asked Sue.

Meade thought for a moment. 'I don't want anyone to go to prison because I couldn't do my job,' he said.

* * *

'How d'you think that went?' Sue was standing beside Raf in the lift as he escorted her back to the ground floor.

'Good, good.' Raf smiled. Sue felt happy he was on her side once again. 'I think he likes you.'

'So, do you think I got the job?' she asked.

Raf grinned, shrugging his shoulders. 'I guess so,' he said.

DISCOVER AND DISRUPT

DISCOVER AND DISRUPT

20. The Cartographers

'They must be getting serious if they want us to sign non-disclosure agreements,' said Coops staring at the signature she'd just left at the bottom of the document.

'Just a precaution,' said Sue.

'Yeah, but we're in the door right?'

'Yes Coops. We're in the door.'

Coops smiled at Sue. 'Not a bad result for a chick with a hangover.'

It was another Saturday and the two women were back in Sue's apartment. Although Michelle Yim had agreed to keep Roper out of their hair, Sue didn't trust Roper to keep his side of the bargain. Sue wanted to work away from prying eyes and had just opened a package of documents she'd received from Raf. The contents of the package were fairly thin, just some background information on Wentworth's network security and some biographies of the project team members.

Coops had also been digging. She'd found some content published by both Robert Meade and the CEO, Craig Martin. She'd also downloaded some of Martin's presentation talks and TV interviews.

'Meade comes across as very people-focused,' said Coops. 'He's published a lot about HR and team-building. But, when he was helping Wentworth develop their mobile apps he also wrote a lot about the whole process of getting to market. He's right across new product development from go to whoa.'

'I got the same impression,' said Sue. 'His ears really pricked up when I started mentioning process. I think he's great with people, but I think he likes to roll his sleeves up and get involved.'

'Sooo,' said Coops, leafing through the stakeholder archetype cards, 'do you reckon he's our Champion?'

'Pretty sure,' said Sue, 'in his journal, Doug mentions that the Champion is the only change agent who's practical, hands-on and project-oriented. I also think he's a champion because he's keen to defend the entire organisation. He's a protector. He's the one who advised the CEO to stay out of the press. He said he doesn't want anyone to go to jail because he couldn't do his job.'

Coops let out a whistle. 'He said that? Well, he could have a point…'

'You think?' said Sue.

'Sure. There's now some stiff penalties in place for large companies who don't disclose security breaches like cyberattacks. They can even fine individuals or slap them in jail.'

'But Wentworth disclosed the attack.'

'Even so, the ACSC and the Federal Police can still fine or imprison individuals for negligence, for not protecting their customers, if they can prove it. And you can bet, if Wentworth's customers were left out-of-pocket, they'd be pointing the finger straight at the bank's C-suite.'

'But has anyone ever been imprisoned?'

'Not yet, but there's always a first time, right?'

Sue was writing. 'You know, this could have the whole C-suite running scared. Fear could be an important factor.'

'In what way?'

'I don't know yet…' Sue looked up from her notepad. She picked up a clipping from a financial magazine about Craig Martin. 'Do we have anything more on the CEO?'

DISCOVER AND DISRUPT

Coops opened her laptop and played some of the interviews and presentations she'd found. Martin was certainly charismatic. He was a spritely man in his mid-fifties with the kind of sparkle in his eyes that suggested he always got a good night's sleep. Sue knew the type: it was usually because they just didn't *need* sleep. He was a dynamo. He fielded every question with a thorough knowledge of the topic and a smile. Often, he disarmed his audience with humour. But it was on the subject of technology that he became most animated. His enthusiasm was infectious. Sue could see it in the eyes of his audience and his interviewers, he'd create a brave new world of technical possibility for them.

'Good, isn't he?' offered Coops.

'He's wonderful on his feet.'

'So what's his archetype you think?'

'Definitely a change agent.'

'Another Champion?' asked Coops.

'No, Robert Meade said Martin doesn't often get too involved. He's not that hands-on. To me, he's got the look of a Sage about him. A communicator, a visionary.'

Coops reached for the Sage archetype card and began to read. 'It says here that the Sage focuses on *communicating the idea.*'

'That's him, he's an ideas man,' said Sue.

'Could explain why he brought Meade in to handle the mobile development products?' said Coops.

'Yeah, Martin needs someone interested in technology and digital innovation, just like him. But he also needs a hands-on manager to see the job through. I think it could be the reason Martin gave Meade the CISO role.'

They returned to the package Raf had sent over and began reading through the biographies, trying to understand the personalities behind them.

'So there's a total of four people in the project team,' said Sue. 'Apart from Raf and Robert Meade, there's also these two: Sally

McCrae, Customer Experience Manager, and Bryce Nichols, the Senior Operations Manager.'

'We need to interview them, right?'

'Right,' said Sue.

'I'm glad they've got someone from customer experience on the team,' said Coops, pointing to Sally McCrae's name on the project team org-chart. 'The whole customer side of things is something we can really help them with.'

Sue smiled. 'Exactly, that's our trump card.'

'So you'll tell her, right? This Sally McCrae?'

'Tell her what?'

'That their crummy CBIS firewall is stuffing up the digital experience for their customers? That the Tesico product is cloud-based, so it doesn't just monitor the hackers, it can monitor the customers' interactions too and help improve them?'

'Ah,' Sue raised a finger. 'But we're not going to tell them that, are we?'

'Why the hell not?' asked Coops, dumbfounded. 'It's our trump card, like you said...'

'That's right Coops, but think back to this EDVANCE process in Doug's book. He says there's a need to take the prospect on a *Journey of Discovery...*'

'Yeah, and?'

'Well, they need to *discover* something, don't they? They need to understand the full extent of the problem for themselves and the impact it's having on customer experience.'

Coops pulled a bewildered face.

'It's all part of Doug's approach Coops. We need to help Wentworth *discover* that their firewall isn't just sub-standard in terms of security, we need to help them *discover* that it's ruining the experience for their customers, and possibly their brand and their business as a result.' Sue could see the wheels turning in Coops's head. 'What was that insight you dug up in the market

DISCOVER AND DISRUPT

research? The insight you wanted to use for your YouTube show?'

'Oh, oh,' said Coops, excited, 'eighty-three percent of companies cite firewall software as a major hindrance to digital innovation.'

'Yep, that's certainly a hot button we can press,' said Sue, 'both Meade and the CEO will be onto it like a flash. And so will the customer experience people.' Sue placed her finger on the org-chart. 'And once they make this discovery for themselves, once they're all aligned on the problem, where do you think they'll head for the solution?'

'Right through Tesico's front door,' said Coops, understanding.

'Exactly,' said Sue.

'So, let me get this right,' said Coops, her face quizzical. 'We're going to *not* tell them about the biggest benefit of our system, so they can figure out what kind of a problem they've got...' Her forefingers began criss-crossing in the air. 'And that the solution to that problem was the benefit of our system all along, so that they'll think they're the smart ones who have figured it all out and lead themselves to our product without us having to push them into it?'

'That's about it,' said Sue. 'It's about taking them on a journey so they can understand the value for themselves. Otherwise, all they see is a salesperson pushing a product.'

'Understood,' said Coops. 'I like it Sue, this discovery thing, it's like planting an idea in their heads. We should update the stakeholder map.'

'Sure.'

Coops crossed the room to Sue's sliding glass door, drew the two axes again and split the map into quadrants. She pointed to the centre of the map and turned to Sue. 'This is where we left Raf. Do we think he's moved?'

'I think so,' said Sue. 'He really helped out by getting me back in front of Meade, so I think we can say our relationship is improving.'

Coops moved Raf further along the relationship axis but kept his level of influence the same. 'And what about Meade?' she asked.

'Well, I guess we have a relationship now,' said Sue. 'But we've only just started.'

'Right,' said Coops, moving Meade from left to right along the relationship axis. She also drew Peter Ludick, the CIO, where they'd left him in their last session. Coops stood back to study the map. 'I guess the next step is to interview these two characters Sally McCrae and Bryce Nichols?'

'Yes.'

'What about Meade? Do we need to interview him again?' asked Coops.

'Not just yet,' said Sue. 'We know enough for now. We know something of his criteria, his fears, and what he's after. We just have to keep developing a relationship there.'

Coops pointed with her pen at Raf's name. 'What about our Accomplice? Do we need to interview him too?'

'Hadn't thought of that,' admitted Sue. 'Yes, he's part of the project team so we need a formal interview with him as well.'

'So what's he after?' asked Coops.

Sue remembered her first meeting with Raf in Cordelia's when she'd asked him the same question. He'd said one word: *change*. He'd looked away as he spoke.

'Honestly,' said Sue, 'I have no idea.'

DISCOVER AND DISRUPT

This book comes with free access to an online reference companion.

By scanning the QR code or by navigating to edvance.sale/recap/discover1/ now, you will gain a deeper understanding of the EDVANCE process and the methodology applied by the characters in the preceding seven chapters, including:

- Identifying Archetypes
- Finding the Champion
- Gap Discovery
- Updated Stakeholder Mapping
- Applying these methods in your own business

21. View From the Inside

'The gaps between our various infrastructures are a kind of blind spot for the firewall,' said Raf, pouring coffee for Coops. Coops smiled in thanks. It was the first time the two had met.

'And the employees' laptops?' asked Sue.

'Yes,' continued Raf. 'They're a weak link too. Once someone takes a laptop out of the office, they're beyond the protection of the central firewall and are only as safe as the network they're connected to.'

The three were seated in a small meeting room in Wentworth Tower. Raf had cleared his diary for the afternoon and was taking Sue and Coops through a detailed appraisal of Wentworth's position. Michelle Yim had been good to her word and had packed Tony Roper off to Melbourne to oversee Tesico's deal with a brokerage firm. Word around the office was that it should proceed without a hitch. The Melbourne-based salesperson had a great relationship with the prospect and the deal was as good as struck. Now Sue and Coops could concentrate on Wentworth.

'But the whole issue with this cat-and-mouse game,' said Raf, 'is that we don't know what the hackers will target next.' He set the coffee pot down with a sigh. 'There's just so many ways to get inside.

Where we choose to upgrade or strengthen the firewall is just guesswork.'

'And what about the places in the firewall exploited by the recent attacks?' asked Sue. 'Have they been patched?'

Raf's eyes met Sue's. 'As best we can,' he said.

'What about CBIS?' asked Sue. 'They have a presence within Wentworth, don't they? Have they been helpful with the patches and upgrades?'

'Sure,' said Raf. 'It's their product. They've got a duty to service and repair it. They're good people but they're as frustrated as our IT security staff. They know the CBIS product has had its day. I know for a fact many of them have updated their resumes and are looking for positions elsewhere.'

'So why does Wentworth stick with CBIS? What's the appeal?'

'There's a few factors,' admitted Raf. 'Their product may be showing its age, but their account penetration is huge. Many of our C-suite execs are finance people. They can't grasp the technical issues. All they understand is that CBIS is still number one in cybersecurity, so that's got to be a good thing, right? It's just herd mentality.'

'You said there were a *few* factors?' queried Sue.

'Yes,' said Raf, 'and the other one is that our CIO, Peter Ludick, is a big supporter of CBIS. He brought them in.'

'And he doesn't want to be proved wrong?' offered Sue.

'Yes,' said Raf. 'Among other things...'

'What other things?'

Raf seemed reluctant to answer. 'Well a lot of people believe he has a bigger goal.'

'Such as?'

'Not really my place to say,' said Raf. 'Besides, it's just speculation.'

Sue and Coops looked at each other and Sue made a mental note. Instincts told her to tread carefully. There was something here,

DISCOVER AND DISRUPT

something important and dangerous. Raf wasn't ready for full disclosure yet. He was too principled, and too loyal to Wentworth to indulge in rumour.

'What about Brenda Huffington, and her relationship with the CIO?' asked Sue, taking a different tack.

'Well, they're very close,' said Raf, 'both personally and professionally, but...'

'But?'

'Well, Brenda, she's a player. She won't deal with people like me. She concentrates on developing relationships with the C-suite. She bypasses the technical staff, the people with a real axe to grind and puts all her effort into dialogue with the higher-ups.'

'So, apart from Peter Ludick, your CIO, who else does she have a relationship with?' asked Sue.

Raf pulled a face. 'That's hard to say. She has access to Robert of course, they have a relationship but I'd say Robert tolerates her. She also has access to the CEO and to our Client Services Director, Jenny Liu, but I have no idea how strong their relationship is. I assume it's good.'

Sue nodded and studied the project team org-chart once again. 'So, we won't have the chance to interview the CIO or the COO until we know they're part of the DMU. But the next step would be to interview the last two members of the project team.' Sue pointed to a pair of names on the org-chart.

'Sure,' said Raf, glancing to where Sue's finger lay. 'Sally McCrae is the Customer Experience Manager. She reports directly to Jenny Liu, the Client Services Director. The other person is Bryce Nichols. He's the Senior Operations Manager and reports to Maria, our COO.'

'What can you tell me about them?'

'Sally is very helpful. You'll learn a lot from her.' Raf's expression became serious. 'But be careful with Bryce.'

'Why?' asked Sue.

'Let's just say he's not much of a team-player.'

Sue noted the warning. 'Can we talk to Sally and Bryce? Soon?'

'Sure,' said Raf. 'I'll set something up.'

'Thanks.' Sue tapped her pen on her notepad for a while, thinking. 'When I asked Robert Meade what he wants out of this process, he said that no-one would go to prison because he couldn't do his job. What do you think he meant?'

Raf studied Sue. 'What do *you* think it meant?'

'I think,' said Sue, 'it means he's worried about the new provisions in the Privacy Act. I think he's worried that senior execs can now be personally prosecuted for being negligent with their customers' data. I think he's trying to protect the whole of the C-suite, and the CEO in particular.'

A faint smile appeared on Raf's face. 'Well, you'd be right. Robert feels it's his job to keep not just the senior execs safe, but the entire company too. He's worried about jobs, reputations and the safe operation of the bank itself. I think it's because he sees what's happening here more clearly than most, he feels the need to move the company towards a safer, more secure solution. But he just keeps butting heads with Ludick and Kutcik.'

'Because they're pro-CBIS?'

'Partly,' said Raf, 'and because Ludick used to be Robert's boss. He still doesn't see Robert as an equal. The two hardly talk, even though their responsibilities overlap.'

'And does Ludick talk to you?'

Raf shrugged.

'But you work in Ludick's department, don't you? Does your relationship with Robert upset him?'

'You'll have to ask him yourself,' said Raf. 'If you ever get the chance to meet.'

'And what about you Raf?' said Sue. 'I know what you fear, but what is it you want out of this process?'

Raf avoided Sue's eyes. 'Like I said before: change.'

'Yes, but what kind of change Raf?'

Raf looked at Sue. 'Change for the better.'

* * *

'He's not playing us with a straight bat, is he?' said Coops to Sue in their Uber back to Tesico.

Sue had been studying the view outside through her sunglasses. It was a hot day in the city. Sunlight bounced from the glass-walled buildings into the streets below. People waiting to cross the road crammed into every available inch of shade and businessmen threw their jackets over their shoulders. She turned to Coops. 'In what way?'

'When you asked him what he wanted out of the whole process...' explained Coops.

'Yes, it's odd,' replied Sue. 'I asked Raf the same question that night in Cordelia's and he said the same thing: change. Of course he wants change, that's obvious. But there's something more. And I can't quite put my finger on it.'

'You reckon he's ridgy didge?'

Sue smiled at Coops. 'Yes, I believe he's being honest with us. I just think he's a professional and a gentleman. When the conversation strays too close to gossip and rumour, I think he gets uncomfortable. He clams up.'

'He didn't want to tell us what he thinks of Ludick, the CIO. He clammed up right there,' said Coops. 'And what does he mean when he says Ludick is supporting CBIS because he has a bigger goal? He didn't want to go into that either. What the hell is that all about?'

'No idea. But it sounds like part of Ludick's informal criteria. We'll have to uncover that ourselves.'

'And this Bryce fellah sounds like a worry,' said Coops.

Sue shot a smile at Coops. 'Welcome to the cut-and-thrust world of sales Coops.'

Coops laughed. Sue's phone rang and she retrieved it from her bag.

'Sue speaking.'

'Sue, it's Raf. I've got you a meeting with both Sally and Bryce.'

'Thanks, that's great, when?'

'Wednesday, eleven am.'

'At the same time? Raf is there any way I can interview them separately?'

'Not if you want to get to them this week. They're at a management seminar, more of a *management retreat* actually. You know how they fill every minute of your day at those things.'

'There's no way I can get to them individually?'

'No. They've got a full day, every day, for the next week. Eleven am Wednesday is their only break. You'll get thirty minutes with both of them.'

Sue let out a sigh of frustration. Interviewing people together was fraught with difficulties.

'I could get them into separate rooms though,' added Raf.

'Why? What do you mean?' asked Sue, confused.

'Well, there's two of you, isn't there? You and Coops? You could still interview them separately.'

Sue shot a look at Coops. Coops raised an eyebrow in question.

'And there's something else you should know...' said Raf.

'Yes?'

'The seminar is out-of-town.'

'Where?'

'A vineyard—in the Hunter.'

'The Hunter Valley?'

'Yes,' said Raf. 'If you want to stay on track with these interviews, it looks like you'd better get yourself up to the wine country.'

Sue hung up and directed a look of alarm at Coops.

'Chin up,' said Coops, offering a timid smile. 'Maybe they do a cheeky little Prosecco?'

22. Divide and Conquer

As Wednesday approached, Sue became more and more of the opinion that Raf was right. The only way to interview both Bryce, the Senior Operations Manager, and Sally, the Customer Experience Manager was for Sue and Coops to split up.

Time was marching on and Sue wanted to achieve as much as possible while Roper was in Melbourne. That window of opportunity would soon come to a close and Sue had no idea what would happen when it did. She also needed to report some kind of positive progress to Michelle. Sue was glad she had Robert Meade's seal of approval to conduct interviews with the project team but knew it was foolish to be complacent. Other security vendors would already be touting their services to the very same people they were interviewing, and Sue was sure that Brenda Huffington was hard at work, somewhere in the higher echelons of Wentworth, securing support for CBIS.

Sue had to keep moving forward.

Splitting Bryce and Sally into separate interviews was the safest way to proceed. That's what Doug always did. He'd helped Sue understand how the dynamic changed in joint interviews. There would always be a dominant interviewee, he'd taught her, one who led the direction of the meeting. The other would remain quiet, even though their answers might be more revealing. With two interviewees in the room, informal criteria remained hidden. People feared disclosing the deeper issues in such environments.

In the lead-up to their Wednesday meeting, Sue coached Coops on her interview technique and together they role-played a variety of different scenarios. With the help of Doug's journal they learned what to look for: all the tell-tale signs that would reveal their interviewees' stakeholder archetypes and their likely motivations. It seemed logical to assume that both Bryce and Sally would be Advocates although nothing could be certain. Remembering Raf's warning, Sue opted to interview Bryce. Then she helped Coops develop her personal story and her own version of a company story.

By the time Wednesday arrived Coops had arranged a hire car. Because Sue's leg was still in a boot, Coops drove them the two and a quarter-hour drive north from Sydney to the Hunter Valley. Coops was clearly nervous but managed to take her mind off things with the country music playlist on her phone. It wasn't Sue's favourite music genre, but she endured the songs of loss, drought, love and land for her friend's benefit, her sacrifice made even greater by the fact that Coops sang along to every single word.

They left the highway and soon the broad, fertile valley of the Hunter wine-making region unfolded before them. Rolling hills were lined with vine trellises and a multitude of tourist road-signs made invitation to a multitude of wineries.

Coops drove through the entrance to Bannerman's Estate Wines and along an avenue bordered with slender poplars. She stopped the car on the white stone-chip drive and leaned forward over the steering wheel. 'Jeez Sue, would you just look at this place.'

They were on top of a hill that offered sweeping views north toward the Hunter River. Spreading below them, terraces of manicured gardens sheltered the chalets of the winery's accommodation. Beside them on the hilltop, an old weatherboard

DISCOVER AND DISRUPT

chapel surrounded by roses served as the cellar door and main tasting area. Whether it was part of the original property or transferred from another site was anyone's guess. Ahead of them was the winery's main building: a modern, sandstone design with floor-to-ceiling windows that took full advantage of the view. A broad, cantilevered balcony shaded with vines projected from one side of the building and seemed to hang in the air above the vineyard.

'Impressive,' said Sue.

'Bloody oath,' agreed Coops. 'Must be good money in grog.'

* * *

While Coops was ushered by winery staff to her meeting with Sally McCrae, Sue was guided to a table on the cantilevered balcony. She now saw it formed the alfresco dining area of the winery's main restaurant.

Bryce Nichols stood to meet Sue. He smiled warmly enough and gestured in invitation to a chair beside him. 'Please,' he said. 'Is there anything I can get you?'

'No, thank you,' returned Sue, propping her elbow crutch against the table. 'Thanks for making the time.'

'Of course.'

'I'll be brief as I can.'

'If you could, they don't give us much downtime here,' said Bryce. 'I've seen the articles you've written that Raf sent through but perhaps you'd like to tell me a little of yourself?'

'Of course, I...'

'In say, sixty seconds?' said Bryce, looking at his watch. He fired another smile at Sue and settled back.

Sue delivered a short version of her personal story. She tried to make it sound as informal and unrehearsed as she could. Bryce seemed nothing less than attentive and smiled throughout.

'So what about you? How did you come to be at Wentworth?' asked Sue, as she'd learned from Doug's notebook.

'Oh, you don't want to hear about me,' said Bryce with a dismissive wave.

'Oh, but I do,' confirmed Sue.

Bryce agreed with a little reluctance and then launched into a lengthy account of his career. After graduating with a double first in economics and a Bachelor of Business, he topped the intern list to secure a strategic role at one of Australia's big four banks. Dissatisfied with the bank's direction, he began looking for a role that better suited his capabilities. Once the finance sector headhunters got wind of this, he was inundated with a range of job offers. As a consequence, he worked briefly in London, Zurich, Hong Kong and Stockholm before being approached by Maria Kutcik at Wentworth. Kutcik needed a protege, he explained, a pair of safe hands in which to leave the bank should she ever leave.

Bryce Nichols seemed very young to be second-in-command to the COO at Wentworth. His rise would have been meteoric. He looked to be in his early thirties, about the same age as Sue. He was slim, fit and obviously took care of his appearance. He was the kind of man who had a skin regime. Sue had no reason to suspect his story was anything but the truth, however, his confidence in its telling seemed a little overplayed.

'Tell me,' began Sue, 'in what way did the attack affect the operational side of Wentworth's business?'

'In no way at all,' replied Bryce.

'Really?' asked Sue, surprised. 'That's the consolidated view of the operations department?'

'Yes.'

'Including the COO, Maria Kutcik?'

Bryce gave Sue a smile. It was a condescending one. 'I speak for Maria,' he said. 'We are of the same opinion.'

'But there must have been some impact on business? Your security people were in a panic, your internet system was taken offline for repair...'

DISCOVER AND DISRUPT

Bryce smiled again. 'Our technical people tend not to see far beyond their own dramas. They are competent at what they do, don't get me wrong, but they fail to see the bigger picture.'

'Which is?'

'The bank is in safe hands.'

Sue considered. Was he referring to Maria Kutcik, himself, or CBIS?

'Do you mean CBIS?' probed Sue.

'Yes, I suppose, in part.'

'Then you believe their firewall provisions are adequate?'

'I believe they are.' Bryce swept his gaze over the vineyards below as if they were his own. 'All this patching, repairing and upgrading, it's just maintenance, isn't it? It's just part and parcel of any security system.' His gaze rested on Sue. 'You can't tell me that the Tesico product never needs upgrading?'

Be careful Sue. It was as if Doug had just whispered in Sue's ear. Bryce was luring her into an argument, to defend Tesico; to reveal the salesperson behind the facade. She wanted to tell Bryce that the AI within the Tesico product would update and manage itself but she resisted. 'I'm not here to sell Tesico product Mister Nichols, I'm here to help identify how the attack affected Wentworth.'

Bryce studied Sue with a spreading smile. His ploy had failed but he'd enjoyed the exchange. Perhaps he even held Sue in higher regard now?

'So, if there was no threat...' continued Sue.

'I didn't say there wasn't a threat,' interrupted Bryce. 'I'm just saying it was discovered and contained.'

'Not by the firewall. It was picked up by your accounts management system.'

'I hadn't realised,' said Bryce. 'But however you look at it, the threat was still addressed. It's proof that our current system works.'

Sue thought of the millions of dollars Wentworth had potentially lost. Nichols was either ignorant or he simply didn't care. Sue could have made the point but she chose not to. It would sound like an attack on CBIS. 'So how do you view the formation of this project team; of the appointment of Mister Meade as CISO? Surely you believe this all points to a degree of concern inside Wentworth?'

'I see this as a case of exercising due diligence,' said Bryce. 'It's a move to pacify the board and the shareholders. And, as for the appointment of Robert Meade as CISO, well...'

Sue waited. 'Yes?'

'I think that's been done for similar reasons.' He paused for emphasis. 'I believe the one person who understands what's best for Wentworth in terms of information security is our CIO, Peter Ludick.'

'So, the recommendation you'll make to the DMU,' concluded Sue, 'is that your current arrangements with CBIS are adequate?'

'Yes.'

'Do you know if Maria Kutcik agrees?'

Bryce gave another of his condescending smiles. 'As I said Miss Novak, the Chief Operating Officer and I are of the same opinion.'

* * *

Coops remained very quiet as she slipped herself into the driver's seat of the hire car. She was like a bottle of soda someone had given a good shake: about to burst.

Sue let her drive back along the avenue of tall poplars, and out through the gates of Bannerman's Estate in silence.

'So, how'd it go?' asked Sue, as they reached the main road.

Coops turned towards her with a broad smile, 'Mate, you wouldn't credit it... she went off! I got all the goss on what the customer relations people reckon, her boss Jenny Liu, what they think of the IT mob and how the firewall has stuffed any chance of them innovating or developing any new product lines and that, and how they had to take the customer portal down when they got hacked because the bloody firewall needed patching and I couldn't shut her up and she just carried on and on like a pork chop about how CBIS need their arses kicked but no-one'll do it because they're all shit-scared of Ludick and Kutcik and losing their jobs...'

Sue was amazed that Coops sometimes didn't need to breathe as she spoke. The car had begun to wander across the white lines onto the opposite side of the road. Sue pointed through the windscreen. 'Coops, watch the road.'

'Sorry,' said Coops, hunching behind the wheel and steering them back to safety.

Sue didn't want to admit it but she was still nervous while riding in cars. She suggested they stop somewhere for lunch. They found a cafe which doubled as an antique shop. After they'd each ordered and handed their menus back to the waitress, Sue let Coops unload.

'That whole business about starting with a story, like Doug said, it worked like a charm Sue,' said Coops. 'I told her that I came from Coota and she said she came from outside Orange and suddenly we're best mates. She's even invited me out for a drink when she gets back to town.'

'That's great,' said Sue. 'You should take her up on that.'

'And then she just started up. Honestly Sue, I couldn't get a word in,' Coops smiled. 'Which, as you know, is pretty unusual for me...'

Sue laughed. This much was true. 'So what did you learn?'

'Well,' said Coops, scanning the cafe to make sure they weren't overheard. 'The key point is that the attack *did* affect customer relations—*big time*. They had to take the customer portal offline to fix it. It was down for some time and many of their customers couldn't get to their money and investments. So, of course, there was a shit-storm. The customer relations people tied themselves in knots trying to calm everything down. They emailed, and snail-mailed and phoned their clients, just to keep a lid on things. But that's not the real problem...'

'Oh?'

Coops leaned over the table, her voice a whisper. 'I hit her with that insight I dug up from the research, you know, about how firewall software holds back product innovation?'

'Sure, I remember...' said Sue.

'Well,' said Coops, rolling her eyes. 'That's when she really went off. She said that's what she's been saying all along but no-one takes any notice. She said she's been trying to push the issue upstream and her boss, Jenny Liu, the Client Services Director, agrees but she won't do anything about it.'

'Why not?' asked Sue.

'They're all running scared of Kutcik and Ludick.'

'The COO and CIO?'

'Yeah,' said Coops. 'Like we guessed, Ludick is behind CBIS all the way and he and Maria Kutcik are thick as thieves. Kutcik is powerful, second-in-command to the CEO, and she sounds like a real hardarse. Kutcik and Ludick gang up on anyone who opposes them or CBIS. Jenny Liu isn't on the C-suite, so she just cops it. And all the customer service people who work for her just pull their heads in.'

A pot of tea arrived and Sue poured.

'And it's a good job we interviewed them separately Sue,' said Coops, stirring her tea.

'Why?'

'Because Sally doesn't like your Bryce fellah one bit. She really spilled on him. Word is, he's a bit of an arse-licker. He just falls in behind his boss, Kutcik. And he's got tickets on himself too: when Kutcik is away, he calls himself the acting COO, telling everyone what to do and whatnot.'

'Acting COO?' said Sue.

'Yeah,' said Coops, 'As if.'

'Do Sally or her boss Jenny have any kind of relationship with Robert Meade?'

'Not really,' said Coops.

'That's a real shame,' said Sue. 'He'd be on their side.'

'What I hear from Sally,' added Coops, 'is that they see Meade as powerless against Ludick and Kutcik. He's a new appointment, he has no department and he even reported to Ludick back in the day. So he lacks the clout. I get the feeling they don't want to be seen siding with him.'

'But he's got a job to do and he has the support of the CEO. Perhaps that's something we should point out?'

'Maybe,' said Coops. 'But I don't think they see him as having the same kind of power as Kutcik or Ludick. Sally even dropped a hint that Ludick has plans to extend his power.'

Sue remembered. 'That's what Raf was hinting at too. He said Ludick has a *bigger goal*. Did Sally clue you in on what that might be?'

Coops shook her head.

'This is how companies shoot themselves in the foot,' said Sue.

'How's that?'

'Well, look at the factions, the power-plays,' explained Sue. 'Wentworth is a service organisation but the customer service people are running scared and their ability to do their jobs is undermined. The real power lies with operations and IT. The bank's focus is lopsided.'

'S'right,' said Coops. 'They've fallen behind all their competitors when it comes to customer service and providing newer and better products. They've been tied down by the firewall and they can't innovate. Their customers have had it up to the eyeballs with the standard of online service they get and it's the main reason they're leaving in droves.'

Sue was surprised. 'Sally told you this?'

'Yep.'

'Does she have any evidence?'

'She said they've got some research—they've done a number of consumer surveys over the last few years.'

'Have they shared the findings? Within the bank?'

'Not yet.'

Sue thought for a moment. 'We need to request that research.'

'I already did.'

'Oh?'

'Sally won't hand it over.'

'Why not?'

'She said Jenny wouldn't let her. It's sensitive. I guess they're scared of the fallout. There's another reason...'

'What's that?'

'She said,' continued Coops, 'that the belief is, Tesico is too small to implement change for a bank the size of Wentworth. That's why we won't get our hands on it.'

'But it's not about us, it's about them understanding the challenges for the bank. The findings of that research needs to be a part of their discovery.' Sue was frustrated. 'And why the hell does everything keep coming back to change management?'

'Do you think we could ask Robert Meade for his help?' suggested Coops. 'We could tell him about the research and ask to see it?'

'Not sure,' said Sue. 'Could be dangerous.' She thought for a moment, then dug into her bag, pulling out a notepad and Doug's stakeholder cards. 'Let's take a look at Sally, what archetype do you think she is Coops?'

'Well, she's definitely no Change Agent.'

'Why?' asked Sue.

'Well, she's powerless. She pushes everything up to her boss, Jenny Liu.'

'So she's an Advocate?'

'I reckon.'

'Which one?' Sue spread the stakeholder cards in front of her.

'I'd say she was an Accomplice, like Raf.'

'Why's that?'

'Well,' mused Coops, 'she's helpful. She's invited me out for a drink—that's a bit like you and Raf catching up at Cordelia's, isn't it?'

'Maybe,' said Sue. 'But remember, Raf shies away from gossip. I don't think Sally does. Sally seems to thrive on gossip, on sharing inside information and her personal opinion. And just think about that whole thing with the consumer research—why would she admit its existence if she won't let us see it?'

Coops's face was a puzzle. 'She likes being in the know?'

'Exactly,' said Sue. 'She makes up for a lack of influence by controlling the flow of information. Information makes her feel of value.' Sue pointed to one of the archetype cards. 'I think this is her.'

Coops stared at the card. 'A Messenger? I hadn't thought of that.'

'I think Sally McCrae could be a big help to us if we keep her on side. You should definitely meet up for that drink in Sydney. She might give us more on Ludick's big plans.'

Coops nodded gravely, accepting the mission.

'And, if Sally is a Messenger,' continued Sue, 'I think asking for Robert Meade's help in getting hold of the consumer research could backfire. It'll be a betrayal of Sally's trust—of what she's told us in confidence. And we don't want a negative Messenger.'

'Oh?' said Coops. 'Because the flow of information will stop?'

'More than that,' said Sue. 'It'll flow the other way. She'll use information against us, to discredit us within Wentworth. We need to keep her on-side. Somehow we need to include that consumer research in Wentworth's journey of discovery.'

'But Sally isn't just going to hand it over,' said Coops.

'Perhaps there's a way to buy it.'

'Buy it how?'

'She's a Messenger, information is her currency, remember?'

'We offer *her* information?'

'Something privileged. Something that won't be common knowledge within Wentworth,' said Sue.

Coops studied the archetype cards on the cafe table for a time. 'And what about you Sue? How'd you go with *your* interview, with this Bryce fellah?'

'Well, he certainly loves to talk about himself. He's worked for at least five different companies in around seven years and I get the impression he's never had loyalty for any of them, Wentworth included. The money Wentworth lost doesn't seem to worry him in the slightest, nor the fact that their customers suffered. I think the only thing that does worry him is how he's perceived. He's a corporate climber.' Sue flipped over one of the stakeholder archetype cards to reveal its face. 'This is him, our Mister Nichols.'

'Oo,' said Coops. 'A Mercenary?'

'Yep,' said Sue. 'It's written all over him.'

23. The Usurper

Sue had just hit the 'call' button on her laptop's teleconference app when Roper marched into her cubicle. Sue and Coops were huddled in front of Sue's webcam. Roper's eyes flitted between the two women as the ringtone sounded.

'We need to talk,' he said, turning away. 'My office.'

'But Tony,' protested Sue, 'we've got a meeting.'

'It can wait,' said Roper over his shoulder.

'But it's with Michelle.'

Roper turned back. 'About what?'

'About Wentworth,' explained Sue. 'We're updating her.'

'Good,' said Roper. 'We'll do it in my office.'

Sue sighed and hung up before Michelle had a chance to answer. Then she and Coops dutifully made their way to Roper's office.

'Not you,' said Roper from his desk, glaring at Coops. Her jaw clenched and she turned on her heel. 'And close the door,' he added as she left.

'Tony, she's been working hard on this too. If we don't land Wentworth, she has the same to lose as me,' said Sue. She could have told him she needed Coops to debrief Michelle on her interview with Sally, that she wanted Michelle to see what a great job she'd done, but she knew Roper wouldn't approve.

'She's in enablement,' said Roper, impassive, staring at his laptop screen as he placed the call to Michelle. 'She's not a salesperson.' Then, under his breath as the ringtone sounded: 'And I doubt she ever will be.'

Michelle answered and Roper led the meeting, as if it had all been on his initiative. Sue stifled her annoyance. She was supposed to be reporting to Michelle directly; that was the arrangement. Roper just couldn't let it alone. But this was not the forum in which to complain.

'I thought you were in Melbourne this week Tony?' quizzed Michelle.

'I fly back in a few days,' he replied.

'Everything going okay?'

'As well as can be expected.' Roper's expression gave nothing away. 'I'll fill you in on the details later.'

Sue gave a brief account of her recent meeting with Robert Meade. She tried to make it sound like it wasn't a roaring success, that it was productive and businesslike, but Roper still glowered in silence. Then she debriefed them on the meetings with Bryce Nichols and Sally McCrae. When Sue revealed the existence of the consumer surveys, Michelle zeroed in.

'These surveys,' asked Michelle, 'do they support what we know to be true?'

'Apparently,' said Sue. 'The CBIS firewall has crippled their chance to innovate, the way firewalls always do. Their customers are fed up with the poor online service they're getting and are looking elsewhere. Wentworth is losing customers, and they'll continue to do so.'

'This is key,' said Michelle. 'So why isn't Wentworth taking notice of these surveys? Why aren't they listening to their customers?'

DISCOVER AND DISRUPT

'I guess,' offered Sue, 'because they're only surveys. Just a few angry emails from some disgruntled customers. It's not like quantitative research.'

'But surely they must have more accurate data on their customers and the quality of their experience?' questioned Michelle.

'I don't know,' admitted Sue. 'There's another reason Wentworth isn't taking these surveys seriously...'

'Oh?' said Michelle.

'Only the customer experience department knows about them.'

'They haven't shared them?' asked Michelle.

'I think they're scared,' explained Sue. 'There's a difference of opinion in Wentworth's management. The CIO and COO are CBIS supporters and they tend to gang up on anyone who threatens that position. The customer experience department is scared—scared they'll be seen as troublemakers, that they'll be discredited.'

'Then we need to help them,' said Michelle. 'Wentworth needs to understand the extent of the problem they're faced with.'

Of course Michelle was right. This was the discovery Wentworth needed to make for themselves. This would be their disruption; the coin on the track that would derail their train of thought. Sue now saw why Michelle and Doug had worked well together, why they had relied on each other. Even though Michelle had never read Doug's journal, she and Doug saw things the same way.

'It'll be an eye-opener for Robert Meade and Raf Singh,' said Sue. 'And if we get them to agree with the customer service department that this is the crux of the matter, then we'll drive consensus between at least three of the four people on the project team. The only outsider will be Bryce Nichols.'

Michelle nodded. 'Sue, please go through the survey responses and put together some kind of summary. Then let's circulate this among the project team members as quick as we can, making sure Robert Meade understands the implications.'

'I would if I could...' stammered Sue. 'But Jenny Liu, the Director of Customer Services won't release the survey results to Tesico.'

Michelle was stunned. 'Why not?'

Sue took a deep breath. 'She believes we're not the solution for Wentworth. That we're too small to offer change management for a bank their size.'

Roper gave a grunt of amusement. 'She might have a point,' he said.

Michelle shot a look of disapproval in Roper's direction. 'Tony, I think it's time you contacted Jamie DeSouza at Onicas. Just as a courtesy. He needs to be ready to work with us on Wentworth if this progresses.'

Roper's expression gave nothing away. 'The Melbourne deal is taking up a lot of my time,' he explained.

'I'm happy to call Jamie and bring him up to speed,' offered Sue.

'No you won't,' said Roper. 'When I get time, I'll do it.'

'But if you're tied up with Melbourne and I'm taking point on Wentworth then it makes sense that I call them...' said Sue.

'No it doesn't,' said Roper, controlling his anger. He laid his palms flat on the desk and turned towards Sue. 'I will make the call and I want you to keep your nose out of it.'

'How about,' began Michelle, bringing the discussion back to business, 'we try to get to the Client Services Director, Jenny Liu, and persuade her of the importance of her customer surveys, not for us, but for Wentworth.'

'I think that's exactly the stance to take,' agreed Sue. 'But at the moment, she won't talk to us.'

'Do we need to talk to Robert Meade?' asked Michelle. 'Should I step in?'

Sue shook her head. 'No, not just yet. I have an idea that might get her to meet us willingly.'

Michelle nodded. 'Very good Sue, your call. Tony, update me on our Melbourne prospect when you can.'

'Of course,' said Roper. 'Bye.'

Michelle's face disappeared from the screen. Roper closed the lid of his laptop and turned to Sue. His face was a thundercloud. 'You will not go anywhere near Onicas, do I make myself clear? You will not speak with Jamie-bloody-DeSouza...'

'But Michelle has asked us to...' Sue pointed out.

'She's out of touch with what's happening here. This isn't Singapore or New York. She doesn't have a clue. Onicas will bring us nothing but trouble, believe me, I've seen it all before.'

Sue stared at him. *What had he seen before?*

'I will not have Onicas anywhere near this office. Get Wentworth to understand they need to look at change management themselves under a separate contract.'

Sue didn't answer. She didn't know how to.

'Or you can kiss your job goodbye.'

DISCOVER AND DISRUPT

24. At the Bottom of the Hole

'You'll love this place,' said Raf to Sue. 'It's one of the few places they cook with a clay tandoor.'

Sue surveyed the lunchtime patrons of the Amritsari restaurant. They looked as eclectic as the restaurant itself. It was one of those East Sydney eateries that seldom made its way into the tourist guidebooks. It was a clash of bright, Indian colour and Sydney minimalism. A soft groove of Indian club music thrummed in the background. On one wall, a projector cast black and white footage of dance sequences from old Bollywood movies. The place oozed a confident modernity, but in an oddly traditional way.

Sue wasn't a particular aficionado of Indian cuisine so trusted Raf to order for her. He looked different today: rested, more relaxed. Sue studied him as he handed their menus to a waiter, ordering in Hindi. He wore a light suit over a crisp white shirt, unbuttoned at the neck. The white shirt accented the coal-black waves of his hair and the chocolate of his eyes. He turned to face her with a bright smile. Sue imagined that if Raf Singh were standing on the face of the sun, he'd still look cool and comfortable.

The food arrived quickly and Sue was pleasantly surprised. She often found Indian food too rich, particularly at lunchtime. There was a platter of assorted curries in miniature bowls which Raf called *thali*. Tandoori meat sizzled on an iron plate and, instead of rice, there was some kind of chapati or roti bread that Raf told her was called *kulcha*. It was a serving designed to please by variety, not by size.

'Here, you have to try the *makhani*, it's a classic...' said Raf, pointing with enthusiasm. Sue let the meal pass without talking business but simply enjoying Raf's company and listening to him explain the nuances of Indian culinary art.

'It's delicious,' said Sue with genuine appreciation.

'Yeah,' said Raf, wiping a *kulcha* through the thick sauce on his plate. 'I miss good Punjabi cooking...'

'Is that where your family's from? Originally?' ventured Sue.

'Oh, heavens no,' said Raf. 'I'm from Goa. My father still lives there. He's an optometrist, *was* an optometrist. Then he became a lens grinder, made his own lenses for spectacles, then he opened a factory and made lenses for everything from microscopes to magnifying glasses. He did pretty good for a Goa boy.'

'So did you.'

Raf blushed a little. 'Me? Oh no. It was all my old man's doing. He made enough money to send my sister and I to school in the UK. Then I went to university there and took a degree in cybersecurity.'

Sue listened to the genteel chime of Raf's accent. 'Where was that Raf, Oxford, Cambridge?'

Raf laughed. 'No, no...' He leaned towards her with a smile. 'Portsmouth,' he said. 'And what about you? *Novak*, is that a Russian name?'

'Ukrainian,' said Sue.

'Uh-huh...' noted Raf with interest.

'That's where my father's family came from,' said Sue. 'But my mother's side are Irish. They met here.' It dawned on Sue how great it was to be alive in this city; to be sitting here, an Irish-Ukrainian-

DISCOVER AND DISRUPT

Australian, sharing a meal with an English-educated Indian. It felt as if all the problems in the world could be solved at tables like these.

'So we're both immigrants,' said Raf.

'It's Australia,' observed Sue. 'We're *all* immigrants.'

Raf smiled. 'That's what makes the place special, no?' He gestured towards the food on the table. 'Here we can embrace what's best in our different cultures rather than letting it divide us.'

Sue regarded the food absently. 'What about Wentworth's culture Raf? What about the divisions there?'

Raf placed his napkin on the table, sensing lunch was over. 'You mean between the C-suite and the technical staff? That they don't have the knowledge to do what's right and we don't have the influence?'

Sue shook her head. 'That's a divide, it's true. But I was talking more about the divide between the customer service department and the rest of the bank.'

Raf turned in his seat to face her with a look of concern. 'There's a divide there?'

'Sure,' said Sue. 'The cyberattack hit everyone hard, we all know that. The customer portal went offline while the firewall was being patched and customers began to panic. This was a huge blow for the customer experience people, but it's just part of a much bigger grievance.'

'Oh?'

'Keeping the CBIS firewall in place means they're finding it hard to bring new online consumer products to market. The digital touchpoints, the products your customers use to access and manage their money through the internet are just—*clunky*. They glitch, they break—and Wentworth's customers are disillusioned.'

'But isn't it the customer service department's responsibility to fix that?'

'Yes, but the firewall holds them back. They're trying to offer an online experience that's slick, interactive and reliable—but from behind a network-embedded firewall that's almost impossible. It's like trying to design a flashy new car around a steam engine. No matter how hard they re-style and re-engineer, it's still a steam engine.'

The penny was slowly dropping, as was Raf's jaw.

'Wentworth's competitors are way ahead,' continued Sue. 'And that's why you've been haemorrhaging customers. It's been a slow, steady drain. This is a much bigger issue than security Raf. It's bigger than protecting your customers' funds and their data. You're losing business, you're losing money, your share-price is tanking and it's all because of your security arrangements.'

Raf sat back. 'Did you get all this from Sally?' he asked.

Sue nodded. 'Most of it, yes.'

'Why haven't we heard this before?'

'Because Jenny Liu and her department are scared...'

'Of what?'

'Of the CBIS camp. Of Kutcik and Ludick,' said Sue. 'I also think they're scared to raise it because they lack any hard evidence. They have some responses to customer surveys, but that's it.'

Raf stared at Sue for a moment, wide-eyed. Then he sat upright. 'We have to talk to Robert. He should know about this. He should see these surveys...'

'In time, he will. But Jenny is reticent to share the surveys and it's not a good idea for Robert to talk to Jenny about them. It could drive a wedge between them both and put Sally offside.' Sue took a long breath. 'Raf, if you'll let me, I think there's another way. I think I can get these surveys without ruffling feathers. Will you trust me?' The word *trust* rang with significance for Sue. She had asked for Raf's trust before in order to get back in front of Robert Meade. Now she was asking for his trust again.

'I guess,' agreed Raf, 'but we need to move quickly.'

'We need to move *carefully*, Raf. Don't you see what this is?'

Raf looked puzzled.

DISCOVER AND DISRUPT

'Remember what I said to Robert about driving consensus on the problem first?'

'Yes,' said Raf, still puzzled.

'Remember what I said about going down that hole to uncover the deepest problems and challenges?'

'Yes?' said Raf.

'Well, this is it Raf,' said Sue. 'We're standing at the bottom of that hole right now. And we've found the biggest problem facing Wentworth. It's a problem that no-one can ignore. If we handle this the right way, it will drive consensus in the project team. It will drive consensus and close the divide between the IT staff and the C-suite. It will close the divide between the CBIS camp and those outside it. It will close the gap between the customer services department and the operational side of the bank...'

Raf's face showed a glimmer of understanding.

'This is your *discovery* Raf,' said Sue.

Raf nodded now, comprehending. 'I see, I see,' he said, 'but we still need to move quickly...'

'*Carefully*,' Sue cautioned him again.

'I was going to tell you this after lunch,' said Raf. 'But you see, the DMU is being announced tomorrow. Robert needs a recommendation from the project team—and he needs it now.'

The Wentworth Prospect

This book comes with free access to an online reference companion.

By scanning the QR code or by navigating to edvance.sale/recap/discover2/ now, you will gain a deeper understanding of the EDVANCE process and the methodology applied by the characters in the preceding chapters of the story, including:

- Gap Discovery
- Current State vs Desired State
- Updated Stakeholder Mapping
- Applying these methods in your own business

DISCOVER AND DISRUPT

25. The Evil Empire

'Will I ever dance again doc?' asked Sue.

Sue's physiotherapist was a woman in her forties with the forearms of a professional arm-wrestler. She re-fitted the soft cast on Sue's leg and smiled. 'You'll be fine,' she said. 'But I wouldn't audition for the Australian Ballet just yet.'

Stretching and exercising the ligaments and tendons in Sue's damaged body was an ordeal. The pain inflicted by the hands of her burly physiotherapist was excruciating but Sue was grateful for the increased mobility she felt afterwards. The swelling on her cheek had gone and her doctor had concluded that the cheekbone had healed, even though it still felt tender to the touch. She was also less dependent on her painkillers: her cracked ribs had healed enough to allow her a good night's sleep although they still sent her into spasms of pain if she coughed or sneezed. She felt some of her old energy returning and it helped her deal with things: with Wentworth, with Roper, with the loss of Doug. She was on the mend, but felt frustrated that the process was taking so long.

It was mid-morning when Sue limped into the Tesico office on her elbow crutch. She cast a cautious glance through the glass wall of Roper's office as she passed. It was empty.

'It's alright,' said Coops, leaping up from her workstation. She continued in a loud whisper: 'He's in Melbourne till the end of the week.' A few of the sales assistants looked up from their desks and smiled.

Sue could now see that Coops was almost hopping with excitement. 'You okay?' she asked.

'Better than okay,' confirmed Coops with a grin.

Sue nodded towards the glass-walled breakout room and Coops followed.

'Guess what I've just swung?' said Coops, closing the door.

'No idea,' said Sue, sitting.

'I just got us a meeting with Jenny Liu,' squealed Coops.

'The Customer Services Director?' Sue was incredulous.

'Yep,' said Coops. 'Sally McCrae just texted me. Our plan worked.'

'That's great Coops. You finally caught up for drinks then?'

'Sure did, last night,' began Coops. 'We went over to some new place near King Street Wharf which was all done up like a tree at Christmas. I never guessed having a drink with Sally would be such hard work. She sat on the same bloody glass of white wine *all night*, and there's me, one drink in, with an empty glass, dry as a chip, listening to her carry on and on like a pork chop...'

'Coops,' said Sue, attempting to get her friend on-subject.

'Sorry,' said Coops. 'Anyway, she kicks off telling me all about the pressure the customer services division is under. The bank knows there's a revenue drain and the COO and the CIO are pointing the finger at customer services...'

'Ludick and Kutcik are blaming them for the losses?'

'S'right,' confirmed Coops. 'The *evil empire* Sally calls them. She says Ludick and Kutcik are giving her and Jenny the rough end of the pineapple with some very tough KPIs. Customer services are under the pump Sue, but they know the real problem is in IT, they know the CBIS firewall is the problem but Ludick won't have it.'

'Did Sally mention anything about Ludick's plans?' asked Sue.

DISCOVER AND DISRUPT

'Did she ever,' said Coops, rolling her eyes ceilingward. 'I think it's mostly water-bubbler talk but there's a strong feeling that Ludick wants control of all information, including customer data.'

'But that's stepping into Robert Meade's area of responsibility,' said Sue.

'Not the way Ludick sees it,' said Coops. 'He's the Chief *Information* Officer and he sees his role as governing *all* information, not just security and corporate information but client data management too. Word is, he's planning to set up a separate system to control client data and place himself in charge of it.'

'And force Robert Meade out of a position?'

Coops gave a wide-eyed nod. 'And you know who he'll get to secure this new network?'

'CBIS?'

Coops nodded again. 'I bet Ludick and the Huff are plotting right now.'

'It's crazy,' said Sue. 'They'll just be compounding the problem. And surely the CEO won't leave Robert Meade exposed? He's the one who appointed him.'

Coops shrugged. 'Hard to say what'll happen. This Ludick fellah sounds cunning as a dunny rat and who knows how the politics will play out.'

'It's our job to understand the politics and get the stakeholders working together, for their own benefit,' said Sue.

'Sounds like herding cats to me.'

'So, tell me about getting this meeting with Jenny Liu.'

'Oh, oh,' said Coops, waving her hands in excitement. 'This is the best bit—I told Sally about the changes in the Privacy Act, all very casual, like we planned, and about how some of the Wentworth C-suite are worried they'll go to jail. I mention that Meade is trying to protect the C-suite and the CEO in particular. I make it sound like it's all hush-hush, the way we discussed, and she shouldn't tell anyone. Course, she's on it like a shot. She asks me, could Jenny, her boss, go to jail if customer data is breached? I say *maybe*, and she's like *shit-a-brick*. I sort of suggested in a round-about way that if Ludick and Kutcik were already pointing the finger at Jenny and Sally for the revenue drain, then they'd likely do the same if there was a serious data breach too.'

'You could be right on that score,' said Sue. 'How did she react?'

'She went for it like you said she would,' said Coops. 'I told her to keep it under her hat and that the best way she could help Jenny is to convince her to meet with us and discuss how we can help protect them from prosecution *and* the evil empire.'

Sue sat back in her chair with a sigh. 'So she took that bit of gossip back to Wentworth...'

'And she's let Jenny in on the secret,' said Coops. 'You're right about her being a Messenger Sue, she loves to traffic in gossip.'

'And now it's got Jenny worried.'

'Worried enough to meet with us,' concluded Coops.

Sue flashed Coops a broad smile. 'Great job Coops. You're really getting the hang of this.'

Coops beamed. 'All thanks to you Sue,' she said.

'And Doug.'

'And Doug,' agreed Coops. 'And there's something else you should know...'

'Oh?'

'Raf just sent us both an email,' said Coops. 'The DMU has been announced.'

Sue booted up her laptop. 'Does it say who's taking part?'

'Sure does,' said Coops. 'The CEO, Ludick, Kutcik, Meade and Jenny Liu.'

'Jenny Liu is on the DMU, even though she's not part of the C-suite?'

'That's right,' said Coops.

'Then our meeting with Jenny will be more important than ever,' said Sue.

DISCOVER AND DISRUPT

26. Southerly Buster

A rough wind had blown in from the Southern Ocean bringing cooler air and mountainous clouds that hid the sun. It was the kind of wind that blew umbrellas inside-out and formed white-caps in the harbour. It overturned the bistro chairs and menus on blackboards at the restaurants in East Circular Quay and chased litter through the narrow, convict-brick alleyways of The Rocks.

Sydneysiders call this kind of wind a *Southerly Buster* after its legendary ability to break shutters and crack windowpanes. Sue watched the darkening sky through the window of her Uber. It had been bright blue only a few hours before. The drop in temperature had broken the heat of the day but an electrical storm was gathering behind the high wall of cloud. Sue had left the office early, eager to reach the sanctuary of her Potts Point apartment before the storm broke. She also had some research she wanted to complete in private.

The first, fat drops of rain hit the glass of the windscreen and the traffic began to slow. Sue decided to make use of her time by calling Raf. He was glad to hear that Sue now had an appointment to meet Jenny Liu, the Customer Services Director. Sue asked Raf to pass this onto Robert Meade, to let him know she was making progress, that everything was moving in the right direction.

'Don't worry,' said Raf. 'I haven't told him about the surveys yet.'

'Thanks Raf,' said Sue. 'When I get my hands on them, you'll be the first to know. Has Robert mentioned anything more about the project team's findings?'

'Yes. He's getting very anxious. Now that the DMU has been announced, he needs a recommendation from the project team—like *yesterday*.'

'I'm moving as fast as I can Raf, but this is delicate.'

'I know, I know. So does Robert, but he needs this wrapped up.'

'The recommendations will be far easier to put together once I've got all the project team to see the problem the same way,' said Sue. 'Can you tell him that?'

'He understands,' said Raf. 'Perhaps I could tell him about this problem, about our discovery?'

Sue was glad to hear Raf using her terminology, Doug's terminology. 'Maybe not just yet. I still need those surveys as proof, and I need the customer services people to stand up and be counted.'

'Okay, I'll try to buy you some more time.'

The rain unleashed itself. It was carried sideways by the gusting wind, striking the Uber like a volley of arrows. Sue plugged a finger in her free ear. It was getting difficult to hear Raf.

'I've another favour to ask,' said Sue.

'Oh yes?'

'I need to meet the other members of the DMU,' shouted Sue. 'Any chance you could help set up meetings with the CEO, the COO and the CIO?'

There was a long pause from Raf. 'Okay, I'll try,' he said.

In the short walk from the Uber to the door of her apartment building Sue was drenched. She took a hot shower and changed. Although it was dark outside, it was still only late afternoon and there was plenty Sue wanted to do. She knew that, with Coops's help, she'd planted a seed of fear in the minds of Jenny Liu and Sally

DISCOVER AND DISRUPT

McCrae. She knew that the forthcoming meeting with Jenny would be centred on the threat of prosecution for the bank's senior officers under the Notifiable Data Breaches Regulations of the Privacy Act. Questions would be fired at her and Sue needed to know the answers.

She began by phoning one of her contacts at the Australian Cyber Security Centre, someone she'd met at the conference on that fatal trip with Doug. She learned that cybercrime was still one of the top four most likely threats to Australian business, along with extreme weather, climate change and natural disaster. Sue listened, riveted, as she watched the wind-driven rain outside her window. In the previous year, Sue learned, nearly one in three companies had experienced a data breach of some kind, yet over thirteen percent of these were unaware any kind of breach had taken place. Corporate data policies were in disarray and less than ten percent of the corporate sector had any kind of defined data risk statement. Data was being looted and customers of service organisations such as Wentworth were left largely in the dark that their precious data had been stolen. The emphasis was on defence, on protection from the threat, rather than response or the notification of authorities and customers alike.

It was against this background that the Notifiable Data Breaches Scheme had been passed. Much like the General Data Protection Regulations in Europe, its objective was to make the corporate sector sit up and take notice. The provision for mandatory reporting and harsh penalties for non-disclosure were designed to make companies monitor their network security more closely.

Sue wanted to know how cases of negligence were brought against individuals. She wanted to know if anyone had, in fact, been jailed or fined under the provisions of the Act, or whether anyone was in the process of being so. Her contact gave her the phone number of a senior constable in the Australian Federal Police Cyber Crime Division who was seconded to the ACSC. He turned out to be taciturn, probably sticking to a departmental script. No, nobody had been jailed. Yes, a long list of individuals had been fined. Yes, he could send her the details of offending organisations. No, he could not say whether the AFP was planning to make an example of any one organisation. He did elaborate on the penalties though: up to ten million dollars for an organisation or ten percent of their annual turnover, and a jail term and a fine of up to half a million dollars for individuals.

The call ended and Sue sat in thought for some time. She booted up her laptop and filled a fresh document with everything she'd just learned. She re-read it and was struck with an idea. Sue navigated to Doug's EDVANCE journal and hit open. Again, she read the first section of the EDVANCE process: Engage. As Doug explained it, the *Engagement* step was an ongoing process. It would attract new leads and even help with the *Discover and Disrupt* step for ongoing prospects.

Navigating back to the document she'd just written on the Notifiable Data Breach Scheme, it occurred to Sue that this was of greater importance than mere background for her meeting with Jenny. It was something she could use as an ongoing part of her *Engagement* strategy. She copied and pasted the notes into a separate document and began writing a blog on the subject. She had no plans, and made no conclusions as she wrote. She tried to keep the piece informative, balanced, and objective. Within an hour she had a detailed appraisal of the Scheme and the need for captains of industry to pay careful attention to its provisions and, more importantly, its penalties.

She searched the corners of her brain for a suitable title and sat, fingers hovering over her keyboard. Giving up on the laptop she picked up a pencil and scrawled onto a notepad, letting her mind wander. She lifted the pencil and found three letters underneath: CCC. It was an initialisation, an abbreviation: *Cybercrime Complacency*.

DISCOVER AND DISRUPT

She knew the title now and wrote at the top of the document: *The Harsh Penalties for Cybercrime Complacency.*

The piece was finished and Sue was pleased with the result. She thought about posting it on social media straight away. She hesitated. Was it too controversial? Too alarmist? She thought back to Doug's journal: *Use your viewpoints as starting points for articles. Get known for them. Don't be frightened of being controversial. Challenge the status quo. That way, when the status quo changes for your potential customers, you'll be there to help them.*

Sue looked up. The darkness outside made a mirror of the glass door to her balcony. The wind still raged, bowing the glass in and out. It distorted her reflection: a woman seated at her laptop, her face lit by the glow of the screen.

But, if a storm is coming, thought Sue, *don't people have a right to know?*

27. The Door That Melted

'I'm only agreeing to this meeting on Sally's recommendation,' said Jenny Liu, the Customer Services Director. She threw a look in Sally's direction. Sally seemed less comfortable with the reasoning.

Sue couldn't make up her mind whether Jenny's po-faced expression was her *resting meeting face* or whether she was wearing it exclusively for this appointment. Either way, the poker expression would make it hard to decode Jenny's archetype. Sue had brought Coops along to the meeting for continuity reasons, and because she and Sally were developing a relationship. Sue wanted that to continue.

'Sally tells me that we have to be careful, that there are risks—*legal risks*,' began Jenny.

'Yes there are,' returned Sue.

'But we're in the clear, surely? The cyberattack only breached our core systems. The firewall certainly causes us headaches from time-to-time but in this case it did its job. The attack was deflected by the firewall before it breached our customer accounts.'

'That's not strictly true,' said Sue. 'The attack was detected behind the firewall by account monitoring software. Your firewall had already failed.'

There was a softening in the po-faced expression which looked a little like nervousness. 'I don't believe you.'

'You can confirm with Raf Singh or Robert Meade if you like,' said Sue.

'It's true,' said Sally.

The po-faced expression was back. 'But I've seen no evidence that the government is taking legal action against companies for data breaches. There's been no comment on the subject or coverage in the press.'

'Oh, there will be,' confirmed Sue. She thought about the blog article she'd written and decided now that it was morally correct to publish. 'Several individuals have been fined, very heavily, for non-disclosure of data breaches. Whole companies have been hit with stiff penalties too.'

'Who? Who?' demanded Jenny.

Coops handed Jenny and Sally a sheet of paper each.

'This is a list of the prosecutions made by the AFP last year,' said Sue.

Jenny read the long list, disquieted.

'Now, fortunately, Wentworth went public with the attack and full disclosure was made—so no infringement there,' said Sue. 'But there's also negligence to consider. Cases of negligence are harder to prove but they can't be ruled out.'

'But the only negligence here lies with the IT department and their insistence on this—*firewall*,' pleaded Jenny.

'The government, the AFP, won't look at it that way,' said Sue. 'No single department is more negligent than another. Negligence is proved when someone, anyone within an organisation, has failed to act when in knowledge of an obvious threat.'

Jenny and Sally looked at each other.

'I'm interested,' continued Sue. 'You say the firewall causes you headaches from time-to-time. Do you mind telling me what these are?'

DISCOVER AND DISRUPT

Jenny and Sally seemed unwilling to answer.

'I'm guessing you're talking about the headaches caused for customer services?' prompted Sue.

'We're being left further and further behind,' said Jenny. 'Every month our competitors come out with some new digital product or phone app that allows consumers to slice and dice their investment portfolio, to analyse, make projections and cross reference with the market in real-time.' Jenny sighed. 'Gone are the days when investors relied on the share-prices in the back of a newspaper to make their decisions. Everything now needs to be up-to-the-second, it needs analytical depth and it needs to be mobile.'

'And you can't compete?' asked Sue.

Jenny shook her head. 'We're struggling to maintain a basic customer portal. Innovation is impossible when your online, customer-facing products sit behind a firewall. In the last cyberattack the portal was taken down and everything went offline with it. Our customers had no way to access their investments. But it's not just in consumer innovation that our competitors are ahead—all these apps and online tools they're able to develop give useful data on what decisions their customers are making, how they make these decisions and why. It's real-time consumer research that helps an organisation understand what their customers are looking for. It helps them develop newer and better products, and drives customer satisfaction. We don't have anything like that.'

'Surely, an investment bank the size of Wentworth must have some kind of data on its customers?' probed Sue.

'Sure, we've got customer research, but it's looking in the wrong areas. We've got data on the call centre efficiency, customers' faith in the strength of the brand, of our partners; we've got data on fund manager satisfaction and investment recommendations, even on returns. But we've got nothing on the online service.'

'Nothing?'

'Nothing concrete,' said Jenny.

'But you must get feedback from your customers in other ways? Don't you write to them, call them or email them?' Sue was pushing hard now.

'Well,' said Jenny, blinking. 'We do run email surveys from time-to-time.'

Bingo thought Sue. 'And?'

'They're nothing to be relied on,' said Jenny.

'Why not?'

'Because they're not accurate. Every few months we send out an email to selected customers inviting them to take part in an online survey. We can only email customers who haven't unsubscribed from email marketing, so that represents less than a third of our client base. Of these, many view the emails as soft spam and it prompts them to either delete or unsubscribe; for many more, it simply ends up in junk folders never to be seen. Our click-through on email surveys like this is low, less than two percent.'

'But it must give you an idea of some of the issues?' said Sue.

'Some of them,' admitted Jenny.

'Could you tell me what they are?'

'Our customers are frustrated with hit-and-miss online access to their investments and a lack of meaningful digital products. They only need to look at our competitors to see what they're missing. And then, they leave.'

'Do you know that for sure?'

'It's an educated guess.'

'Do you think this is the main reason behind Wentworth's declining revenue and loss of customers?' asked Sue.

'I believe it is. But I can't prove it,' said Jenny. 'These surveys are inconclusive.'

'But still, there's no reason not to share them, within Wentworth I mean?'

'Perhaps, but they wouldn't be taken seriously, they'd be seen as divisive, a weak attempt to discredit the CBIS firewall,' said Jenny.

DISCOVER AND DISRUPT

Sue paused for thought. 'Jenny, if there was a solution to all this, what would you like to see? What would be the best possible outcome for you?'

'I suppose,' said Jenny, 'that I'd like to be able to sleep at night, knowing that our customers are protected and that they're happy. I'd like to not be in permanent damage control. I'd like to not lose any more good people.' She looked at Sally with a smile. When she turned back to face Sue, the po-faced expression was replaced with one of sincerity. 'And just for once, I'd like to hear someone say *well done.*'

'Jenny, will you let us see those email surveys?' asked Sue. 'Will you let us share them with Robert Meade and the project team?'

The sincerity left Jenny Liu's eyes. She stared at Sue. 'No,' she said.

'Why not?'

'I will never support a Tesico solution for Wentworth. I know all about you and your company Miss Novak. I've heard from colleagues in the industry that you're not to be trusted.'

Sue was shocked.

'Tesico is too small to provide change management,' continued Jenny. 'That's what you told WestInvest and that's why they broke contract with you, isn't it Miss Novak?'

Sue was at a loss to reply.

'If you can't supply change management for WestInvest, how would you provide it for a bank the size of Wentworth?' concluded Jenny.

Sue gathered her thoughts. 'I'm not here today to sell you anything,' she said.

'But you're salespeople, aren't you?'

'Yes, yes we are,' said Sue. 'But there's no point in us forcing a product down your throat that'll make you unhappy.' Sue looked Jenny in the eye and spoke with quiet emphasis. 'And I think we both know a lot about unhappy customers right now.'

Jenny Liu gave a small nod.

'Our job is to help you understand the problems yourselves,' said Sue. 'I've been tasked by Robert Meade to help the project team agree on the challenges you face. Because, if you can't agree on the challenges, then you'll never agree on the solution. And this, this challenge you're refusing to admit and share, it's a vital piece of the puzzle that others in your organisation need to know about.'

'And what if it leads to a solution Tesico can't deliver?' asked Jenny, eyes narrowing.

'Then so be it. We walk away,' said Sue. 'But right now, this isn't about Tesico, it's about you, it's about Wentworth, it's about understanding the problems with your customers, your security and your business.'

'And how do we protect ourselves from prosecution Miss Novak? Tell me that,' asked Jenny.

'The best way to protect yourselves is to do the right thing by your customers. And the first step is to acknowledge the problems,' said Sue.

The room remained quiet. Jenny Liu turned to Sally McCrae. 'Sally, what do you think?'

'I think we should share the surveys. People need to know,' murmured Sally. She regarded the floor sheepishly.

'I've made my feelings plain Miss Novak,' said Jenny Liu. 'I will support any value statement that solves our customers' problems and I will support any proposal that protects our employees from prosecution. But I will never support Tesico as chosen supplier.'

Sue nodded in acceptance. 'Understood. But the email surveys?'

'I'll have Sally send them over,' said Jenny.

* * *

Sue and Coops followed Sally McCrae back through the corridors of the customer services department. When they reached the lift, they said their farewells.

'It's a good result,' said Sue, trying to reassure Sally.

'We'll see,' said Sally with a curt smile. 'Thanks for not ratting me out,' she said to Coops.

As Sally left, Coops leaned close to Sue's ear. 'And I thought we'd be leaving empty-handed.'

Sue let out a long breath, relieved. 'We got what we came for Coops.'

'True enough, but Jenny Liu was hard yakka,' whispered Coops.

'She's no fan of Tesico,' agreed Sue.

'And we're the ones who can help her!' pointed out Coops, her whisper becoming loud. 'We're the ones who can solve all her woes by putting their security in the cloud and letting them innovate. On top of that, we'll give them all the precious consumer data they want.' Their lift was a long time coming. Coops was studying Sue from the corner of her eye. 'So why didn't you tell them?'

Sue turned to Coops, 'Tell them what?'

'That we're the answer.'

Sue looked around, making sure she wasn't overheard before whispering close to Coops. 'It's like Doug said, the Discovery has to be theirs to make...'

'I know, I know,' said Coops. 'But she attacked Tesico Sue, she said we couldn't supply change management services, then she dug up all that WestInvest shit again. Why didn't you tell her that we *can* include change management, that our product is scale-able, that we can bring in Onicas to help?'

Sue looked her friend dead in the eye. She was about to speak just as her phone rang. She dragged it to her ear. 'Hello?'

'Sue, it's Raf.'

'Oh, hi?' said Sue.

'I heard you were in the building. Have you got time to swing by?'

'Sure.'

'Good. See you soon.'

Sue hung up and the lift arrived. As the doors closed, leaving them in private, Sue had enough time to finish her conversation with Coops.

'You know Coops, getting hold of those consumer surveys? Doug helped us do that...'

'He did?'

'In his journal he stresses the need to keep it about the prospect, about *their* issues.'

Coops's eyebrows knotted in confusion.

'If I had leapt to Tesico's defence in our meeting with Jenny,' explained Sue, 'then the discussion would suddenly have been about *us, our credentials, our product*. It would have been a defensive argument with me trying to convince Jenny that we're the right people for the job. Honestly Coops, I've seen Roper go down this same path and Doug is right, *it doesn't work*. If I'd done the same thing, those consumer surveys would have remained behind a locked door.'

Coops nodded, unsure.

'But the trick, as Doug explains, is not to be drawn into that fight. Because you can't win. What I did was bring the discussion back to Wentworth; to their needs, their problems. So there was no need to break that door down...'

Coops smiled, understanding. 'It just melted away.'

28. Running Into Walls

'I wish I had better news,' said Raf. He and Sue were seated in a small breakout area in the IT security department. Coops had returned to the Tesico offices to await delivery of the consumer surveys from Sally.

'So there's no way I can get to Craig Martin?' asked Sue.

'Nope, the CEO has pulled himself out of the DMU for now. He's got a lot of holes to plug,' said Raf.

'Understandable,' sighed Sue.

'As Robert pointed out initially, Craig often stays out of the process and will rubber-stamp decisions made by the DMU,' said Raf. 'He likes them to reach a decision on their own.'

'It's a shame,' said Sue, 'I was looking forward to meeting him. And the CIO, Peter Ludick, he's out too?'

'Well no-one knows for sure. He just hasn't responded to Robert's request.'

'Ouch,' observed Sue.

'Exactly,' said Raf. 'So I'd take that as a *no*.'

'There's no love lost between those two, is there?'

Raf leaned back in his seat, unwilling to comment.

'Sorry,' offered Sue.

Raf smiled. 'It's okay, I've just never been one for politics.'

'But this whole business,' Sue reassured him, 'the bank's response to the cyberattack, the differences in opinion and the different factions. It's *all* politics, isn't it?'

Raf studied Sue for a while. 'Yes, yes it is.' He leaned forward in his chair again. 'As I mentioned before, Peter Ludick used to be Robert's boss. Now they're both part of the C-suite; level peggings so to speak.' Raf's response was typically reserved but his implication was clear.

'Well,' offered Sue. 'If Peter won't respond to a meeting request from Robert Meade, why can't you ask him?'

'Me?' Raf was surprised.

'Well, you report to Peter Ludick, don't you? He heads your department.'

'Technically I'm a few levels below Peter, I don't report to him directly,' explained Raf.

'But surely his door is open to people in his department?' suggested Sue.

'Well, some people yes, but not...' began Raf. Sue remembered Doug's advice to resist filling the silence; that when someone was about to reveal something it was best to have patience and wait.

Raf sat quietly for a while before continuing. 'Robert has the authority to recruit a project team from all departments and have them report to him directly. This includes staff from the IT security department—like me.'

'So, having his own people report directly to someone else has put Peter Ludick's nose out-of-joint?' asked Sue.

'I have no idea,' replied Raf. 'I only know he won't talk to me.'

Sue gave a sympathetic nod. 'And Maria Kutcik, the COO, she won't talk to me either?'

'No, but it's not about you,' explained Raf.

'Well, that makes me feel better,' smiled Sue.

DISCOVER AND DISRUPT

Raf smiled back. 'What I mean is, she's very busy and she often refuses to see any outside vendors.'

'But I'm here as an industry commentator, to help Wentworth reach a solution. Has she been told that?'

'I'm sure Robert explained everything to her,' said Raf.

'And you're sure it doesn't have anything to do with her relationship with your CIO, Peter Ludick?'

Raf frowned. 'In what way?'

'Well, Kutcik and Ludick are joined at the hip, aren't they? That's what Jenny and the customer services people say. That they're CBIS supporters and that they oppose change...'

Raf shook his head. 'That's not strictly true. Peter wants a CBIS solution, for sure. He recommended CBIS from the start and oversaw the original installation, so he has a vested interest. Maria is different. She's not technically-minded, she relies on people with the credentials, people like Peter Ludick...'

'So she lets *him* call the shots?'

'In the area of IT, yes, because she doesn't have the knowledge herself. She sees Peter as being best qualified for the job and so she supports him on that. That's about as deep as their relationship goes. I don't think you get to be as senior in an organisation as Maria by doing everything yourself. You have to trust others to do their job too.'

'Then do you think,' ventured Sue, 'she could be persuaded there's a problem with the CBIS firewall?'

'Perhaps,' said Raf. 'I'm sure she's aware of the revenue drain and customer dissatisfaction, that's all part of her job—but she hasn't joined the dots to the CBIS firewall. If she knew, she could be torn on the subject.'

'Then that's what we need to help her understand. She needs to make this discovery for herself.'

'That's a tall order,' said Raf. 'You'll need evidence, and tonnes of it, before changing Maria's mind on anything. And this is all assuming you could actually get in front her, which you can't, remember?'

'Well, pretty soon we're going to have the customer surveys Jenny Liu has promised us. That should be enough to get her thinking,' said Sue. 'And I know someone who might like to present them to her.'

'Who?'

'Someone in her department. Someone who loves to be seen as a hero, saving the day—all by themselves.'

'Bryce Nichols?' asked Raf.

Sue nodded. 'The one and only.'

'Then be very careful,' warned Raf.

29. Friends in High Places

Sue scrolled through the long document on her laptop. Coops sat beside her.

'What do you reckon?' said Coops.

Sue took a long breath. 'Well, they don't pull any punches,' she said.

'They call Wentworth *a bunch of dinosaurs*,' said Coops.

Sue pointed to her laptop screen. 'This one is calling them *luddites...*' she said.

'*Ostriches with their heads stuck in the sand*,' added Coops. 'That's another.'

'How many of these survey replies are there?' asked Sue, looking up.

'Oh, around sixty or seventy,' answered Coops.

Sue was pensive. 'It's not enough,' she said.

'But if this is what Wentworth's customers, *ex-customers* think, they're pretty damning,' countered Coops. 'Didn't Jenny tell us they only get a click-through of around two percent? What about the customers who've unsubscribed or the ones who were too busy, or the ones who never saw the email in the first place? This could be the tip of the iceberg Sue.'

'But, putting Maria Kutcik's hat on for a moment,' theorised Sue, 'I could say there will always be a dissatisfied minority and these are just the kind of people who love responding to surveys like this. The vast majority have remained silent because they're largely happy.'

'And I'd say,' Coops sat upright, stabbing the air with her finger, 'pull your head out your arse girl and listen to your consumers. Why the hell do you think they're leaving you?'

'Because they fear another cyberattack?' replied Sue. 'That'd be the obvious assumption. Nothing to do with the online experience.'

A frown gathered on Coops's face. 'Are you thinking she won't go for it?'

'I don't know,' said Sue. 'Raf said we need hard facts, evidence, to sway Maria Kutcik. These surveys aren't concrete enough.'

'She sounds like an Inquisitor...' murmured Coops, studying the surface of Sue's desk.

Sue looked at her friend with a smile. 'I think you're onto something there.' She pulled Doug's stakeholder archetype cards from a drawer and laid the Inquisitor in the middle of the desk.

'The Inquisitor is a powerful Change Agent,' Coops read aloud. 'And focuses on *interrogating the proposal.*' She looked up. 'Told you.'

'And look here,' offered Sue, pointing.

Coops craned her neck and read where Sue's finger lay. *'Responds to truth, quantifiable evidence.'*

'You're right Coops, Maria Kutcik sounds like an Inquisitor. She has the power to drive change but she needs proof. I don't think we can position these surveys as any kind of evidence, but as a theory only. A formal study is the best way to examine and pressure test, to find the reasons for the customer drain. An Inquisitor should respond to that.'

'We tell her she needs to commission research?' asked Coops.

'Well *we* can't, because we may never get to meet with her. But

DISCOVER AND DISRUPT

somehow we need to get the message to her that research is the way to go,' replied Sue. 'A detailed study with clients past and present. On all aspects of customer service.'

'And you're betting this research will find the online experience is the main cause for the customer drain?'

'We know it's a fact. What was the research you found? Eighty-three percent...'

'...Eighty-three percent of companies cite firewall software as a principal hindrance to digital innovation,' Coops recited.

'And that fact will lead us right to the problems with the CBIS firewall,' said Sue.

'And to security in the cloud as the answer?'

Sue nodded.

Coops mulled this over for a time. 'So, if we never get to meet Kutcik, how are we going to get the surveys and our theory in front of her?'

'I have friends in high places,' said Sue.

'Robert Meade?'

'Actually, I meant Bryce Nichols, her direct report, but perhaps Robert could help too, if he's amenable and he agrees with our thinking.'

'That way, we can hit Kutcik from both sides, like a double-pronged attack,' observed Coops, jabbing two opposing fingers at each other.

'Raf is bringing Robert up-to-speed on the surveys now. Perhaps we should give him our perspective, and ask him to share with Maria Kutcik?'

'Sounds like it's time to call our Champ,' said Coops.

* * *

Raf had already delivered the customer email surveys to Robert Meade and briefed him on the background. Meade had even finished reading the majority of the surveys by the time Sue called him.

'So, casting my mind back to our previous meeting,' said Robert Meade, 'you said we must drive consensus on the problem first? This is the way to align everyone's thinking?'

'Correct,' said Sue.

'And you think this issue, this *problem* with digital innovation is it?'

'I do,' said Sue. 'It's not the whole of the problem, your exposure to cyberattack is an obvious threat, and so is insulating you from the provisions of the Privacy Act, but this is significant and it should drive the consensus we need.'

'Well, our customer retention rates are a serious problem, no-one will argue with that. But your belief is that it's driven by a lack of digital innovation?'

'Not *my* belief,' corrected Sue. 'Jenny Liu's and the customer relations department's. But what I do know from experience is that a lack of digital innovation is often a result of a company's security arrangements,' said Sue. She heard the long pause on the other end of the line and supposed Robert Meade was looking out over the city again, lost in thought.

'I agree that the customer surveys seem to support this,' he said at length, 'and I agree it's worth investigating.'

'So you agree further research is needed?' asked Sue. She heard a long intake of breath from Robert Meade.

'Of course, it's imperative,' he said. 'Without it we'll have a hard job making people see the connection. The two areas seem so unrelated. It's astounding. It'll be a revelation for many.'

Sue heard Doug's words in her head: *When these deepest needs and realisations are evident, this will be their Discovery.*

'It's a discovery,' said Sue. 'It's your *discovery*. You can thank Jenny and Sally in customer services for that.'

'If the research supports the theory?' added Robert Meade.

'If the research supports the theory,' confirmed Sue. She heard another long intake of breath. Sue sensed a degree of reticence.

DISCOVER AND DISRUPT

'My only concern is how this will affect our timeline,' said Meade.

Sue waited awhile. She knew that Robert Meade was thinking, probably assessing the consequences of a delay. 'Want to hear my opinion?' she offered.

'Of course,' said Meade.

'I believe, when all this is over and done, no-one will look back and say *if only we kept to the deadline*. All they'll care about is whether the right decision was made.'

Sue heard the warmth in Robert Meade's voice and imagined the smile appearing in the corners of his eyes. 'Of course, you're right,' he said. 'If the project team are unanimous that further research is required, then I'll recommend any presentations to the DMU be put back until we are clear on the findings and a way forward.'

'Thank you.'

'Do you think the project team will be unanimous on this? Will they come to a consensus on the problem?'

'I believe so,' said Sue. 'Except I'm not sure about Bryce Nichols. I've yet to tell him about these customer surveys.'

'Would you like me to do that?'

'I'd prefer to follow up with him, if you don't mind?'

'Not at all,' said Meade. 'You're the one driving this. In the meantime I'll talk to Jenny Liu, to thank her for the input and to reassure her this business with the surveys will be handled sympathetically. As soon as you've spoken with Bryce I'll talk to Maria, our COO, and our CFO too—we'll need budget for the research. It shouldn't be a problem but it'll need to be approved at C-suite level.'

Sue felt his energy. It was the drive of a Champion in full pursuit of a quest.

'I might also have a quiet chat with Craig...' offered Meade.

'Craig Martin, your CEO?'

'Yes,' said Meade. 'Digital innovation is a bit of a hot topic for him. He's even set up a separate think tank to look into it. It might be worth bringing him up-to-speed on our...' he paused, '...*discovery*.'

'That,' said Sue, 'is a great idea.'

* * *

Sue placed two calls to the landline number listed on Bryce Nichols's business card. She left messages in both instances but received no call in return. Then she called his mobile but it went straight to voicemail. She texted him and waited for a few hours. Nothing.

It was very late in the afternoon when Bryce Nichols finally answered his mobile phone. Sue could hear music in the background and suspected he had already left work and answered by accident.

'Miss Novak, what a pleasant surprise. How may I be of service?' said Bryce. Sue detected the oily undercurrent of pretence.

'Actually, perhaps it's I that can help you,' offered Sue.

'Oh?'

'Something I've just learned that may be of value—to the operations department.' Sue felt like she'd just cast a fishing line into a lake.

'And what might that be?'

'You're aware of Wentworth's steady decline in customers?' asked Sue.

'Yes.'

'And that this decline is eating into your profit?'

'Yes, this is a very real concern for Maria and myself.'

'What if I told you your security arrangements are responsible for this decline?'

There was silence from the other end of the call. Then a short laugh. 'That's preposterous, how can our security arrangements...'

DISCOVER AND DISRUPT

'I have something you might want to see,' interrupted Sue.

'And what is that?'

'The results of a series of consumer surveys,' said Sue.

'Really?' Sue felt the piquing of Bryce's interest, a nibble on the fishing line.

'Yes,' said Sue, 'and they indicate that your customers' online experience with the bank is sub-standard. It's driving them straight to your competitors.'

'But the customer services department is responsible for customer retention. It's a part of their job description,' said Bryce.

'Not if the lack of digital innovation for your customers is a direct result of your current security arrangements.'

'Is that so?' Sue felt a tug on the line.

'Yes, I'd love to go through these surveys with you if I could,' said Sue. 'And with Maria too, if possible.'

'Exactly where did these surveys come from?' asked Bryce.

'From the customer services division.'

'Then why is this the first we've heard of them?'

'There's a story to that,' said Sue. 'One I'd be happy to share with you both when we meet.'

There was a hesitant pause from Nichols.

Sue recalled the Mercenary archetype card. *Responds to: vanity, personal advancement.*

'In the right hands, these surveys could be instrumental in solving the bank's problems,' added Sue. 'I feel you have the influence to make this happen.'

'I'll see what I can do,' said Bryce Nichols. Sue felt the line tighten. The hook was set.

DISCOVER AND DISRUPT

30. Spitting Chips

'I think you're leading Wentworth towards a value proposition similar to the one adopted by China Prestige,' said Michelle. Sue and Coops sat in the Tesico breakout room, updating Michelle via teleconference.

'You mean that big Hong Kong bank?' asked Sue.

'That's the one,' said Michelle. 'We helped them create a Networks Operation Centre, a NOC, to monitor their network around the clock.'

'Sounds great, and having Tesico security in the cloud has freed them up to create a suite of customer-friendly products?'

'Yes, they're delighted with the results. Customer satisfaction is running at an all-time high. They're even up for some consumer awards,' said Michelle.

'Wonderful. And what about customer research, can they monitor interactions on the portal and gain insights to their customers' online behaviours and needs?' asked Sue.

'Yes they can,' said Michelle. 'I can't remember the architecture exactly but I know customer services were highly involved from the value proposition onward.'

'Sounds very similar to our experience with Wentworth,' confirmed Sue.

'Yes,' said Michelle. 'We're seeing a regular pattern here. Now tell me about these consumer surveys. Have you sifted through all the data yet?'

'Yes, we have. There's enough to support a theory but Wentworth needs more research to prove there's widespread customer dissatisfaction and that it's linked to a lack of digital innovation.'

'Will we see a green light on that research?'

'Meade is behind it, he's pushing for it.'

'Good,' said Michelle.

'Michelle...' began Sue, hesitating.

'Yes?'

'Change management is going to be a big issue for Wentworth. Jenny Liu said for a fact that she'd never support Tesico on account of the way we handled WestInvest.'

Michelle Yim sighed. 'We made a rod for our own backs there,' she said.

'If all goes well, and we make it to the proposal stage,' said Sue, 'then we're going to need a strategy to handle that.'

'Has Tony been in contact with Onicas? He needs to bring Jamie and his team onboard,' said Michelle.

'I don't know,' stammered Sue. 'I haven't heard...'

Michelle's frustration was obvious. 'Is he there?'

'Uh no. He's in Melbourne this week.'

Michelle sighed.

'Michelle,' began Sue, summoning courage, 'Tony and I talked about this...'

'On second thoughts,' interrupted Michelle, 'why don't *you* call Jamie? It's better that way. After all, you're handling Wentworth as we agreed and I should probably let Tony concentrate on the Melbourne job.'

'Okay...' agreed Sue, unsure.

'I'll send you Jamie's number. Call him. He'll be happy to help

DISCOVER AND DISRUPT

out. He's a good operator and a valuable friend to Tesico. He was a tremendous help on the China Prestige Bank win for us.'

'But—here, in Australia, are they the best, I mean can we rely on them for Wentworth?'

Michelle's expression was puzzled. 'Of course Sue, no-one's better qualified. Onicas know our product better than anyone. And they have the scope to handle a customer as big as Wentworth, they've already demonstrated that.'

Sue was scrambling to order her thoughts. 'Then should I tell Jamie that Onicas will need to act independently?'

'Why would you do that?' queried Michelle. 'Sounds to me Wentworth is looking for a team approach. The best way to overcome criticism like Jenny Liu's is for Tesico to partner with a big, respected player like Onicas, right from the start. And you can bet CBIS will be making a big deal of their all-in-one, single-company solution.'

Sue nodded.

'In the meantime, keep the momentum going. Interview whoever you can on the DMU and get them behind this research proposal. I suggest you include Robert Meade, he's becoming our *go-to* guy on these matters.'

'Will do,' said Sue.

'Oh, and Sue...'

'Yes Michelle?'

'Tell Tony you'll take Onicas off his plate. And you should probably give him a bit of an update on where you are—just as a courtesy.'

Sue looked at Coops and read the look of alarm on her face. Michelle hung up.

'What are you going to do?' asked Coops.

Sue opened a fresh email and began writing.

Hi Tony, tried calling you to bring you up to speed on Wentworth...

'Did you?' asked Coops, reading the email over Sue's shoulder. Sue shook her head and continued.

The CRM has been updated and Wentworth is almost at the value proposition stage.

'Shouldn't we call him?' asked Coops.

'Do you want to?'

'Nope,' admitted Coops.

Sue kept the email brief. She included Wentworth's discovery that the firewall was hindering digital innovation and impacting customer services but referred to it as an *insight* not a *discovery*. She didn't want Roper to know anything of Doug's method. When she was done she hit *send*.

Her inbox refreshed itself and a new email appeared.

'Holy crap,' whispered Coops. The email header revealed the sender's name: Bryce Nichols. Sue opened it.

Maria and I will be available to meet you from 7.30 to 7.40 am tomorrow. Please confirm. Bryce.

'Maria and I,' muttered Coops. 'What a nong.'

'Ten minutes?' uttered Sue.

'You got your meeting though,' offered Coops. 'It's a result.'

'I guess,' replied Sue, unsure.

'Your Mercenary friend took the bait.'

Another email appeared in Sue's inbox. It was from Roper. The contents were typically terse: *Have you told Wentworth there will be no change management from Tesico?*

Sue began a reply. She sat for several minutes with her fingers poised over the keyboard.

'What you going to tell him?' quizzed Coops.

Sue clicked out of the email and closed the lid to her laptop. 'Nothing,' she said.

Coops's eyes were like saucers. 'He's going to spit chips,' she said.

31. The Rarefied Air

'You sure it was right to bring me along?' asked Coops, surveying the expansive reception area where they sat waiting.

They were on one of the uppermost floors of Wentworth Tower, a level that housed the bank's most senior officers. Sue reflected that companies usually planned their interiors this way. The lower levels were teeming with open-plan workstations and filled with the noise of the corporate worker-ants. The higher you took the lift, the more the headcount thinned. The offices became more spacious, more tranquil. This far up from street level is where you found elaborate flower arrangements, art on the walls and a selection of *eau de toilette* in the marble-lined restrooms.

'Well, there's two of them, and there's two of us,' said Sue. 'It's equal.'

'I feel like a sheep in the shearing shed,' whispered Coops.

'You'll be fine,' Sue reassured her. 'You don't have to say anything. It'll be an education.'

Sue guessed this floor contained not only Maria Kutcik's office but perhaps that of the CIO, Peter Ludick, and even the CEO Craig Martin. Robert Meade's office was a few floors below them, and humble by comparison.

Somewhere a door opened and Sue heard voices. Several lanky men carrying folders and laptop bags emerged, hovering in the broad hallway. A meeting had just concluded. Sue now heard another voice, a woman's voice, shrill and commanding, that cut through the low murmur of the men. The owner of the voice appeared in the hallway. The high heels she teetered on did nothing to conceal the fact she was very short. Her stockiness was made even plainer by the retinue of tall, gangly men who followed behind as she made her way back towards the reception area where Sue and Coops sat. The woman caught sight of Sue and changed direction towards her. She was now bearing down on Sue with a look of stern intent. The high heels click-clacked across the polished parquetry and Sue now recognised the pile of over-coiffured hair balanced on top of the woman's head.

'Bugger me, it's the Huff!' whispered Coops, her eyes and mouth all circles. She looked like a Venn diagram in a PowerPoint presentation.

Sue felt sure this would be an attack. How did Brenda know who she was? She must have done her homework. What had Brenda heard? Had Sue said anything defamatory about Brenda; about CBIS; about the firewall? Maybe, but to who? And who had relayed it to Brenda? Sue rifled the filing-cabinet of her memory for a reason that would provoke Brenda's hostility. She reached for her elbow-crutch and hauled herself up. If she was going to defend herself, she was going to do it on her feet.

'Sue? Sue Novak?' demanded Brenda Huffington, marching up to Sue. Her lanky entourage came to a halt behind her.

'Yes,' said Sue. She hoped her answer didn't sound weak, but she knew it did.

Brenda Huffington stared Sue in the eyes for a moment and Sue did her best not to look away. Then, without warning, Brenda's hands shot out and grabbed Sue's. Sue did her best not to appear startled at the odd gesture. The two women stood, holding hands, in the centre of the reception area.

'I was so sorry to hear about Doug,' said Brenda Huffington, squeezing Sue's hands. The thick layer of make-up creased around Brenda's eyes as her expression softened. 'We were always in opposite corners, he and I. But I never had anything less than the utmost respect for him. I never got the chance to tell him myself. So I'm telling you. Please accept my deepest sympathies.'

Sue didn't know how to answer. She thought she mumbled a polite thank-you, but she wasn't sure.

'He was a credit to our profession,' said Brenda, then she smiled. 'And he could charm the birds from the trees.'

A small laugh passed between the two women and Sue felt the sting of tears in her eyes. The two adversaries continued to hold hands, heads bowed. It was a temporary truce. A ceasefire. Christmas day in the trenches.

'Good luck Sue Novak,' said Brenda Huffington, releasing her grip on Sue's hands with a smile. Then she turned on her oversized heels and made for the lift. Her lanky entourage made passage for her, then fell into step behind her.

'And may the best woman win!' called Brenda Huffington over her shoulder.

* * *

Bryce Nichols swept Sue and Coops into Maria Kutcik's office. It was a different office from the one they'd seen Brenda Huffington emerge. Bryce remained silent and Sue had the impression he was either angry or putting on the appearance of detached formality for the sake of his boss.

Maria Kutcik was on the phone. Without a glance in their direction Kutcik pointed at a meeting table in one corner of her vast office. It was an instruction to sit and wait. From the tone of the call, Sue guessed Maria Kutcik wasn't one for small-talk or pleasantries. This was not the place for an introductory personal story. Sue had learned from Doug's journal that introductory stories could sometimes annoy a time-poor Change Agent, especially an Inquisitor. Instead, Sue placed her business card and Coops's on the table where she guessed Maria Kutcik would sit. This was as much of an introduction as they had time for.

The call ended and Maria Kutcik joined them at the meeting table. She didn't even look at the business cards in front of her.

'Bryce requested this meeting on the basis of some kind of *information* you want to share?'

'That's right,' said Sue. 'Based on the consumer email surveys we sent over last night.'

'I've read them,' said Maria Kutcik. 'Frankly I don't know why I bothered.'

Coops had turned white. Sue could now see that Bryce was avoiding her eyes. He was simmering. Kutcik had probably torn strips off him.

'Do you have anything else?' asked Maria Kutcik.

'Not at this stage...' stammered Sue.

'And you are recommending, I understand, that we put the DMU on hold until further research is done into this—lack of consumer innovation?'

'Yes,' said Sue. 'It's key to finding a way forward.'

'It's a very big ask on the basis of some very flimsy evidence,' said Kutcik. 'These surveys are soft measures at best. They're just a forum for whingers to hop on their soapboxes and criticise the bank.'

'That may be true,' said Sue. 'But if they point to a larger, more general problem, can you afford to ignore them?'

Kutcik remained silent.

Sue continued. 'We agree that the surveys are not as accurate as quantifiable research, but they've still been conducted for good reason. And they're in line with other statistics uncovered by our industry.'

'Such as?'

Sue swallowed. 'Eighty-three percent of companies cite firewall software as the principal hindrance to digital innovation.' Beside her, Coops was nodding.

'I don't much care for other companies and their problems,' said Maria Kutcik. 'Nor do I care for wishy-washy statements about the industry in general. Our circumstances are entirely individual. And so are the problems we face.'

'But it's a trend, Miss Kutcik, one the whole of the finance sector is experiencing. And one Wentworth may be experiencing too.'

'Here's the trend,' said Maria Kutcik. She walked back to her desk and collected a copy of the *Financial Review*. Returning, she deposited it on the table while reading the headline. '*FinTech eats big banks' lunch,*' she said, pointing to the article. 'This is the real issue, these new entrants to the finance sector are nimble, they're entrepreneurial. Wentworth could lose almost thirty percent of its market share over the next five years to FinTech start-ups offering solutions like peer-to-peer payment. Our customers are looking elsewhere and they're attracted by all this...' Kutcik made a theatrical wave at the newspaper headline, '...glitter.' She sat down. 'That's the reason they're leaving, that's the reason for the dissatisfaction, not our firewall. The two issues are unrelated.'

'Other people in this organisation would disagree,' said Sue.

'Who exactly?'

'If you talk to customer services or to Robert Meade, or people in the technical division.'

'In that case, why would I not talk to the most *senior* person in our technical division, Mister Ludick, our CIO?' said Kutcik with a smile.

Sue was stumped. It was a difficult rationale to out-argue.

'I'll be frank Miss...' Maria Kutcik picked up the business card in front of her. '...Novak.' Sue wondered if she'd been anything less than frank in the conversation so far. Kutcik continued: 'I see this as a smoke-screen, a tactic, a way for salespeople such as yourselves to confuse the issue in order to sell your own product.'

'That's quite untrue.' Now it was Sue's turn to be firm and it caught Kutcik's attention. 'You mentioned that your circumstances and the issues you face are *entirely individual*?'

'Yes,' responded Kutcik.

'Well, our job here is to act as security advisers, as industry experts to dig as deep as we can and uncover all those *individual issues* created by your digital exposure, from security, to your relationship with your customers, to innovation and legal liability...'

'Legal liability?' interrupted Kutcik with concern. 'Surely, there's no connection there?'

Sue shrugged. 'Who knows?' She was being disruptive, challenging Kutcik's ingrained thinking. In the back of Sue's mind was the unpublished article she'd written. 'You have to dig to find out. This is no time to sweep stuff under the carpet but to discover the truth—and to arrive at the solution Wentworth ultimately needs.'

Maria Kutcik turned Sue's business card over in her hand. Her eyes narrowed. 'Are you and this solution mutually exclusive?' asked Kutcik.

'I'm sorry?' said Sue.

'By that I mean, what if we accept your recommendations Miss Novak, but we don't accept...' Kutcik looked again at Sue's business card. '...Tesico?'

'That's entirely at your discretion. We're currently helping the project team formed by the CISO to interrogate the problem and report. Helping Wentworth understand the deeper issues is our only concern at present.'

Kutcik studied Sue for a while, then nodded. 'Well, I'm not a fan of partnering with organisations I know little about Miss Novak. However, for a couple of salespeople, you seem to have your priorities in the right order.'

'And you agree part of that priority is to support further research?'

'I'm undecided,' admitted Kutcik. 'I need to think. I might need some advice.'

Sue shuddered. She knew exactly whose advice Kutcik was talking about.

DISCOVER AND DISRUPT

32. A Bird in a Cage

Sue was finding it difficult to concentrate on anything relating to work. She gazed over the lid of her laptop at the view outside her apartment. It was a glorious Saturday morning and Sydney sparkled in the sunshine. Reflected light shone from the water in the harbour and from the windows of the buildings that fringed the shoreline.

On days like these she usually found it impossible to stay indoors. She would bound down the stairs and into the streets of Potts Point. Then she'd simply walk, just happy to be outside. She'd find herself walking past the stylish eateries and bars on Finger Wharf, towards the grassy expanse of the Domain. Here she'd skirt the classical sandstone architecture of the Art Gallery of New South Wales and wander through the cool green shade of the Botanic Gardens, all the way to the steps of the Opera House. Some mornings she'd walk this route to the Tesico office on Kent Street. It took less than an hour and it never failed to clear Sue's head and put a smile on her face.

She frowned at the soft cast on her leg. There would be no long walks for a while yet. Sue felt as if she'd been chained to a desk for weeks; shut away from the light; locked inside offices and conference rooms. She felt like a caged bird.

A document was open on her laptop. It was her article: *The Harsh Penalties for Cybercrime Complacency.* She'd been editing and revising most of the morning. Sue had an idea that the way to make it feel less alarmist was to write it in a way that was utterly factual; without bias and supported with as many references as possible. She peppered the piece with links to relevant sections in the Privacy Act and the Notifiable Data Breaches Scheme. She'd asked her contacts in the Federal Police and at the Australian Cyber Security Centre to go *on record* and they'd agreed. They too, felt a need to highlight the importance of taking data protection seriously. Sue wanted her article to be an accurate representation of the issues; unassailable and iron-clad in its reporting; the kind of article even an Inquisitor would not dismiss. After all, Sue had a particular readership in mind—and it was a readership of one.

By lunchtime Sue had uploaded the article to LinkedIn. With difficulty she resisted the urge to stare at her screen and watch the number of views accumulate. Instead, she updated the stakeholder archetype map she and Coops had been working on. Then she wrote a halfhearted first draft of Wentworth's *desired state*; a visualisation of the future waiting for the bank at the end-point of the *Gap Discovery*. Both Robert Meade and Jenny Liu had given Sue enough of an idea as to what kind of outcome they wanted to see for Wentworth, but Sue struggled to express it convincingly. Until they had the findings of formal research, any statement of Wentworth's true desired state would be a stab in the dark. It was premature. Sue wondered what Doug had written on the subject and guessed it would be in his journal under the third section of the EDVANCE process: *VALUE PROPOSED.*

Opening up Doug's journal on her laptop, Sue skimmed the opening of the section on *Value Proposed.* Her mind wandered and she clicked open her browser window again. Four views only. She was distracted and the processing and retention of the lessons in Doug's journal were becoming impossible. She re-read a few of the sentences again, then looked up, trying to make sense of their meaning for Wentworth. The Manly Ferry flashed green and gold between the buildings opposite. It would be carrying people to the Northern Beaches, to the sheltered sands of Fairy Bower, or a leisurely lunch on the Corso.

Sue groaned. *Give up girl, you're getting nowhere.*

After ten minutes hobbling around her apartment on her elbow-crutch, Sue finally found her Android tablet. She connected it to her computer and copied over the entirety of Doug's journal. It would be easier to read this way; more portable. Then she checked the newspapers, popped the tablet into her handbag and ordered an Uber. She was pushing the cage door open and, just for a while, she'd spread her wings.

There was a new British rom-com at the cinemas she'd been meaning to watch. She bought a ticket for one and sat in the darkness where she laughed and wiped the tears from her eyes all on her own. When she emerged, the brightness of the day was blinding. She donned her sunglasses and made her way down to East Circular Quay, searching for a table outside one of the bars or restaurants. Most had been claimed by patrons too immersed in the laziness of their afternoon to move on. Sue exaggerated her limp until a waiter at a seafood restaurant took pity on her, and waved her to a table. She ordered half a dozen Sydney Rock Oysters, a side of antipasti and a glass of Prosecco. Then she pulled the Android tablet from her bag and made an attempt to continue reading Doug's journal.

Perhaps it was the movie she'd just seen but sometimes it can appear to a single person as if the entire world is made up of couples. Tourists sauntered, hand-in-hand beside the quay, posing for photos and laughing at each others' jokes. Young people drank in twos, oblivious to the glory of the day. Older couples smiled at each other over their menus, communicating in an unspoken language learned over years.

Was Sue still alone because she worked too hard? Was it because of her job? Was it because real relationships, unlike the ones in rom-coms, were too messy and too time-consuming to accommodate? She thought of Coops, another single woman, younger yes, but approaching thirty. Then her mind strayed to Raf. Was there a significant other in his life or was he too, all alone?

Sue's phone buzzed in her bag and she fished it out.

'Sue speaking...'

'Sue, it's Raf.'

Sue was briefly tongue-tied by the coincidence of his call. 'Raf, it's Saturday. Do you ever stop working?'

Raf laughed. 'Do *you*?' he countered. 'I just read your blog post.'

Sue sat upright in her chair. 'Oh, really? What did you think?'

'Wow!' said Raf. 'It's a brave piece.'

Sue chewed her lip. 'You don't think it's going too far, do you? That it's too *sensational*?'

'Oh no, it's very well researched,' he said. 'The point you're making is important, but it'll set off alarm bells for many. You've already got some tongues wagging.'

'I have?'

'Sure, haven't you seen? You're up to a hundred views already and there are quite a few comments,' said Raf. 'And it's still only the weekend!'

'I didn't realise...'

'Robert's already read it.'

'He has? How did he react? I hope it didn't upset him.'

'No, not in the slightest,' said Raf. 'He thinks it's important enough, serious enough, to share internally, with the rest of the C-Suite as a kind of wake-up call.'

'He does?' Sue was stunned, but flattered by Robert Meade's reaction. It meant he was fully in support of her view. Now she felt certain: she had a Champion fighting for her cause.

'*Cybercrime Complacency*,' laughed Raf. 'Love it…'

Sue smiled. 'Thanks.'

'By the way, how did your meeting with Maria Kutcik go?'

'Not as well as I'd hoped.'

'In what way?' asked Raf.

'She doesn't believe the customer and revenue drain has anything to do with the CBIS firewall. She thinks it's due to competition from elsewhere in the sector. FinTech mostly.'

'Because she's listening to Ludick?'

'Highly likely,' said Sue.

'But will she support further research?'

'Hard to say.' In her mind's eye, Sue could see the stakeholder archetype map. 'I haven't been able to drive consensus as far as I'd like within the project team,' she admitted. 'It's likely you won't have Bryce Nichols onside. But there's you and Robert, and Sally McCrae is definitely on-board.'

'That's three out of four,' said Raf. 'Isn't that enough to recommend further research?'

'I don't know,' admitted Sue. 'If they're going to convince the DMU, their finding needs to be unanimous.'

'The other problem is,' said Raf, thinking out loud, 'the DMU will be split down the middle with Robert and Jenny on one side and Maria Kutcik and Peter Ludick on the other.'

'I know, but don't forget your CEO,' said Sue.

'Craig Martin?'

'Yes, Robert plans to speak to him, apparently digital innovation is one of his hot buttons.'

'It certainly is,' agreed Raf.

'And I think he'll take notice of the legal issues if Robert decides to share my article with him too.'

'So we might have a slim majority on the DMU?'

'Perhaps. But it's still not enough. We need to get everyone to agree on the problem before we can find a solution.'

'Can you debrief Robert on all this Monday sometime?'

'Yes, I was planning to,' confirmed Sue.

There was a low sigh from Raf's end of the line. Sue knew there was something more.

'What's up?' asked Sue.

'It's such a shame we couldn't get Maria Kutcik on side,' said Raf. 'I was quietly hopeful she might come round.'

'Sorry,' offered Sue.

'No matter,' said Raf. 'Enjoy the rest of your weekend Sue.'

'You too.'

Sue's order arrived at the table just as she put down her phone. She took a sip of Prosecco and decided she would indeed take Raf's advice. She would enjoy the rest of the weekend. She would not work. She would not read Doug's journal. She would begin by enjoying her oysters and her quayside view of the Harbour Bridge and the Opera House.

Then her phone buzzed a single alert. It was a text message.

Sue didn't recognise the number and the message was short.

Tomorrow. 8.30 am. Callan Park Oval. MK.

33. The Soccer Mum

Within the grounds of the disused Rozelle Hospital lies a well-tended expanse of sports field known as Callan Park. To the south and east of the park are strewn the many nineteenth-century sandstone outbuildings of the old psychiatric hospital, now empty but protected as part of the city's heritage scheme. To the north, the park overlooks Iron Cove, one of Sydney Harbour's larger inlets and part of the Parramatta River. A flat, seven-kilometre track runs around the cove known locally as the *Bay Run*. On the weekend the area comes alive with fitness enthusiasts. Outdoor gyms are set up and thousands of Sydneysiders cycle, run, or walk the Bay Run.

    As Sue struggled from the back seat of her Uber, she wondered where she needed to go. The text message had given no clue. The car pulled away, leaving her standing beside the Bay Run. Sue watched groups of Lycra-clad cyclists whizz past. Runners, sheened with sweat, pounded their way across her field of view and middle-aged ladies in designer tracksuits and sun-visors sipped their takeaway coffees as they sauntered in front of her. Not here.

    Sue narrowed her gaze against the early sunlight and turned to look out over Iron Cove. Rowing teams of eights, fours and single sculls were slicing the calm water to Iron Cove Bridge and back. Would her contact be among them? Sue thought not.

She turned back towards the playing fields of Callan Park. Teams of primary school-aged children were taking part in soccer matches on two separate pitches. Sue scanned the cheering parents on the sidelines. One of them was turned towards her—a woman. She stood, legs apart, one hand on her hip, the other held aloft in a wave. It took Sue a moment to recognise her in the floppy, broad-brimmed hat and sunglasses. It was Maria Kutcik.

'Thanks for coming,' said Maria. Sue came to a stop beside her, resting her weight on her elbow crutch. 'You need a seat?' added Maria with a concerned nod towards Sue's leg.

'No, I'm fine,' replied Sue.

Maria Kutcik looked away, casting a critical gaze over the soccer match in progress. 'Come on, mark up. Mark up!' she shouted at the top of her lungs.

Sue's ear rang. 'I never picked you for a soccer mum,' said Sue.

'Manager,' corrected Maria, still watching the game.

'Manager?' said Sue, impressed.

Maria gestured to one of the players. 'My youngest plays midfield. The team's manager dropped out at the beginning of last season.' She glanced at Sue. 'I figured I'd be standing on the sidelines anyway, so why not take the job? I've been their manager ever since.'

'You must know a lot about the game?' suggested Sue.

'Not really,' admitted Maria. 'It's more about leadership.' Her attention moved back to the players. 'Besides, you can learn a lot about running a company by coaching a soccer team of nine year-old boys…'

Sue grinned and looked towards the players. Excluding the two goalkeepers, the sum total of players from both sides was massed in a clump in the middle of the field, kicking and hacking at the unseen ball that lay at their centre. 'They're all going for the ball at the same time…' observed Sue.

DISCOVER AND DISRUPT

'Spread out!' roared Maria Kutcik. 'Give yourselves someone to pass to!' She turned to Sue with a wry smile. 'Because they're not playing as a team. They get fixated easily, and that stops them seeing the bigger picture.'

Sue wondered if this was how Maria saw Wentworth: a bunch of boys with a ball. 'They need to rely on each other more,' ventured Sue.

'Exactly,' agreed Maria. She shot Sue a sidelong glance. 'And what about you Miss Novak, can we rely on you?'

'Yes,' said Sue, trying to sound as honest and as forthright as possible. Maria Kutcik's sidelong look rested on her a while longer.

'Can you truly be relied upon to do the right thing by Wentworth?' pressed Maria.

'I can,' said Sue.

'No ulterior motives?'

'No,' said Sue. 'I admit, I'd love to secure your business, nothing would please me more, but that's not my current objective. Right now my only aim is to help you understand the issues you face for yourselves. As I see it, this is the only way you'll arrive at a solution.' Sue lifted her chin in the direction of the soccer match. 'Wentworth needs to work as a team too.'

'Do you know why I invited you here today?' asked Maria Kutcik.

'I'm assuming you wanted to talk in private?'

'That's right. I read your article about Cybercrime Complacency.'

Sue remained quiet, waiting for Maria to continue.

'You've touched a nerve Miss Novak. My first reaction was that you are stirring the pot, using scare tactics to force your agenda. But I checked your sources and I've checked many of the claims you made in our last meeting. I have to say, you know your stuff. Your article is confronting but it's accurate. Perhaps it's timely also.'

This is what Sue had hoped for: to pass the scrutiny of Maria Kutcik's inquisition. 'Changes need to be made in your industry, customers need to be protected,' said Sue. 'This legislation is in place to encourage that.'

Maria Kutcik nodded grimly. 'Do you know we're being downgraded?' she asked.

'Wentworth? By who?'

'Moody's Investor Services,' said Maria Kutcik. 'We're being downgraded from stable to negative. We're not the only ones though. Other banks will suffer too. Current indicators point to mounting debt, robust lending competition, interest rates at a record low and little or no growth because wages aren't increasing. Do you know what this all adds up to?'

Sue shook her head.

'Fear Miss Novak. Fear within the walls of Wentworth. Our analysts are scared, our executives are scared. There's fear of change, there's fear of failure, there's fear of being proved wrong. There's fear of the FinTech menace. There's fear we're falling behind our competitors, there's fear we're losing revenue and fear we're losing customers. Now there's this—a new fear, the fear of prosecution. I know you want me to ask you if you think Wentworth is guilty of Cybercrime Complacency, but I won't ask that, not even here. I don't want to know the answer. What I do know is that fear is a breeding-ground for accusation, insecurity and resentment. And if we don't break free from this cycle of fear, this bank will struggle at best. At worst, it will fail. Fear makes sheep of people. Or it makes them do stupid things...'

Maria Kutcik moved her attention back to the soccer pitch but Sue sensed she was elsewhere. 'I fear another attack,' continued Maria. 'I fear what it may do to us. We can always minimise the impact it has on brand image with PR but it could cripple us as an institution.'

'You know, when I spoke with Robert Meade, he felt the same way,' said Sue. 'He spoke about fear too. He said his greatest fear would be that someone went to jail because he couldn't do his job.'

DISCOVER AND DISRUPT

'He's right, it's a governance issue that worries me greatly. It may never come to pass that anyone is actually jailed, but another attack could destroy a great many careers. We can't afford to be exposed like this.' Maria turned back to Sue. 'You know, I've always had faith in our CIO, in Peter, I've always *relied* on him like a good team player should—and I remember the last security overhaul. It was a nightmare I don't wish to repeat. But...'

Now Sue understood Maria Kutcik's need for privacy. She was in doubt, a doubt she did not want to be made public, and Sue's article had nudged her towards the tipping point. All Sue needed to do was remain silent, and listen.

'But,' continued Maria, 'if you're right on this, if our firewall is driving our customers away and putting us in danger of prosecution, then I'm all ears. We need a solution.'

'Then you'll agree to place the DMU on hold until we get more consumer research?' asked Sue.

Maria Kutcik drew a long breath. 'Think of it this way Miss Novak, I'm giving you one shot at goal. Yes, I'll agree to further research. But if you're wrong on this, you leave the field. You will walk away. Do you understand?'

'Yes,' said Sue. 'And if I'm right?'

Maria Kutcik fixed her gaze on Sue. 'Then I'll be the first to welcome you to the team.'

DISCOVER AND DISRUPT

34. The Waiting Game

'Sounds as if you had a busy weekend Sue,' observed Robert Meade.

'And a productive one too,' added Raf.

Sue and Coops were seated in Robert Meade's office in Wentworth Tower. Sue smiled at Raf's compliment.

Raf turned to Meade. 'It's as we thought Robert, once Maria was across the facts, she saw the sense in further research.'

Robert Meade nodded. 'It's a good outcome. And as far as the project team is concerned, we should have some kind of consensus there to push for research.'

'You may not get a vote of confidence from Bryce Nichols though,' offered Sue.

Sue saw the smile in Robert Meade's eyes. 'Oh, I wouldn't worry about Bryce,' he said. 'If Maria is in favour of our recommendation, Bryce will fall in line.'

Sue had been losing sleep over this particular issue. It was likely Bryce Nichols had become negatively disposed, and a negative Mercenary could be a destructive force. But Maria Kutcik's support would now insulate them. Bryce would now be unable to influence Maria against Sue and the rest of the project team. As an advocate, a Mercenary, he'd served his purpose in bringing Sue closer to Maria Kutcik. Things would take their own course now.

'And what about Mister Martin, your CEO?' asked Sue. 'Did you get to share the consumer surveys with him?'

'Not in any detail,' replied Robert. 'I did inform him of their existence and I gave him a brief rundown. From his standpoint, any lack of digital innovation is a serious concern. But he won't jump to any conclusions until the research debrief is in.'

'So he's in favour of the research?' asked Sue.

'Yes,' said Robert Meade with a smile. 'Very much so.'

Sue let out a long breath. It was a genuine relief that her recommendation had been accepted at the highest level in Wentworth.

Robert Meade cocked an eyebrow at Sue. 'And I showed him your article on Cybercrime Complacency.'

'Oh,' said Sue. 'What did he think?'

'He found it very interesting,' said Meade, his tone becoming grave. 'Not to mention *very scary.*'

* * *

Jamie DeSouza was an olive-skinned man in his early forties; his dark hair beginning to grey at the temples. The crow's feet at the edges of his eyes told Sue he worked hard. Or that he smiled a lot. Sue learned he had a large family and it was possible he'd simply been tugged and pulled by his children into a more tired but happier version of himself. On the table of the Clarence Street cafe in front of him lay the *Opportunity Synopsis* Sue and Coops had prepared earlier and which they were now sharing as background to the project.

'Michelle is right,' said Jamie, tapping the documents on the coffee table. 'Your prospect's situation is a familiar one. I don't think there's a company out there that hasn't had customer service issues because of in-house firewall security.'

DISCOVER AND DISRUPT

'Was it the same with China Prestige, when you first worked on their business?' asked Sue.

'Sure was,' said Jamie. 'Moving their security to the cloud turned them around.'

'And how did it all go, the change from firewall software to cloud security?'

'There were a few last-minute dramas, as you'd expect, but things went okay. The old system stayed in place until the Tesico cloud went through its testing phase and then went online. The change from one security system to the other was a bit like flicking a switch.'

'That's good to hear,' said Sue. 'Some of the people at Wentworth still have nightmares about the last security upgrade. They'll be comforted to know there won't be a repeat performance.'

'Moving to the cloud is far more seamless,' explained Jamie, 'at least, it *should be*, technically. The real job is teaching their people to drive the system, adapt to new processes and to understand the possibilities.'

'And that's where you come in?'

'That's where Onicas comes in, yes.'

'So how big a job is it?' asked Sue, 'change management?'

'Well, we need to be involved right after you get a Request For Proposal. Then we'll work closely with your solutions architects to understand all the ins and outs of the system and what the customer wants from it. It'll be broad brushstrokes at first, feasibilities, that kind of thing. But there will be a full overview and an accurate budget for your proposal. Then, if you win the contract, we really get down to the nitty-gritty—planning change, adapting business processes, designing training programs and helping build the interface between your product and the people who'll be using it. It's a long process, but it has to be.' Jamie's look became quizzical. 'Hope you don't mind,' he said, 'but I have a question...'

'Please,' said Sue, 'go ahead.'

'Don't take this the wrong way but, on a project the size of Wentworth, I usually work directly with the sales manager. You guys are reps, right?'

'Sales consultants, yes.'

'Have you done this kind of thing before?'

Coops gave Sue a concerned glance. 'No,' said Sue, 'not really.'

Jamie DeSouza nodded, contemplating. 'Your National Sales Manager is Tony Roper right? Should I give him a call, to introduce myself?'

'Uh, no,' stammered Sue. 'He doesn't like to be involved with change management. Besides, he's tied up with another really big prospect at the moment.' Sue pointed a finger at Coops and herself. 'We'll be handling this one.'

At that moment Sue's phone rattled on the surface of the coffee table, alerting her to a new text message. 'Sorry Jamie, can I get this?' asked Sue, grateful for a way to close this line of discussion. She opened the message. It was from Raf.

Research budget approved. Well done. It's a waiting game now.

* * *

'*Three* bloody weeks?' exclaimed Roper.

'Yes,' said Sue. 'And that's just till we get the topline. The full research debrief will take another week and then they'll probably need another week upfront to recruit the right mix of respondents.'

'So, it's five weeks then? Is this what you're telling me? Five bloody weeks of research until you even get within a flea's dick of a proposal?'

Sue nodded.

'I can't believe this. What's taking so long?' continued Roper, staring at Sue across his desk. 'You should have wrapped this up by now, you should have closed.'

It occurred to Sue that Tony Roper was still working on the Melbourne sale. The project was taking just as long as Wentworth, and it was a smaller prospect. 'This is a critical step Tony,' she said. 'If the research findings support what we already know, then they'll lead themselves to a Tesico solution.' She knew she was exposing Doug's thinking here. She hoped Roper would understand the reasons, even if he couldn't get his head around the process.

Roper raised the palm of his hand towards Sue and looked down, shaking his head. 'Hang on, hang on just a second...' He looked up. 'What do you mean *if* it supports what we know? Are you telling me that an entire sale is hanging on an *if*? And what do you mean *they'll lead themselves to a sale*?' He aimed a finger at Sue. 'That's your job! You're the salesperson, you're the one who's supposed to lead them to a sale...'

Sue sighed. 'Tony, it's a big company and there's a lot of politics. There's many players and they all have different agendas. This is the one piece of evidence that'll bring them together and help them understand the problem for themselves.'

Roper sat back, both palms now laid flat on his desk. 'I don't know what kind of game you're playing here. It's a simple bloody task, you just have to get to the opinion leaders and get them onside. Wine them, dine them, flutter your eyelids—hell, show them a bit of leg if you have to!'

Sue swallowed her ire.

Roper continued. 'But you and your friend...' He waved a finger in the direction of Coops's desk outside the glass wall of his office. 'You and your little friend are making a pig's ear of this. You're complicating everything. You're leaving everything to chance, to *research* for God's sake. And you're letting *them* decide for themselves what's right. That's not how things are done Novak. I want you to buck up and take the lead. Tell them why their current system is screwed and why Tesico is the best solution out there.' He sat back, both hands raised. 'It *is* the best system out there, isn't it?'

Sue didn't answer.

'Isn't it?'

'Yes,' admitted Sue.

Roper continued holding his hands up with a look of mock bewilderment. 'Then why the hell can't we just tell them that? Feature, function, benefit? Why are we prolonging this?' He was silent for a time, thinking. 'I know what you're doing here. You're dragging this out on purpose, aren't you?'

'Why would I do that?' replied Sue.

'It gives you more time to hang onto your job, doesn't it? More time to get chummy with Michelle Yim. You think she'll save your arses if the Wentworth deal goes bad.'

Sue was struggling to stay professional with Roper. She was hurt and she was furious. 'Tony, that's not...'

'Mind you...' interrupted Roper, suddenly thoughtful. 'It could be a blessing in disguise.'

Sue stared at him, open-mouthed.

'I should have the Melbourne deal wrapped up in a couple of weeks,' said Roper. 'Then I can take over Wentworth again.'

Sue felt sick.

'Yes, it could all work out fine,' mused Roper, nodding to himself. 'The research will be in and, if it confirms what we already know, I should be able to push them over the line.'

Sue saw the ploy. It would be easy for Roper to think he could step in at the last minute and steal the glory. 'But we agreed Wentworth was *my* prospect,' countered Sue. 'It's what Michelle wants...'

'There you go...' replied Roper. 'You and Michelle, you and Michelle, it's all about you and bloody Michelle, I'm right aren't I? Well I don't give a damn about Michelle, she's not here—I am!' He pounded his chest with his fist. 'I'm the one who carries the can for the failures of this office and so I will make sure we land Wentworth!' He sat back with a thin smile. 'All things come to he who waits, Novak.'

35. Into the Light

Cook and Phillip Park Pool was situated halfway between Sue's apartment and the office. If she made an effort to leave work at a reasonable hour she could walk through the city to the pool, swim for half an hour and walk the rest of the way home.

Her soft cast had now been off for more than three weeks and Sue was enjoying the increased mobility and the chance to exercise. Her physiotherapist had suggested swimming to strengthen her leg and redress any misalignment to her posture caused by her use of the elbow crutch. The crutch was now gone, replaced with a collapsible walking-stick, but Sue still walked with a limp. Sue had asked whether the limp would disappear in time but her burly physio had been non-committal. Sue put it down to professional prudence, but she was also reaching the unhappy conclusion that the limp might be permanent; something she'd just have to live with. In the water, at least, Sue felt normal, moved normally. She took a stroke correction class to sharpen her technique and she now looked forward to her time in the pool.

It was after one of these visits to the pool that she got the call from Raf. She'd walked through Cook and Phillip Park and had just crossed the road into the Domain when her phone rang.

'The topline's ready tomorrow,' said Raf. Sue could hear a schoolboyish excitement in the genteel chime of his voice.

Sue was taken by surprise. 'Ahead of schedule? I thought it'd be another week or so?'

'Well,' said Raf, 'we've been pushing them to expedite the process. The findings are pretty clear, so that's made it easy too.'

'Do you know what they are?' asked Sue, nervous.

'Sure I do. I've sat through all the research, so has Sally McCrae. The full debrief will be out by the end of the week but we have a pretty good idea what it'll say.' He paused to take a breath. 'Sue, the firewall is the problem. It's killed our chances of providing the digital experience our customers are looking for and it's driving them to our competitors.'

Sue couldn't speak. Her legs felt like jelly after her swim. This news made them even weaker. She found a park bench and sat down heavily, collecting her thoughts.

'Sue, Sue? You there?'

'Uh, yeah, I'm here Raf.'

'Do you know what this means?'

'Uh-huh.'

'It means you're right—that there's a huge problem with the CBIS firewall we never saw.'

Sue's thoughts scrambled together. 'It's not me that's right...' she said.

'Not you? What do you mean? Of course it's you, you saw it...'

'No, said Sue,' focused now. 'Sally saw it, Jenny Liu saw it. You all dug deeper and deeper into that hole to uncover the truth. Now you've found it. It's *your* discovery, *Wentworth's* discovery.'

Raf remained silent for a moment, taking the point on-board. 'So what happens now Sue?'

'Now we climb out of that hole, up into the light. And towards a solution.'

* * *

DISCOVER AND DISRUPT

The rest of the walk home was a blur. Sue had been lost in thought the entire time. She hurried into her apartment and placed her phone on charge. She'd take a shower later. Sue checked the time: good. Singapore was three hours behind. Michelle might still be in the office.

Sue scraped a chair over to her phone and sat. She hit the video call icon on the screen and Michelle answered. She was still at her desk.

'Sue, good to see you. Haven't heard from you in a while.'

'No, we've been in a bit of a holding pattern while the research has been happening. But I've just heard the topline will be in tomorrow.'

'Excellent, any clues as to what that might look like?'

'Yes, Raf tells me it'll pinpoint the CBIS firewall as a major cause of their customer drain.'

'That's a relief. Will you be able to help them scope their future state and value statement?'

'That's the plan,' said Sue. 'But the full debrief won't be in until the end of the week. I don't suspect they'll finalise a value statement until then.'

'No, but you might want to get working on one yourself as a thought-starter and share it with Robert Meade. I'll send you the one used by China Prestige.'

'Great, thanks Michelle.'

'And Tesico will get an RFP?'

'No reason why not. I believe I've developed a good relationship with Raf and Robert Meade, they'd want us to present our proposal for sure.'

'Good. Any way you could confirm with Robert when you share your thoughts on their value statement?'

'Sure, of course. But it'll only be whether he wants to include us. He won't be able to speak for the rest of the DMU.'

'I realise that,' said Michelle, 'but he seems adept at influencing others over at Wentworth. If he wants our proposal, he'll push for it.'

Even without the benefit of Doug's journal, Michelle understood Robert Meade's archetype. As far as Sue was concerned, Robert Meade was proving to be the best Champion they could wish for. He had taken their cause to heart, and now he would rally the troops.

'I'll talk to him tomorrow then,' said Sue.

'Good,' said Michelle. 'And have you spoken to Onicas?'

'I have, yes. Jamie is ready to be briefed the moment we get the RFP.' Sue wondered if now was the right time to broach the matter of Roper's issues with Onicas. She hesitated. Wasn't the matter premature until they secured the RFP? And if they didn't, wouldn't it be a dead issue anyway?

'Sue?'

'Uh, yes?'

Michelle waited, her head to one side, curious. 'I said is there anything else?'

'No,' said Sue. 'Nothing at all.'

36. In the Back of the Net

It should never be forgotten that there are two steps to the 'D' in EDVANCE.

The first is DISCOVERY, the uncovering of all the deep-seated problems and their implications. This is the laborious digging down, down, to the bottom of the hole where all the real issues have lain hidden. By now your prospect will see their situation for what it truly is. By these means you will have driven them towards consensus on their CURRENT STATE. They will be aligned and ready for you to lead, their trust in you will have grown.

Now we are at the second step, DISRUPTION. From here you will guide your prospect into the light, towards the solution they need—not the solution they thought they wanted. In this way you are leading them to a new paradigm, a future they never considered. This is the derailment of their fixed train of thought, this will be their DISRUPTION.

DISRUPTION is about helping them paint a bold picture of their future, a future to which they all aspire.

A future of broad brushstrokes and possibilities, a future where all their issues are addressed, all their problems solved. This will be their DESIRED STATE.

Once they reach agreement on their DESIRED STATE, then urge them to make it their goal, regardless of the technicalities, or how it can be realised. In this way it will become their most important objective and help them envision the value they need.

In turn, this will become the value you must help them realise.

'So where the hell is the part where we propose a value prop?' asked Coops. The two women were at Sue's desk reading Doug's journal on a laptop.

'Nowhere. We don't need to.'

'Then why the hell did Michelle tell us to take a look at the China Prestige value statement?'

'For inspiration,' said Sue.

'You've lost me...'

'Look at it this way,' said Sue. 'The China Prestige value statement was a description of the value they'd see by reaching their desired state. This is what Doug means when he says that their desired state will help them envision the value they need.'

'So is that the same as their value statement? Is that what you're saying?'

'That's what Doug is saying, yes,' said Sue. 'We help them paint a picture of where they want to be, a kind of wished-for tomorrow without any of their current problems. They'll imagine this future for themselves and, if they all understand the broad value it delivers, they'll all be in consensus.'

'And that value is what they'll write down in their value statement?'

'Correct. So we don't really need to recommend a value statement and wrangle them into agreement. All we need to do is help

DISCOVER AND DISRUPT

them imagine their desired state and the value it'll deliver. They'll do the rest. This is what I'll be suggesting to Robert.'

Coops was nodding. 'You know, I thought sales was all about *pushing* stuff. But it's not, is it? This whole process, Doug's process, is a way to help the customer sell themselves on the solution...'

Sue smiled, glad that the lights had come on for Coops. 'This is what the *Gap Discovery* is all about—letting them figure out exactly where they are and where they need to get to. The bit in the middle, the gap, is the next part of the process, it's how we move them from one state to the other, how we help them realise that value in real terms.'

'Sure, but first we need a Request For Proposal, right?' added Coops.

'Yes. And the DMU needs to agree on us getting one.'

'You think there's a chance we won't?'

'Robert Meade will do his best to get the DMU onside. He's probably got into the CEO's ear. Maria Kutcik should have come around by now too. Ludick will be the wild card. And so will Jenny Liu...'

'Shouldn't she be thankful we helped out with the consumer research?' asked Coops.

'She *should*. But she might still be thinking we're too small to offer change management.'

'What if we set her mind at rest?'

Sue looked at Coops. 'How can we do that?'

'Well, I could invite my mate Sally out for a night on the tiles,' said Coops, a smile spreading across her face. 'And what if I casually drop that Onicas will be working with us on Wentworth?'

Sue grinned back.

'Just you watch. She'll be in Jenny's ear quick smart,' said Coops.

'*Devious* Coops...' said Sue. 'It could help change Jenny's mind on Tesico.'

'And agree to us getting an RFP,' added Coops.

'I'm going to meet with Robert too. He'll have news to share from the DMU members.'

Sue's phone buzzed with a new text alert. She scooped it up and read the message.

Looks like you scored. Welcome to the team. MK.

'Wentworth must've got the full debrief on the consumer research,' said Sue.

'How'd you know?' asked Coops.

'Looks like I just kicked a goal,' said Sue.

Coops's eyes were wide with surprise. 'Some stunt with a busted leg,' she said.

37. The Bush Telegraph

Robert Meade looked up from the document in his hands and regarded Sue and Coops with a look of mute astonishment. Then he turned to Raf who lingered by the window overlooking the city, sipping from a mug of tea. 'Have you seen Sue's take on this Raf?'

'I have,' said Raf with a smile. 'I agree. It's just what we need.'

Meade cast his attention back to Sue and Coops. 'You know, a lot of people within Wentworth will believe this is an impossible ask. It's a very bright future you're describing here—but it's the *right* future.' A playful smile crept into the corners of his eyes.

'It's up to you to reach your own conclusions. It's a draft, a suggestion,' said Sue. 'But we believe it's where Wentworth should be heading. We believe this could well be your desired state—the best possible future for Wentworth.'

'In theory, I can't foresee anyone in Wentworth objecting to a future like this. I'll share it with everyone involved and I'm certain they'll agree. It's a great starting point for our vision.' Meade smiled openly now. 'And I have a feeling it's just the kind of future Tesico is able to deliver.'

Sue was glad to hear the vote of confidence. 'So does that mean we'll get an RFP?'

'As far as I'm concerned, yes,' replied Meade. 'I'm very thankful for all the progress you've made here, the way you've helped align our thinking—and the way you're partnering with a reputable provider such as Onicas to provide the change management we need.'

Sue smiled. Meade the Champion. Sue realised that, if things went well, she'd need to spend a lot of time with this man to move Wentworth along the path to change.

'But mine isn't the only opinion here. The RFP process must be agreed by the DMU,' said Meade.

'And will they agree?' asked Sue.

'I know that Craig Martin will accept my recommendation, and I've spoken with Maria—she's happy with the work you've done too. She seems to trust you.'

'Which is no small thing,' added Raf with a smile over the rim of his mug.

'No small thing indeed,' agreed Robert Meade.

It was as Sue thought: the only real opposition would come from Ludick, the CIO, the staunch ally of CBIS. But did Sue have enough support within the DMU to outflank him?

'I can't speak for our CIO, Peter Ludick,' said Meade, as if reading Sue's mind. 'And I don't know if Jenny will support your involvement. I should talk to her...'

'She will...' began Coops, quietly.

'I know she wasn't in favour of Tesico at the outset...' continued Meade.

'She's okay...' said Coops, a little louder.

'She could prove difficult to convince...'

'She'll agree,' said Coops, summoning the bravado to be heard.

Robert Meade swivelled his chair in Coops's direction. 'I'm sorry Miss Cooper,' he said. 'You were saying?'

'Jenny Liu will agree to Tesico getting an RFP,' said Coops.

Raf placed his mug of tea on the corner of Meade's desk.

DISCOVER AND DISRUPT

'How do you know?' asked Robert Meade, surprised by the revelation.

'I had a yarn with Sally a few nights...' Coops coughed and corrected herself. '...A few days ago. She said Jenny will support an RFP for Tesico, on account of the support we gave them. And the fact we're partnering with Onicas.'

Robert Meade glanced at Raf. A smile passed between the two men. The smile was still on Meade's face when he turned back to Coops. 'Well Raf, it seems our friends at Tesico have a better handle on our people than we do!'

This book comes with free access to an
online reference companion.

By scanning the QR Code or by navigating to
edvance.sale/recap/discover3/ now, you will gain a deeper understanding of the EDVANCE process and the methodology applied by the characters in the preceding chapters of the story, including:

- Gap Discovery
- Gaining consensus on the Desired State
- Updated Stakeholder Mapping
- Applying these methods in your own business

VALUE PROPOSED

VALUE PROPOSED

38. The Flying Dutchman

'V' stands for VALUE PROPOSED and is the third step in the EDVANCE process.

This step matches ASSESS OPTIONS in the Buyer's Journey.

VALUE is always a trade. It represents what a prospect must pay or give up, in return for what they receive. What they give up can be anything from money, to peace of mind, to operational ease or comfort, product lines, people and suppliers. What they stand to gain may include increased revenue, greater market share, brand awareness or reduced costs or risks.

The more they gain, while the less they give up, all adds up to greater VALUE.

VALUE is always to be looked at through the eyes of your customer. It must be understood in their terms and what it means for their business, never what the salesperson thinks of as VALUE.

Without seeing VALUE, your prospect will never

invest in your service or product. And VALUE must be agreed before the price of that investment is ever discussed.

Sue sat in her partitioned cubicle at Tesico reading Doug's journal. She looked up to see Coops motioning towards her from the breakout room, pointing dramatically at her wristwatch. Sue nodded, collected her laptop and made her way over. It was time for their scheduled call with Michelle Yim.

'Well done the both of you,' beamed Michelle from the screen of Sue's laptop. 'Wentworth is a huge prospect and you two should be very proud of yourselves for getting to this stage.' Robert Meade had been good to his word and had sent Sue the formal Request For Proposal. Now she and Coops were one step closer to winning Wentworth, one step closer to keeping their jobs.

'Thanks Michelle,' said Sue.

'But now we have an RFP, this is where the hard work really begins,' said Michelle. 'How long till we present to the DMU?'

'I'm sending you the schedule now,' said Sue.

'Good,' said Michelle, checking her screen.

'Michelle, is there any chance you could be there for the final presentation?' asked Sue. 'It would really help us.'

Michelle frowned. 'I'd love to but we're booked to present to a Dubai financial services firm around the same time. It's a very large deal. I'll have to juggle my time. Let me see what I can do.'

'Thanks,'

'If I can't make it,' said Michelle, 'you could always invite Tony.'

Sue and Coops exchanged a wary glance. 'I guess...' said Sue.

Michelle noted the reaction. 'Sue, you're lead on Wentworth. Nothing changes. But if you want a senior Tesico salesperson to add some weight to the presentation, to show we're taking this seriously, then Tony can help.'

'He just hasn't had much involvement,' said Sue.

'Well, in Wentworth's eyes, nor have I,' argued Michelle. 'I'll

VALUE PROPOSED

make sure he doesn't get in your way. Where is he by the way? I can't seem to raise him.'

'Still in Melbourne.'

'Still?'

Sue nodded.

'But he's been there for weeks.'

'I know,' said Sue, trying not to appear too relieved.

Michelle sighed. 'If you get to him before I do, tell him to get in touch.'

'Sure.'

Michelle was cheerful again. 'Now, I'm sending you someone to help out. His name is Jens Hendriks, he's a solutions architect from the Amsterdam office. One of our best.'

'Wonderful. Thanks Michelle...' replied Sue.

'I suggest you get him to meet Raf,' said Michelle. 'Together they can iron out the technical implications of a solution for Wentworth. Jens can design the architecture and map everything out ahead of the presentation. He's a bit of a rising star within our technical division, so you'll be in safe hands. Jens is quite brilliant but you may find him...' Michelle paused to smile. '...Interesting.'

Sue smiled, curious.

'And you might want to bring in Jamie DeSouza from Onicas while you're at it,' said Michelle. 'They'll all need to pick each other's brains.'

'Bring on the nerdfest...' whispered Coops.

'You've briefed Jamie?' asked Michelle.

Sue's expression fell.

'Sue, you've briefed Onicas?'

Sue avoided Michelle's gaze. 'Uh, no. Not fully. Not yet.'

'Well, we've got the RFP. Time to get moving...'

'About that, Michelle...' said Sue, composing herself. There was no way to put this delicately. 'Tony has directed me not to involve Onicas. He wants Wentworth to make their own arrangements for change management.'

Michelle stared blankly for a while. 'Why am I hearing this *now*?'

'I'm sorry Michelle. I tried convincing him. I hoped he'd come round, but...'

'But?'

'He's got some kind of problem with Onicas. He thinks they could be trouble. I don't know why...'

Michelle's expression became grave. 'I think I do.'

'You do?'

'I'd hoped he'd gotten over it, moved on...'

'Moved on from what?' pressed Sue.

'Some time ago he worked with Onicas on a large regional project. The prospect was based in Taipei but their network spread across APAC. Anyway, he and the Onicas management didn't see eye-to-eye on the implementation. It soured the deal and I guess he still blames them.'

'I see,' breathed Sue.

Michelle appeared to be turning this over in her mind. 'But you told me you've spoken with Jamie already? So you've had some preliminary meetings, right?'

'Yes,' said Sue. 'We've shared the *Opportunity Synopsis* and the background. Jamie's clear on the intent but not the scope.'

'And you've done this without Tony's knowledge, against his instruction?'

'Yes,' said Sue. 'I didn't know what else to do.'

'I'm sorry you've been placed in this position,' said Michelle.

'Is there anyone else, another change management contractor Tony'd be happy to work with?' asked Sue.

'We can't manage this deal without Onicas. Brief Jamie. Clearly, Tony and I must have words.'

Michelle hung up and Sue's hands went to her forehead. 'Shit, what a mess,' moaned Sue.

'Like a turd in a ceiling fan,' agreed Coops.

VALUE PROPOSED

39. A Meeting of Minds

Jens Hendriks looked the worse for wear when Sue met him in the arrivals hall at the airport. His winter European suit was crumpled, the skin of his face was waxen and he smelled of canned air. He'd spent a day in the sky travelling from Amsterdam. It looked more like a week.

'Did you get much sleep?' asked Sue.

'No,' was the simple reply.

Jens was tall and skinny. He was young, but something about the way he dressed and carried himself belonged to an older man. His sandy, close-cut hair was thinning and it looked to Sue as if he had never seen much sunlight. They walked together from the shade of the terminal into the blinding, high-contrast light of a Sydney day. Sue pulled on her sunglasses as they walked to the taxi rank. Jens walked with a forearm held over his eyes.

The taxi ride into town was uncomfortable for several reasons. To begin with, Jens was untalkative. Sue tried to be friendly and chatted about the people he'd meet: Coops, Raf, Jamie. He seemed preoccupied with the view through the taxi window or thumbed through messages on his phone. Sue guessed the last thing he wanted was a conversation. He was exhausted. So she left him alone. The other reason for Sue's discomfort was that the taxi took a route through the same intersection on Botany Road where the accident had occurred—where Doug had died. As the taxi waited at the same lights, Sue took in the day outside. The place was bathed in sunlight. It was hard to think anything tragic could have happened here. But it had.

Sue turned to Jens. She thought to explain to him what had taken place on this spot, partly to tell him something of herself and perhaps to exorcise her own demons. But she thought otherwise. She'd keep the events of this place closed in her memory, along with her memories of Doug.

Jens spent the best part of the drive into town staring at the scenery outside. As they passed parks and playing-fields he craned his neck to look. When he finally hauled himself from the taxi outside his Pyrmont hotel his eyes scanned the entire length of the street. Then he turned to Sue.

'Can you see koalas here, in the city?' he asked.

Sue smiled. 'Only in the zoo at Taronga,' she explained.

'Oh,' said Jens, nodding. He seemed disappointed.

* * *

It always gave Sue a great deal of satisfaction to show off her home town in its best light. This was the reason she always booked her out-of-town business visitors into the hotels of Pyrmont. From here the office was just a short walk away but visitors would have to cross the pedestrian-only thoroughfare of the old Pyrmont Bridge. On their morning walk across the bridge they'd take in the views of the Convention Centre, the restaurants and bars of King Street Wharf and the marina at Cockle Bay. They'd witness throngs of tourists on the promenades of Darling Harbour and see the replica of James Cook's Endeavour, sails furled, among the colourful historical ships at anchor beside the Maritime Museum.

The following morning Sue had arranged a meeting in the

VALUE PROPOSED

Tesico offices to introduce Jens to Coops and brief him thoroughly on the project. The afternoon was scheduled to be their first architecture meeting with Raf and Jamie DeSouza's team from Onicas. Roper's office remained empty and Sue had briefed Jamie at Michelle's instruction. Sue hoped Michelle had spoken with Roper on the subject, but she still feared the fallout.

When Jens arrived at Tesico, he looked a little more rested. He was dressed in what only an indoor-dwelling technophile from Amsterdam could describe as *summery*. He wore a white, cheesecloth *Nehru* shirt under a cream-coloured, casual linen suit with sandals worn over tan socks.

Sue suppressed a smirk as she led Jens into the sales meeting room. Coops wasn't as guarded.

'Stone-the-bloody-crows mate, you didn't walk all the way here like *that*, did you?' said Coops.

'No,' replied Jens, unaffected. 'I took a taxi.'

'Just as well,' said Coops openly, then whispered as Sue sat beside her. 'He looks like the cover of one of Nan's old sewing patterns!'

Over the next few hours, Sue and Coops gave Jens the background on the project. He squinted at Coops when she spoke, perhaps finding the strains of her New South Welsh accent difficult to follow. He asked for a pad of drawing paper and ordered unhealthy amounts of coffee. By the end of the meeting he had recorded a mass of notes into a spiral-bound notebook and drawn a maze of diagrams onto the butcher's paper Sue had provided.

'So, Jens,' said Sue. 'You must have a lot of questions?'

'No,' said Jens, closing his notebook. 'I just need to talk more with the Wentworth IT people. I need to understand their current structure.'

'Your first meeting with Raf, the IT Security Manager, is this afternoon,' offered Sue.

'Good.'

'So, reckon you can knock something up?' asked Coops, excited.

Jens squinted again, his internal translator hard at work. 'Of course,' he said with a smug smile. 'Didn't Michelle tell you who you were dealing with?'

'She gave us a little of your background, yes,' said Sue.

Jens steepled his fingers, still smiling. 'Did she tell you I have an IQ of one hundred, forty-seven?'

'No,' said Sue.

'Do you know what that figure means?' asked Jens.

Sue shook her head with a smile.

'It means I'm...' began Jens.

'Too smart for the faaarm!' murmured Coops, her chin tucked into her chest.

Sue failed to stifle a short chuckle.

Jens looked lost. His smile had vanished and his internal translator had malfunctioned. 'Actually it means I'm a borderline genius,' he tried to explain.

'That's great,' smiled Sue, unsure how to react. She signalled the end of the meeting by gathering her notes.

Coops got to her feet and made for the door. 'Don't mind us, just having a lend,' she said to Jens in conciliation. 'You'll get used to us girls...'

Jens stood up. 'Good day Miss Cooper,' he offered. He seemed humbled now. Sue guessed the smug attitude was a mask that hid a lack of confidence.

'Aw, onya borderline genius,' said Coops. She gave Jens a friendly punch in the top of his arm. 'And thanks for leaving your windmill to come help out.'

Coops walked from the room. Jens rubbed the top of his arm with a smile that failed to hide his pain.

'I think she likes you,' said Sue.

*　*　*

VALUE PROPOSED

Over the course of the next week Jens was ferried backwards and forwards between Wentworth Tower and the Tesico office on Kent Street. He met with the IT staff, the data security staff and the network technicians. He spent time with Sally McCrae and the customer services people. He met with the marketing department and the clients' accounts team. He spent a great deal of time at Onicas too, with Jamie DeSouza and his people.

Bit by bit, he put together his series of flowcharts and diagrams: the architecture that would solve Wentworth's problems and reinvent their business.

On the weekend, and with the presentation to the Wentworth DMU looming, Coops dragged Jens through department stores and clothing shops in search of attire more appropriate for Sydney's boardrooms. Jens seemed very happy to tag along, although this had less to do with shopping and more to do with being chaperoned around Sydney by an attractive young woman. As a reward for his patience, Coops even took Jens for a visit to the koala enclosure at Taronga Zoo.

It was halfway through the next week, at the end of several very long days, that Jens asked Sue and Coops to join him in the Tesico sales meeting room. One wall was covered with pieces of butcher's paper, taped together. Across them lay a web of lines, diagrams and notes.

Jens gestured to the collage of paper on the wall. 'It's done,' he said.

Jamie DeSouza was in the room too, photographing the architecture diagrams with his phone. The two men had been hard at work all day and the room was littered with coffee cups and takeaway food containers. It looked like they'd been camping there for weeks.

'Wow,' said Sue, surveying the paper-covered wall. She had no idea what it all meant. 'Looks impressive, will it work?' she asked, turning to Jens.

247

Jens smiled. 'Oh yes, it will *work*,' he said, pleased with himself. Jamie nodded in agreement.

'Good,' said Sue. She looked at the paper on the wall again. 'But will they understand it? It looks complicated.'

Jens rolled his eyes. 'It's very simple, actually,' he said.

'We'll only get a short time to present,' said Sue. 'Can we explain it, easily?'

'Of course,' said Jens, defensively. He got to his feet and pointed to a section of the diagram. 'So, what we're recommending is a virtual data centre in infrastructure-as-a-service mode. It'll be VM optimised with microsegmentation and use adaptive scaling and load balancing. The process flow from the customer will use nearshore keying of metadata, OCR, ICR and IDR to capture in encoded datastreams.' He smiled at Sue. 'I thought about template-based intelligent capture too but we won't need it, this architecture is way ahead of that...'

Coops looked at Sue. 'Was that Dutch?' she asked.

'Jens,' sighed Sue. 'I think you can detail all the technical information in our presentation document, perhaps in a separate annexure, but for the purposes of the DMU, we need to keep it simple.'

'Simple?' repeated Jens with disgust. 'This is as *simple* as I can make it. It's...' Jens gestured at the paper-covered wall. '...Elegant.'

'Elegant it might be,' said Sue. 'But we're presenting to the C-Suite. They're largely non-technical.'

'Just give them the potted version darl,' said Coops. Jens squinted at her.

'Maybe instead of telling them what it *is*, in technical terms, perhaps we tell them what it does, in more human terms. Or what it's *like*,' offered Sue.

'What it's *like*?' Jens's irritation was showing.

'Yes,' continued Sue. 'Imagine you're trying to explain it to a layman, or a child even.'

VALUE PROPOSED

'You mean a kind of *story*?' asked Jens, revolted.

A light came on for Sue. 'Yes, yes, a story!' she said, remembering the importance of storytelling from Doug's journal.

'Well here's a story boys and girls,' began Jens, 'the big bad hacker is coming to blow your house down!'

Sue gave a frustrated sigh. 'Jens, *seriously*?'

'Okay, okay,' Jens picked up a marker pen and crossed the room to a whiteboard. He drew a square with a triangle resting on top and pointed. 'That's Wentworth.'

Sue studied the whiteboard, not comprehending.

'Can't you see? It's a house,' said Jens, voice raised in agitation. 'It's a house with no windows and no door. Because windows and doors are weak spots where bad people get in, so you've nailed them shut and you sit inside, behind your defences. You can't see the hackers so you don't know what they're up to outside, and you can't see your customers so you don't know what they're up to either because you're inside, all alone in the dark.' Now Jens drew a wide circle outside the house. 'This is the cloud, it's like the fence *outside* your house. From *here* you're on the outside looking in. You can see who's trying to break in through a window, you can see them before it happens, you can even see them walking up your garden path! And you can see your customers knocking on the door, so you know who to invite inside. *This* is cloud-based security, *this* is our system, *this* is the Tesico difference.' He threw the marker pen onto the meeting-room table.

Coops applauded.

Jens made a small bow, smiling in return.

'It's certainly a great way to tell our story,' said Sue. 'Michelle could use this to give the DMU an overview of the benefits, then you could explain the technicalities for the CIO and the IT people.'

'Michelle?' asked Jens.

'Yes,' said Sue. 'I've invited her to the presentation.'

Jens cocked an eyebrow. 'I don't think so,' he said. 'I spoke with Michelle last night. She'll be in Dubai when we present to Wentworth.'

Sue and Coops exchanged a concerned look.

'Does that mean...?' began Coops.

'...We have to bring in Tony.' finished Sue.

VALUE PROPOSED

40. A Lot Can Happen in a Lift

The days leading up to the DMU meeting passed in a blur of presentation rehearsals and last-minute adjustments to the presentation deck. The team worked late and started early. Tempers were frayed and tiredness was beginning to show.

Sue dedicated a large chunk of time to coaching Jens. He wasn't a natural presenter and had a tendency to rely on technical mumbo-jumbo when he lost the thread of his argument or his confidence waned. Sue was struggling to keep his section of the presentation on-time, and on-subject.

Night after night, Sue tried to update Michelle on her progress. Her calls went largely unanswered and her emails disappeared into the void. The Dubai project was demanding Michelle's full attention. Even when Sue did manage to raise her, their conversations were brief. Michelle apologised for her lack of involvement and repeated her request that Sue include Tony Roper on the presentation team. Where was he? Had she seen him? Sue was forced to admit she hadn't. She'd called him again and again without success. The Melbourne project had consumed him.

From Sue's perspective it all felt less than organised. No, worse. It was a shambles. *A right kerfuffle* as Coops called it. Sue tried to lead her team as best she could, calmly, with assurance. But she often doubted she was up to the task.

At her lowest ebbs she thought of Doug and took courage from his explanation of the presentation stage.

'When you glide into that boardroom, your customer will see only a swan—all serenity and grace. What they will never see are those little webbed feet, paddling like crazy, just below the surface of the water.'

Sue smiled. How she missed him.

On the day of the DMU presentation, Sue felt anything but swanlike. She limped into the foyer of Wentworth Tower on her walking-stick, clumsy and anxious. Under her arm she carried the laptop which contained their presentation. Coops followed, lugging the paper leave-behinds and ancillary material. Jamie DeSouza was there, his Onicas deployment team in tow and Jens looked ill-at-ease, self-conscious in the sharp new suit Coops had helped him pick out.

From the reception desk Sue called Raf and he made his way down to escort them through security. He greeted the team warmly and the smile he directed at Sue put her a little more at ease. With all the preparation for the meeting Sue had forgotten to turn on her phone. She pulled it from her bag as they waited for a lift to whisk them to the upper levels of Wentworth Tower. The phone buzzed to life and an alert sounded the arrival of a new text message.

'It's from Michelle,' whispered Sue to Coops.

Coops leaned close, intrigued.

Sue read out the short message. 'Plans changed. On my way to Sydney now. See you in the meeting,' she said.

'That's great!' said Coops. 'So where is she?'

'Dunno,' replied Sue, 'On her way I guess.'

Sue pocketed her phone. She felt someone grab her elbow. It was rough; an ungracious, physical tug that nearly pulled her off-balance. Looking round, Sue was surprised to see Tony Roper. He dragged her, limping and hobbling, away from the group into a quiet area beside the lifts. His skin was purple from the neck up.

'What the hell are you playing at?' hissed Roper.

Through her shock Sue managed a reply. 'I'm presenting to Wentworth's DMU.'

'I can see that.'

'We tried to get hold of you,' said Sue. 'Where have you been?'

'I was in Melbourne. But I had to fly back this morning to fix this shitfight, didn't I?' Roper thrust his face close to Sue's. 'I was very clear Novak. I told you, no change management for Wentworth as part of our offer. Separate suppliers, no partnerships. And you're presenting with Onicas!' He lifted his chin towards Jamie and his team. 'I'm trying to stop this office getting screwed over and you go behind my back and play politics with Michelle Yim.'

'Then you spoke with her?'

'Yes!'

'Tony, I was just reporting back to her, that's all, like we agreed. I was just relaying to her what the prospect was asking for—Wentworth *wants* a single team approach.'

'You only needed to do your job and sell *Tesico*—that's all. But I've read your presentation. Every other page is *Onicas, Onicas, Onicas* and how we're going to partner with them. It's bullshit, this is *our* deal, not *theirs*.'

'But we're up against CBIS Tony!' Sue was trying to keep her voice low too. 'And you can bet Huffington's proposal will include firewall, software, change management, training—the whole box and dice—in *one* contract, from *one* company!'

Roper produced a laptop. 'Well I've re-written your presentation and removed all mention of Onicas,' he said. 'That's what I'll be presenting today.'

Sue reeled. 'Then you'll lose Wentworth's confidence, *and* their business,' she said.

'I care more about protecting *our* business, Tesico's business!'

Roper swept his free hand at the building surrounding them. 'Look around Novak, they're a friggin' bank for God's sake. They're huge. They're loaded. You can't tell me they don't have the budget to bring in a change management outfit of their own? Where's the risk for *them*?'

'They're hurting, and they need our help,' said Sue.

'No, we're hurting!' returned Roper. 'And you and your little cowgirl friend have defied me for the last time. As soon as this meeting is done, you can both clean out your desks!'

Roper stormed back to the lift lobby. Sue followed him. She felt robbed of everything: her career with Tesico, her hopes for Wentworth. *And what about the team? What about all their hard work?* It meant nothing now. As she rejoined the group Raf eyed her with concern. Sue couldn't look at Coops.

The ride in the lift was tense, and silent. Sue suspected everyone felt the anger that radiated from Tony Roper and possibly the despair that flowed from her. Raf watched the sequence of floor numbers glow on the display panel. He was avoiding eye contact. The lift stopped and Raf led them to a waiting area outside one of the large conference rooms. Then he excused himself and made his way inside. Sue guessed he was grateful to escape the toxic atmosphere.

It reminded Sue of coming round after the car accident. She felt disoriented. It was shock. Gradually her thoughts pieced themselves together and she turned to Roper. 'Tony, whatever you think, Michelle wants us to help Wentworth with change management. She was the one who suggested we bring in Onicas. *She* made that decision. If you go in there and tell Wentworth that change management is off the table, you'll be going against her wishes.'

Raf appeared in the doorway to the conference room and beckoned the Tesico team inside.

'Don't worry about Michelle Yim,' said Roper under his breath.

VALUE PROPOSED

'I'll handle that bitch.' He tugged his jacket straight and was the first to march through the door into the room. Sue followed, head lowered, but nearly collided with him. Roper had stopped, stock-still, in the doorway. Sue drew alongside him and followed the direction of his stare. Two figures were seated at one corner of the immense boardroom table. They were drinking coffee and chatting. One of the figures was Robert Meade. The other was Michelle Yim.

Meade leapt to his feet and crossed the room towards Sue. His smile was warm, genuine. 'Sue, I didn't realise Tesico would be here in such force today. You should have told me your Global Sales Director would be attending.'

Sue realised her mouth was hanging open. There were no words left in her head.

Michelle read Sue's dumbstruck expression and explained: 'Finding a solution for Wentworth has been our highest priority Mister Meade. Not just for Sydney, but for Tesico as a global company. That's why global has been working closely with our Sydney office to develop the proposal you'll hear today.'

Sue closed her mouth and nodded. Words still evaded her.

'I'm here, as is Mister Roper,' continued Michelle, staring Roper down with a look of caution, 'to demonstrate our commitment to this project at the highest level. But we promise not to get in the way. Miss Novak will deliver our proposal.' Michelle smiled at Sue.

Sue came to, recovering from her disorientation. With renewed purpose she carried her laptop to the lectern at the head of the boardroom table. Raf joined her, helping her set up. She could still feel his uneasiness, so she placed a reassuring hand on his arm with a look that she hoped said: *don't worry, everything's going to be alright.*

Raf returned an understanding smile.

Once everything was ready, Sue swept her gaze across the boardroom table where her audience would be seated. Tent-cards bearing the names of the DMU members were already in position. Sue could read the names of Robert Meade, Maria Kutcik, Peter Ludick and Jenny Liu. Among them was also a tent-card for Craig Martin.

'Your CEO's coming?' whispered Sue to Raf. 'I thought he just rubber-stamped the DMU's decision?'

'He doesn't normally attend these things,' confided Raf. 'But we always leave a spot for him. Just in case.'

* * *

During the next ten minutes the room filled. Maria Kutcik was the first to arrive and took her spot at the boardroom table. She cast the smallest of smiles at Sue. *Welcome to the team*, it seemed to say. Robert Meade took his place beside her and the two fell into conversation. Next came Jenny Liu. The guarded, poker expression was still in evidence although Sue noticed the nod in her direction which she took for a good sign.

Last to arrive was a balding, middle-aged man who wore reading glasses and a stern expression. He sat at the chair reserved for him and Sue realised this was Peter Ludick. He made no greeting but buried his nose in the reams of paperwork he carried with him. After several minutes he glanced at his watch and looked up.

'I think we should make a start,' said Peter Ludick. 'Robert, you're chair?'

'Yes,' said Robert Meade. 'But I did ask Craig to join us, seeing as this is such a critical issue. Let's give him another minute shall we?'

Ludick blinked behind the reading glasses. He betrayed no emotion but Sue could feel his hostility. 'Very well,' he agreed. 'Another minute then.'

The fact that the issue was *so critical*, as Robert Meade observed, was an obvious barb to Ludick. Sue believed Ludick already knew all the answers: that CBIS was the solution, not Tesico.

VALUE PROPOSED

For Ludick, this DMU presentation would be a fiasco. He was simply going through the motions. Sue watched Robert Meade cross to the lectern. He must have been fighting hard for her cause, Sue realised, both openly and behind the scenes. He must have spoken with Craig Martin, the CEO and enlisted his support. Now he was calling his allies to the field. Her Champion.

Ludick looked up from his paperwork with an annoyed shake of his head. 'Robert, I really think we should start...'

'Very well,' said Robert Meade, signalling for the conference room doors to be closed. 'Craig might join us later.'

'How would you like to proceed?' asked Ludick, head down again.

'I'll begin by recapping the project team's findings,' said Meade.

'No need,' said Ludick, without looking up.

The conference room doors swung open and a spry looking man in his fifties entered the room. His eyes sparkled with energy and intelligence. Several of the DMU members got to their feet.

'Apologies everyone,' said the man. He cast a warm smile at the Tesico camp before taking his seat. Sue recognised him. It was Craig Martin, Wentworth's Chief Executive Officer.

'Robert, have you gone through the project team's findings?' asked Craig Martin.

'Not yet,' said Meade.

'Good, I'd like a recap. Please walk us through it,' said Martin, settling back.

Robert Meade began his presentation. He allowed much of the detailed data to be projected on the screen behind him while he summed up the larger implications for Wentworth. He was a calm and measured presenter; easy to follow. He spoke without notes, indicating a thorough understanding of the subject matter. Throughout the presentation Craig Martin gave his undivided attention. Meade detailed the effects of the cyberattack from a security standpoint, then gave an analysis of its impact on customer services. He made brief reference to the email surveys and concentrated instead on the results from the in-depth quantitative consumer research. He then offered the project team's appraisal and recommendation, ending with a statement of the value Wentworth expected to achieve.

At the end of Meade's address Craig Martin sat forward and looked at his Wentworth colleagues on either side. 'So, you all agree this is an accurate reflection of the situation?' he asked. All nodded, except Ludick. 'Very well,' said Martin, taking this agreement as unanimous, 'Robert, please tell us who we'll be hearing from today.'

Robert introduced the Tesico team, then turned to Michelle. 'Would Tesico's Global Sales Director care to open?' he asked.

Michelle took her turn at the lectern but kept her preamble short. She thanked Wentworth for the chance to present and stressed that her presence was to demonstrate Tesico's commitment at the highest level. This drew a particularly warm smile from Craig Martin. Then it was Sue's turn. She limped to the lectern and stood with the aid of her walking-stick. She felt the full attention of Craig Martin's bright eyes settle on her. Raf sat apart from the boardroom table, attempting encouragement with a brief nod.

Sue began to talk. Her words flowed, not from conscious thought but from somewhere deep inside. She'd pictured herself in this exact spot so many times over the past months, and in her mind she'd gone over everything she needed to say. She'd gone over it in the shower, in the pool, or in her bed when the pain of her injuries kept her awake in her loneliest hours. She knew her delivery inside-out, back-to-front and upside-down. She became aware of the reactions from the listeners in the room. She was independent of herself, of the speaker at the front of the room, like some out-of-body experience. She could see the tiny crook of a smile at the corner of Maria Kutcik's mouth, the gleam of understanding in Craig Martin's eyes and the silent approval of Robert Meade. She saw Michelle's enthusiasm, the adulation of Coops, Roper's disdain and Raf's smile urging her on.

VALUE PROPOSED

And there, in her mind's eye, seated at the very back of the room she saw Doug. He smiled at her, proud: proud of all she'd achieved; proud of the person, the *salesperson* she'd become.

If only you were here, Doug.

Her presentation seemed to be over in a heartbeat. Sue handed over to Jens who appeared infected with some of her enthusiasm. He used the story of the house without windows and the fence around it to explain the difference between network-embedded security and security in the cloud. The analogy drew a ripple of amusement from all in the room, except Peter Ludick who sat, arms folded and unimpressed. Jens referred to the more detailed material in the leave-behind document and handed over to Jamie DeSouza. Robert Meade's interest in Jamie's part of the presentation was obvious. Jamie was a seasoned presenter in situations like these and was careful not to sugar-coat the real change necessary to move Wentworth's people towards a new security system. He kept it honest. He made it real in their imaginations. His overview of the task that lay ahead wasn't lost on Jenny Liu either. She also seemed impressed by the credentials of Onicas as a company.

When the presentation was finished, Craig Martin was the first to ask a question: 'So, this approach goes way beyond mere security and can help us improve the customer experience too?'

'It will help us monitor customer interaction and design new ways to meet their needs,' said Jenny Liu.

'It'll allow us to innovate once again Craig, and mitigate the impact of the FinTech startups,' added Maria Kutcik. 'And it won't just halt customer attrition, it'll attract new accounts. It'll put us back in business.'

'So, am I right in thinking we can monitor customer transactions in real-time?' queried Jenny Liu.

'That's correct,' answered Sue, 'through a Network Operations Centre. It'll also allow you to selectively test new products and apps, and measure acceptance and functionality while they're deployed.'

'But just how safe is all this, operating from the cloud I mean?' asked Craig Martin. 'Peter, what do you think?'

'I've never advocated security in the cloud,' said Peter Ludick. 'I see no need. Keeping our security system in-house means it's less exposed, it gives us better control. And we need to remember that next-gen firewall software is within reach. It'll become the new standard.'

'With respect,' said Meade, 'a great many financial institutions would disagree. That's why they've already moved their security arrangements into the cloud.'

'But have our technical people been involved?' asked Martin. 'What's their view?'

'We have technical people here from both Wentworth and Tesico,' replied Robert Meade, indicating Raf and Jens. 'They've been working together on this.'

'Ah, Raf,' said Craig Martin. 'What's your perspective on all this?'

'The system can be implemented organisation-wide and I believe it's infinitely more secure than our current arrangement,' said Raf.

Peter Ludick was staring at the ceiling now. He looked in danger of boiling over. 'It's all pie in the sky,' he said with an edge of derision. 'It's just words on a wall,' he waved a hand at the presentation screen. 'I mean, *Network Operations Centres* and *real-time data monitoring*. How can we know that this—that any of this—will work for Wentworth?'

'Very well Peter,' agreed Craig Martin. 'I think we all remain to be convinced, but I believe we have to start somewhere, with the theory, with the possibility of what can be achieved. And it's a good start, don't you think?'

Spoken like an ideas person thought Sue. *Spoken like a true Sage.*

Craig Martin smiled in her direction. 'Well, you've certainly given us a lot to consider,' he said. 'But as you've just heard, there's still further...' he searched for the right word, '...*reassurance* you'll need to provide.'

'Of course,' answered Sue, but the request threw her. She hadn't planned for any further substantiation of the Tesico product. It felt as if a new pathway had appeared at her feet and she had no idea where it would lead.

Martin glanced at the Wentworth team assembled around him. 'I won't have any smouldering concerns, any lingering objections on this. Whatever the proposal, I want everyone to be on-board.' He looked back towards Sue. 'That's just the way we work Miss Novak.' A smile crossed his face. 'And thank you for your discretion today.'

Sue had to think. *Discretion?* What was she being discreet about?

'Now, if you don't mind, I'd like to invite all non-DMU members to clear the room. We've a lot to discuss.' Martin threw a warm smile in Michelle's direction. 'And thanks so much to you and your team today Miss Yim.'

***

'Thanks for making the meeting,' whispered Sue to Michelle as they walked from the conference room to the waiting area outside. 'You helped in more ways than you can know.'

'Happy to help out,' said Michelle. A question-mark formed on her face. 'What did Craig Martin mean when he thanked you for your *discretion*?'

'I think he was referring to the issues of governance surrounding their current security, that they run the risk of prosecution for negligence if they don't protect their clients.'

'Ah, yes, I see,' said Michelle. 'I think you made that point clear in the article you posted.'

'Yes,' replied Sue. 'It's an informal part of their buying criteria anyway, a hidden mover. Best not raised openly. I think the CEO was grateful we didn't go there.'

Michelle nodded in agreement.

'Let's just get the hell out of here, shall we?' said Roper, suddenly at their side. 'Michelle, we need to figure out how to handle this prospect.'

'Oh,' said Michelle, not taking her eyes from Sue. 'I think Sue's doing an excellent job of handling them…'

'Sue's fired,' said Roper.

'No she's not,' said Michelle with a sigh of exasperation.

Roper's voice was a whisper but it still carried his rage. 'You gave me the run of this office Michelle. I think you should respect the decision I've made.' He drew himself to his full height before continuing. He was attempting to intimidate. 'I feel as if I've been kept in the dark on this project Michelle, that I've been sidelined for some reason…'

'Nonsense,' said Michelle, now angry. 'You've been missing in action Tony. You've been off the air. And as we discussed upfront, Sue was always to lead this project.' She turned back to Sue. 'And I, for one, think she's doing a great job.'

'She's sold us down the river, that's what she's done,' said Roper.

Michelle closed her eyes for a moment. Sue knew she was collecting herself, keeping her cool. When her eyes opened, Michelle's voice was calm. 'Tony, we need to talk,' she said. Then she took him by the elbow and led him away.

'Everything okay?' asked Raf, approaching Sue.

'Sure,' said Sue. 'Everything's fine—now.'

'Presentation was great by the way, you all did a great job.'

'Well, we gave it our best shot,' said Sue. 'But I'll admit I don't know where to start in terms of providing the further *reassurance* your CEO is asking for.'

'Oh,' said Raf with a wry smile, 'you'll think of something. You always do.'

Raf bid Sue's team a warm farewell and guided them into a lift, leaving Michelle Yim and Tony Roper behind, locked in discussion. As the lift headed for *terra firma*, Coops turned to Sue. 'Yay, Sue, you were *great*!' she squeaked. 'And what a bonus, having Michelle rock up at just the right moment.'

'Sure was,' whispered Sue. 'And you know what else?'

Coops raised an eyebrow in question.

'This morning, you and I were both fired.'

'How?'

'Roper.'

'When?'

'Coming up in this lift,' confided Sue. 'And now, going back down again, we've got our old jobs back. Thanks to Michelle.'

Coops considered this turn of events with astonishment. 'Blimey,' she said, 'a lot can happen in a lift, hey?'

This book comes with free access to an
online reference companion.

By scanning the QR Code or by navigating to
edvance.sale/recap/value/ now, you will gain a deeper
understanding of the EDVANCE process and the methodology
applied by the characters in the preceding three chapters,
including:

- Gaining consensus on the Desired State
- The prospect's Value Statement
- Updated Stakeholder Mapping
- Applying these methods in your own business

AUTHENTICATE

AUTHENTICATE

41. Show Don't Tell

Sue was betting that, somewhere in his journal, Doug had explained how to set a customer's mind at rest, how to coax them towards a sale and how to overcome reluctant stakeholders.

She thought of Craig Martin's words, how Wentworth would need further—*reassurance.*

She remembered his insistence that there should be *no smouldering concerns—no lingering objections.*

Then she pictured Peter Ludick, the Chief Information Officer, arms folded, unimpressed. How the hell was she going to bring him around?

Sue had a hunch she'd find the answers here. In the next section: *Authenticate.*

Dropping her Android tablet on the sofa beside her, Sue looked at the nightscape through the window of her Potts Point apartment. Lights danced like fireflies on the harbour: navigation lights on fishing vessels, on ferries, and the pulsating, rainbow hues of party lights that shone from the dance-floors and cocktail bars of the pleasure-cruisers. Sue picked up the glass beside her and raised it in brief salute to the water-borne revellers. She was celebrating too, in a way. She took a sip of Prosecco, set down the glass, and slid deep into the cushions of her sofa. It had been a rollercoaster of a day. She was glad to get the presentation behind her. It was a relief; a load off. But its passing had ushered in a new mix of anxieties. She didn't want to think about them now. She just wanted to close her eyes. She'd tackle things again when she was fresh.

She was sitting in the car with Doug again, driving into town from the airport along Botany Road. The rain was pelting the windscreen and Doug was hunched over the wheel, staring through the slashing wipers into the impenetrable haze made by the headlights.

'How do I do it Doug?' she asked.

Doug gripped the wheel, staring into the night outside the car.

'How do I reassure them?'

Suddenly, his face was turned towards her with that carefree, unguarded smile she always remembered. 'Just show them,' he said. 'Just show them how it works.' Over his shoulder Sue saw the chromed radiator grille of the container truck burst through the haze. She screamed as it hammered into Doug's side of the vehicle. There was a blinding flash and the ringing of bells.

The ringing of bells.

Sue dragged herself from the depths of sleep towards the sound. It was real and it was nearby. As she clawed her way back to wakefulness, Sue realised it was the sound of her phone. She picked it up, answering.

'Sue, it's Michelle.'

'Michelle?'

'Sorry I didn't get much chance to catch up after. Just wanted to say what a wonderful presentation you gave.'

'Thanks Michelle.'

'I needed to spend some time with Tony.'

'Oh?'

Sue heard Michelle's long inward breath.

'Yes, I uh, wanted to hear all about the Melbourne job, seeing as we hadn't spoken for so long. And...'

Sue waited.

'And I wanted to talk to him about you and Coops.'

'Do we still have a job to go to tomorrow?' asked Sue, too tired to be delicate.

'Yes, yes, of course you do,' reassured Michelle. 'You're still Tesico employees so long as Wentworth is a prospect. My agreement with Tony still stands.'

So Wentworth was still the answer to keeping her job. At least nothing had changed on that score. 'What about Onicas?' she asked.

'Onicas will deliver change management services, including the re-engineering of Wentworth's processes.'

'Tony agrees?'

'Perhaps, perhaps not,' said Michelle. 'But I've made it clear it's what I want.'

'Thanks.'

'You've still got a lot of work ahead Sue.'

'I know. I was just thinking about Craig Martin, about his need for the DMU to be completely on-board. I think most of them are on-side but the CIO, Peter Ludick, is going to be impossible to convince.'

'I saw that from the body language in the meeting,' said Michelle.

'He'll be undermining our ability and the Tesico offering every chance he gets.'

'Then press ahead with Jamie's team at Onicas,' instructed Michelle. 'That way you can stay ahead of the competition. You can bet Ludick will make sure CBIS get an RFP. Soon you'll have them to contend with too.'

'Sure, that's all do-able, but I still don't know how we can reassure Ludick.'

'Well,' offered Michelle, 'what we usually do in this situation is prove our proposal with the help of a happy customer.'

Sue heard Doug's words again.

Just show them.

Michelle continued. 'China Prestige would make a great example. Jens worked on their business and so did Jamie. They could present the case study together.'

'It's not enough Michelle. Ludick will need a whole lot more.'

'Well, I could ask if someone from China Prestige could fly down and make the presentation themselves, their CISO would be ideal—if we could get him. It may have to be someone from data security though, or their customer services department.'

'It's not enough,' said Sue. 'A presentation won't be enough. You heard Ludick, *just words on a wall*, that's what he said. He needs more than someone just *telling* him it'll work.'

Just show them how it works.

'Michelle,' said Sue, thinking. 'How good is your relationship with China Prestige?'

'Well, I'd say it was excellent. As I think I told you, they've just won some consumer choice awards off the back of our system. They're delighted.'

'Delighted enough to do us a favour in return?'

'I would think so.'

'Then, instead of flying China Prestige down to present to Wentworth,' began Sue, 'why don't we fly Wentworth up to China Prestige? That way they can see a Tesico system at work, first-hand.'

'You think that'll be enough to convince Ludick?'

'I honestly don't know,' said Sue. 'But it's the best option we've got.'

'Then I'll make a call,' said Michelle.

AUTHENTICATE

42. Stacking the Deck

Sue and Jens checked into their hotel on Paterson Street in Causeway Bay. It was one of the more budget-friendly hotels on Hong Kong Island, converted from one of the city's tall, narrow tenement buildings. From the outside it hardly looked like a hotel at all. A single door led into a tiny, brightly-lit lobby. Above towered twenty-odd floors of compact but well-appointed rooms. The hotel had even done away with the custom of a dining-room on account of its position in the heart of one of the world's denser concentrations of eating-houses.

Michelle had left a note for Sue at reception. It was the address of a restaurant in Soho. They were to meet for dinner.

It would be just the three of them. Michelle was there as point-of-contact between Tesico and China Prestige, Sue was lead on the Wentworth project and Jens was present because he'd designed the China Prestige architecture and would need to answer any of Wentworth's questions. Although Coops had been desperate to attend, Sue couldn't justify the expense. Roper already viewed the trip as a waste of time and money, even though Singapore had booked the flights.

After dropping off their bags and taking a quick shower, Sue and Jens headed into the warm, sticky Hong Kong night. Instead of a taxi, they took the MTR to Central. Sue carried her walking-stick and limped beside Jens along Des Voeux Road. It felt good to stretch her legs after the flight from Sydney. From there they rode the flights of covered escalators upwards, above the colonial-era, precipitous stone steps of Soho. They found Michelle, as planned, in a modern restaurant specialising in Shandong cuisine. It was one of Michelle's favourites whenever she visited Hong Kong.

'So when did you fly in Michelle?' asked Jens, chasing a mushroom around a serving plate with his chopsticks.

'Yesterday,' replied Michelle, eyeing him with concern. 'Do you remember Patrick Leung?'

'The China Prestige CISO? Sure, I remember him,' said Jens, curtailing his mushroom-wrangling and making a stab at the easier target of a chicken dish instead. 'Nice guy.'

'Well I met with him today and their Client Services Director, Valerie Chan. I wanted to give them some background on Wentworth,' said Michelle.

'And they're happy to show Wentworth around, in person?' asked Sue.

'Most certainly,' said Michelle.

'So there's no conflicts of interest?' said Sue.

'Well, they're both investment banks, but their focus and portfolios are very different. They won't be sharing any privileged information. The fact they're an investment bank should be a good thing as far as Wentworth is concerned.'

'Their issues will be similar,' noted Sue.

'Like-for-like,' observed Michelle. She flashed an excited smile. 'Personally, I think Wentworth will find it fascinating. I took a look around today. China Prestige have made a great many improvements to our security system, what they've done with the interface is world-leading.'

'Of course,' said Jens. 'Because it's a world-leading system.'

AUTHENTICATE

'Yes,' said Michelle.

'Designed by a world-leading solutions architect,' said Jens with a grin.

'Don't go patting yourself on the back too quickly,' cautioned Michelle. 'It's worth remembering their deployment wasn't exactly world-class.'

'It wasn't?' Sue was surprised.

'Yeah, but that was their call,' said Jens. 'They admitted it and they wore the cost.'

'But it's not the whole story, is it Jens?' said Michelle.

'Tell me,' said Sue, 'what happened with their deployment?'

'China Prestige's old security system was one we'd never encountered before,' began Michelle. 'Changing over to our system created a few *wrinkles* we weren't prepared for.'

'To be fair, Michelle,' said Jens, 'they decided to separate the SOC and the NOC right at the last minute.'

'Which is why they didn't make a fuss,' said Michelle.

'So they have separate Security Operations and Network Operation Centres?' asked Sue.

'Yes, totally separate,' said Michelle.

'I engineered that for them,' said Jens, popping some chicken into his mouth.

'And,' said Michelle, 'they have moved client services data into a separate monitoring centre as well.'

'My work too,' said Jens, chewing.

'Of course, this was all outside the scope of our original proposal,' continued Michelle. 'But even if they hadn't made the request to separate SOC and NOC, we might still have missed their deadline.'

'Because the outgoing system was an unknown?' guessed Sue.

'Yes, Jens had his work cut out to bridge the two systems and make them work together.'

'Didn't sleep for a week,' explained Jens. 'We were building APIs round the clock.'

'APIs?'

'Application Programming Interface,' explained Jens. 'It's like an app that lets you control the function of a service from the outside. Helps you merge stuff.' He interwove the fingers of both hands like cogwheels.

Sue shook her head. 'And how much of a delay did this cause?'

'Hard to say,' said Michelle. 'The separation of SOC, NOC and client services was the main reason for the delay and, as Jens says, that was their call. But the API build contributed. They missed their original deadline by two months.'

'Two months?' Sue thought for a moment. 'Is this something Wentworth will find out?'

'It's possible,' said Michelle, bringing a teacup to her mouth. 'My contacts at China Prestige tell me Wentworth have asked to bring in a technical team to investigate and report.'

'Honestly guys, it's not going to be a problem,' said Jens, chewing. 'The separation of SOC and NOC is already part of the proposed architecture for Wentworth. We're not making that mistake again.'

'So everything should go smoothly if they decide to deploy a Tesico system?' asked Sue.

'Sure!' said Jens with conviction. 'Although...'

'Although *what*?' pressed Sue.

'We've never migrated a customer from a CBIS firewall either,' admitted Jens, attempting a smile.

'We haven't?' asked Sue.

Michelle shook her head.

'And what if Wentworth's technical team dig this up? They'll worry the situation could be repeated for them. It could be a concern.'

'You're right Sue, but let's park this for now,' said Michelle. 'Our first job is to get Wentworth in favour of a Tesico solution and to sign a contract. We can expect that issues of timing and delivery will resurface in the final negotiations, if we get that far.'

AUTHENTICATE

Sue knew Michelle was right. They were still in the *Authenticate* stage. *Negotiate* was further down the track. Her phone buzzed and she checked the screen. 'It's Raf,' she told her colleagues. 'He's just checked into the Conrad. He's invited me for a drink.'

'Then you should catch up,' said Michelle. 'Our most powerful allies are just friends with different masters.'

'Hmm,' said Jens. 'Sounds like Sun Tzu?'

'Not Sun Tzu,' said Michelle with a smile. '*Michelle Yim.*'

* * *

Sue met Raf at a small bar on Staunton Street. It was decorated with modern art from the mainland and tall arrangements of orchids stood in glass vases illuminated from beneath. The place was filled with well-to-do locals and expat bankers. Raf had secured a table on the stone steps near the front, where the building was open to the narrow street. A bottle of Prosecco was chilling in an ice-bucket.

'How thoughtful of you Mister Singh,' said Sue, propping her walking-stick against a chair.

'My pleasure,' said Raf, getting to his feet. 'When did you get in?'

'This afternoon,' said Sue. They sat down. 'So who's in town from Wentworth?'

'Well, just me for the moment,' said Raf, 'but Jenny Liu will arrive shortly, so will Maria Kutcik. Robert and Peter Ludick will fly in first thing tomorrow. It's confusing, we're all on different flights but that's bank policy. Craig won't be coming though, he's the only DMU member who won't be here.'

'I heard you're flying in a technical team too?'

'More like an operational team,' said Raf. 'They'll stay behind for a week or so, evaluating, fact-checking, that kind of thing. They'll report back to Robert and Peter Ludick.'

Sue nodded. She leaned across the table, keeping her voice low. 'So how'd we do?'

Raf poured two glasses of Prosecco. 'With your presentation, your proposal you mean?'

'Yes,' said Sue. 'How'd it go over with the DMU?'

Raf smiled. He raised his glass to his lips and swept his free hand at the scene around them. 'Well, we're here aren't we?'

'Yes we are,' observed Sue, raising her own glass. 'But you're going to have to give me more than that Raf. I'm itching to know.'

'Well, you already know Robert's a big fan of yours. No question there. But your presentation went over very well with Maria too. She's really coming round to Tesico, but mostly to you I think.'

'And Jenny Liu?' pressed Sue.

'The impression I get is that she liked your proposal too,' replied Raf. 'But what really interests her is the Onicas side of things. I think the fact you're partnering with them was a smart move. Seeing what Tesico and Onicas has done for China Prestige will be important for her.'

'And your CEO?'

'You heard Craig for yourself,' said Raf. 'He loves the idea, and if it can address innovation, well, that's a big plus for him. A big plus for *you*.' Raf sipped his drink and placed his glass on the table. 'What he really buys into is the big picture. And I think he sees that in your proposal. All the really granular stuff, the minor details, won't interest him. He'll trust everyone else to work through that. What he needs now is for the rest of the DMU to be in agreement.'

'That's going to be hard with your boss, the CIO, in opposition.'

Raf sighed. 'Yes, I don't know whether Peter is against Tesico as a company or whether it's a case of security in the cloud...'

'Or whether he's too scared to admit he's wrong, or too stuck in his ways to see the alternatives...'

Raf shuddered. 'If a deal like this went through without Peter Ludick's approval, then working at Wentworth would be hell. There'd be a massive difference of opinion in the C-suite. And if

Maria and Peter no longer see eye-to-eye...' He ended with a whistle.

'That's why we're here, isn't it?' Sue reminded him. 'To persuade *everyone* of the benefit of security in the cloud? Even Peter Ludick.'

Raf seemed unconvinced. 'Well, your presentation certainly raised a lot of questions about the CBIS firewall. There's clear dissatisfaction there now. But you'll have a hard job stopping Brenda Huffington convincing Peter Ludick otherwise.'

Sue thought back to some of the early planning sessions she and Coops had held. They'd guessed that Huffington would use fear as a tactic to keep Ludick in her pocket. Fear of the cloud. Fear of the unknown. It was all part of the fear Maria Kutcik had described so clearly. The fear that Robert Meade felt too. Sue knew now that Wentworth, despite its brave, corporate face, was really an organisation in the grip of fear. And the answer to that fear? *Reassurance*, as Wentworth's CEO had so cleverly insisted upon. And the person who needed that reassurance more than anyone was Peter Ludick.

'So, apart from Tesico and CBIS, who else are you hearing proposals from?' asked Sue, switching the subject.

Raf nearly spat a mouthful of Prosecco across the table. 'You can't ask me *that*...' he said, laughing.

Sue was being forward but she felt she knew Raf well enough by now. 'Come on, spill the beans, who else?' Sue smiled.

Raf wiped his chin. 'All I can tell you is there are three other companies in the running.'

'Do any of them offer a cloud solution?'

Raf drew an imaginary zipper across his mouth.

Sue left it at that. Raf was too important as her contact at Wentworth, and as a friend, to push any further.

They finished their drinks and Raf walked Sue to a cab. As Sue climbed inside the red, silver-topped taxi, Raf stooped to talk. 'Just think Sue, if Wentworth is so unhappy with the CBIS firewall solution, why on earth would we repeat the same problems with yet another firewall system?'

'Ah,' said Sue, understanding. 'So you *have* invited other cloud-based providers for proposals?'

'I never told you that.'

'No. But can any of these *other-companies-you-never-told-me-about* solve your customer experience issues the way Tesico can?'

'Maybe,' said Raf. The smile on his face broadened. 'Maybe *not*.' Emphasis hung on his final word.

'And have you invited any of *them* for a drink yet?'

Raf closed the door for her. He admonished her with a wag of his finger, smiling, as the taxi pulled away.

He hadn't broken company policy by telling Sue directly, but Raf had just given Sue a valuable clue: they were looking at other companies with a cloud-based solution. But could they address the customer experience problems and lack of innovation the way Tesico could? It didn't seem so, judging by Raf's response. Sue smiled, glad the solution and associated value proposition she'd recommended had been approved by Wentworth. It was the differentiation she needed. She'd stacked the deck so the cards would fall in Tesico's favour. Now she had to play it out. The more Sue thought about it, the more it became clear that innovation and customer experience was the ground on which she had to fight, the point she had to prove. It would be a critical part of their session tomorrow.

As the taxi coursed through the electric glow of streets lined with wet-markets, clothes shops, technology stores and hawker stalls, Sue leaned back against the headrest. She thanked Raf for the valuable clue, for being her Accomplice and her friend. Again, she pictured his name on the opportunity synopsis and the stakeholder archetype map. She saw the blank space next to his informal criteria.

Why are you helping me?

What the hell are you after Raf Singh?

AUTHENTICATE

43. The Proof of the Pudding

'Daddy's home,' said Jens, smiling, as he walked into the China Prestige Security Operations Centre.

Sue had seen several SOCs before, but nothing like this. It was like a boutique cinema with tiers of desks arranged in front of a central screen. There was a quiet hum of activity in the room as the IT security staffers went about their work.

'From here,' continued Jens, indicating the screen that dominated the room, 'they'll see what it's like to look at the world from the cloud, and the control they can have. I can show them just how far, and in how much detail they can monitor their entire network. This is what they've been missing.' He turned with a grin. 'This is what they *need*.'

Sue heard Doug's voice, clear as conscience in her ear. The words were from his journal: *value is always to be looked at through the eyes of your customer—never what the salesperson thinks of as value.*

'But,' began Sue, 'I don't think we should suggest to Wentworth that this is what they *need*. We should let them decide that for themselves.'

'I agree,' said Michelle, beside them. 'They're here to understand why China Prestige invested in a Tesico system, what it meant for *them*. They'll come to see the parallels with their own business.'

'Let China Prestige do the talking,' said Sue.

Jens sighed, capitulating.

Their escort for the day was a female IT manager from China Prestige. She replaced a handset on one of the desks and looked up. 'They're here,' she said. 'Your prospect has arrived.'

* * *

Patrick Leung, the CISO of China Prestige, had graciously taken on the role of chaperone to the visitors from Wentworth. As he led Wentworth's C-Suite into the SOC, Sue was pleased to notice he was deep in conversation with Robert Meade—perhaps because they were equals, or perhaps they had already discovered a liking for each other.

The Wentworth party came to a halt and swapped a distracted greeting with the Tesico team—their eyes already scanning the room.

'So this isn't Network Operations?' asked Jenny Liu.

'Oh no,' said Patrick Leung. Sue caught the smile at the corner of his eye and wondered if all CISOs did this. 'I can show you the Network Operations Centre later if you like but it's nothing exciting. Network Operations handles the stability of the whole system: the hardware and the way everything connects. They guard against network failure, outages, brownouts, the kind of thing most IT departments are responsible for. But here,' Patrick Leung swept a dramatic wave around the room. 'Here is our Security Operations Centre, or SOC for short. It's where we protect our customers and our data from cyberattack.'

'But, truthfully, you haven't been attacked yet, not really?' accused Peter Ludick.

Patrick Leung smiled. 'You know, when we relied on a network-embedded firewall, we used to think the same way. The only way to know you've been attacked is when you've already suffered damage. So if you don't see an attack then you believe there wasn't one. But,' Patrick swept another wave towards the screen at the front of the room, 'as soon as we switched to cloud-based monitoring, we could see we were being attacked on a daily basis.'

He was right. This was in line with the facts Sue had unearthed for her article on cybercrime complacency. As much as thirteen percent of companies who'd suffered a data breach were unaware the breach had even occurred. The real number of cyberattacks was likely to be far higher than anyone could imagine.

'A *daily* basis?' scoffed Peter Ludick.

Sue saw the smile in Patrick Leung's eyes. He conducted a brief exchange in Cantonese with a security manager sitting at one of the desks. Then Patrick Leung turned back to Peter Ludick. 'We're monitoring a few security threats right now, if you'd care to look?' he said.

The whole of the Wentworth team took a step forward as the details appeared on the central screen.

'This is our incident log,' explained Patrick Leung. 'The three lines in red are current attacks on our system in three different locations.' The readout on the screen looked more like lines of code to Sue, but she could see each line in the log was timestamped and, sure enough, three of them were flashing, highlighted in red.

The security manager scrolled through them, expanding each in turn to reveal further details.

'So, the first is a trojan blocked at a port in one of our Hamburg servers. The second is a denial-of-service attack intended to shut down some of our core systems by overloading connected machines. Ah, now this is interesting...' He pointed at the third flashing line. 'A keylogger is attempting to report back to the hacker who deployed it. It's a silent keylogger; clever, encrypted to be almost invisible. From here this hacker is hoping to learn more, to hack deeper into our system.'

'No-one seems particularly worried,' offered Maria Kutcik,

scanning the room. She was right, most of the operators watched their screens, idly. The room remained quiet, calm even.

'There's nothing to worry *about*,' said Patrick Leung.

'But shouldn't somebody be doing something?' quizzed Jenny Liu.

'No need. Our cloud-based system is doing all the work for us. In seconds it's already blocked these attacks and learned all about them. It's cloned the keylogger, analysed its code and created a countermeasure to render it harmless. It will never threaten us again, nor anyone else: we'll make our analysis available to the authorities and the security sector.' He looked around the Operations Centre. 'Our people are here to monitor and only step in if the situation becomes critical.' He added with a smile, 'But it never does. And MindCloud works at a speed and efficiency far beyond any human ability, thanks to the inbuilt AI and machine-learning capability.'

'MindCloud?' said Meade. 'You call it MindCloud?'

'Yes,' replied Patrick Leung. 'We gave it a name.'

'I like it,' said Robert Meade.

'But you share your analysis?' asked Ludick.

'Absolutely.'

'Why on earth would you do that?'

'If you witness a crime,' explained Patrick Leung, 'are you not duty-bound to disclose the nature of that crime? MindCloud positions us at the leading edge of cybercrime analysis. It's our moral obligation to share what we know in order to help others. To combat crime.'

'Except that you'd be sharing your advantage directly with your competitors,' said Ludick with derision.

Patrick Leung's only response was to raise an eyebrow in Ludick's direction.

'You said MindCloud works at a speed beyond human ability. So how many transactions can it monitor?' asked Robert Meade, fascinated.

'Today MindCloud is monitoring millions of transactions every hour. Tomorrow this number may be higher. It's important to remember that the cloud offers limitless potential, and MindCloud is scale-able, so it can grow with our business.'

'And what about your customers?' asked Maria Kutcik. 'Has MindCloud helped them in any way?' Beside her Jenny Liu was nodding emphatically.

'Perhaps you'd like to see for yourself?' came a woman's voice from behind them. As one, the Wentworth and Tesico assembly turned in the direction of the voice. Standing in the doorway was a smiling, round-faced woman. 'I'm Valerie Chan, Client Services Director here at China Prestige,' she said. She turned towards the door, beckoning. 'This way, please.'

***

By a series of lifts, corridors and security doors, Valerie Chan guided everyone to an even larger area on one of the floors within China Prestige's marketing department.

The area felt less austere than the SOC and less like a mission control centre. Instead of the focus upon a central screen, the room was divided into six circular tables, each housing a circular array of screens. Around these sat many of the bank's client services professionals. The room was noisier too. People crossed the room to converse with each other or huddled in groups around the tables, deep in conversation.

'Welcome to our CEC,' announced Valerie Chan.

'CEC?' asked Jenny Liu.

'Our Customer Experience Centre.'

'We came to the conclusion,' said Patrick Leung, still with the group, 'that MindCloud's security and customer experience functions were best separated.'

Valerie Chan nodded. 'Different objectives, different data, different staff.'

Patrick Leung gave a wave in the direction of a grinning Jens. 'We can thank Mister Hendriks for helping us with that.'

'So the SOC resides in our IT security department and the CEC within our client services department,' continued Valerie Chan. 'But we both have access to the data MindCloud provides.'

'So what do you monitor here?' asked Maria Kutcik.

'MindCloud can be purposed in so many ways,' explained Valerie Chan. 'The data she gathers can be sliced, diced, cross-referenced and compared for any task we set. She learns, so increasingly, she presents new opportunities or pinpoints areas of concern of her own accord.'

'MindCloud is a *she*?' mumbled Peter Ludick.

Valerie Chan swung her round-faced smile in his direction. 'Of course. How could she be anything else? She's *intuitive*.'

Maria Kutcik and Jenny Liu swapped a smile.

'The CEC is split into two broad areas,' continued Valerie. 'Analytics and Innovation. I like to think of Analytics as telling us what's happening now, while Innovation can tell us what opportunities we can create for tomorrow.' She guided the team towards the side of the room where three of the circular tables were grouped. 'This is Analytics.' She pointed at the three tables in turn. 'Customer Analytics monitors how our customers are using the portal. Product Analytics monitors reactions to new apps and new product development. The Transaction Analytics team monitors global transactions.'

'We heard the SOC can monitor millions of client transactions every hour,' said Robert Meade. 'Is that the same here?'

Valerie Chan pointed to one of the screens. 'The monitor you're looking at is providing general trends based on a hundred thousand global transactions every hour. MindCloud is currently crunching the data for almost two and a half million transactions every day. And the results are immediate. It's the competitive edge we've always dreamed of.' She led the group to the desks on the opposite side of the room. 'Over here are the Innovation teams. The Market Trends and Projections team uses MindCloud's data to formulate projections for Prestige, and the markets in general. These discoveries go straight to the Prestige Financial Analysts. The Touchpoint Innovation team uses MindCloud's data to find ways to improve how customers interface with the bank, and how we can develop new ways to improve their experience. The Brand and Product Innovation team helps reveal truths about Prestige as a brand. They formulate plans for brand development and suggest avenues of exploration for new financial products.'

Jenny Liu rolled her eyes like a child in a toyshop. 'To have access to all this information—what has it done for your business, and managers like yourself?'

'I'm no longer working blind,' explained Valerie Chan. 'I have the information I need and I feel in touch with our customers. It allows me to do my job with an enhanced level of insight. And I'm always ahead of our competition.'

'Not really,' said Peter Ludick, unable to resist the temptation to be contrary. 'Let me go back to security. If you're sharing cybersecurity information, you're placing yourself on the same footing as your competitors. It's information they don't have to pay for. You've developed a superior system to place yourselves in a position of parity. It's a wasted exercise.'

'Well, to be clear, we only share details of the threats themselves, not our business or our customers,' said Valerie Chan. 'But, if sharing security data concerns you, I can assure you, that works in our favour too...'

'How?' argued Ludick, displaying the Inquisitor within.

Patrick Leung fielded the question. 'Industry commentators are very aware of our policy of disclosure. They report it directly to the investor market.'

'How is that a good thing?' pressed Ludick.

'Well, it helps position Prestige at the leading edge of

cybersecurity. In turn, investors see us as the safest bank to deal with,' said Valerie Chan.

Ludick remained silent. The icy hostility was beginning to thaw.

Valerie continued. 'And I don't have to explain what a perception like that does for our share price or investor appeal.'

Peter Ludick's lips pursed in understanding, processing the revelation. Sue wondered if he was actually beginning to come around. Maria Kutcik was at his side, the smile on her face urging his acceptance. She didn't want to play this game on her own. She wanted her team-mate back.

'And what about the change from your old security system?' began Ludick. 'How'd that go?'

Valerie Chan's smile faltered. 'In honesty, it wasn't as smooth as we'd hoped,' she admitted. 'But it all worked out in the end.'

'In what way,' quizzed Ludick, 'was it *not as smooth as you'd hoped*?'

'There were delays.'

'What kind of delays?'

'During the deployment phase we decided to separate the NOC and SOC. This was a China Prestige decision, this caused the delay,' explained Valerie.

'How long?' asked Ludick.

'Two months.'

Sue was quick in her attempt to deflect criticism: 'But in making this decision, you must have understood the consequences, yes?'

'Oh yes,' the smile had returned to Valerie Chan's face. 'The rewards were far greater than the risks involved, and we understood the impact.'

Sue noticed Michelle giving her a tight-lipped smile. She also noticed Ludick's eyes narrowing in suspicion.

The group now splintered into its different factions. Jenny Liu led Valerie Chan back to the circular desks, keen to understand the customer monitoring process. Raf and Jens formed their own miniature technology symposium. Patrick Leung and Peter Ludick began a discussion on security while Michelle Yim shadowed Maria Kutcik. Sue looked on, but was soon aware of someone standing beside her.

'I didn't know what to expect, Sue,' said Robert Meade, taking in the room. 'I guessed we'd see a monitor somewhere, some kind of *device*. I just didn't expect *this*...' He gestured at the CEC around them. 'And you can do this, you can build MindCloud for Wentworth?'

'Certainly,' said Sue. 'The MindCloud we build for Wentworth will be different of course, but we've done the feasibility and the broad design is complete. You can ask Raf about that. But she's waiting Robert. She's ready whenever you are.'

Meade spoke quietly: 'I didn't know what to make of Tesico at first, but Raf was right to recommend you. You've shepherded us to a solution beyond our imagining. And that's largely down to you Sue. I appreciate all your hard work on this.'

'All I've done,' said Sue, 'is help you find a path to the solution you need. Not the one you think you want.'

The words from Doug's journal surfaced in her memory: *your buyer has developed a fixed train of thought. We must derail this train to get them on the right track.*

Valerie Chan called for everyone's attention and the various groups made their way back to the centre of the CEC. 'I should also point out,' said Valerie, 'that Onicas played a very large part in the implementation of the system you see today.' Sue checked Jenny Liu's interested expression. The point wasn't lost on her. 'They helped us rethink our processes, trained our people and made the transition seamless,' continued Valerie. 'And we're only just beginning to understand the opportunities MindCloud offers. Thanks to Tesico and Onicas, our business has gone from strength to strength.' Her round-faced smile shone on everyone in the room. 'Now, questions?'

'Did the change from firewall to cloud-based security aid innovation with new products and the customer experience?' asked Maria Kutcik.

'Most certainly,' replied Valerie Chan. 'We were suddenly able to develop a wide range of new digital products aimed at the customer. Better still, MindCloud guided us towards these solutions and helped us gauge take-up and suitability through a range of different test cells. We'd never been able to do that before.'

'And how did the consumers react?' asked Jenny Liu.

'They awarded us the *Grand Prix* at the Asia-Pacific Consumer Choice Awards two years in a row,' replied Valerie. 'It's done wonders for our brand.'

Sue raised a hand. 'Valerie, perhaps you could explain what it was you thought you needed, before Tesico and Prestige began working together?'

Valerie Chan and Patrick Leung swapped a smile. It was Patrick who answered. 'You know, it's funny,' he said, 'but all we thought we needed was a better firewall.'

44. Bumpy Landing

As soon as she walked back into the Tesico Sydney office Sue had the feeling that something was different. Roper's desk was empty—that wasn't it. She scanned the furniture, the decor, looking for the source of her disquiet. Then she knew.

It was the people.

Many of the familiar faces, the people Doug had appointed and nurtured, were gone. At their desks now sat a different breed: all men, all in the twilight of their careers. They lifted their heads, assessing Sue as she passed.

'How was Honkers?' asked Coops with a smile that didn't suit her.

'Uh, okay,' replied Sue.

'How 'bout you tell me all about it then?' said Coops, a little too loudly, with a nod towards the breakout room.

'Sure.'

Once inside, Coops closed the door and the fake smile left her face. 'Thank God you're back.'

Sue pointed to the office outside. 'Coops, what the hell?'

'Roper's been going at the sales team like a bull at a gate,' explained Coops. 'He's sacked anyone who didn't meet target and he turfed them out the same day. No payout, no notice, nothing.'

'That's just crooked,' exclaimed Sue.

'Tell me about it,' said Coops. 'The bloke couldn't lie straight in bed. He must've been cooking this up for a while though, because the very next day *this* happened...' she cocked a hidden thumb towards the scene outside the door, '...the invasion of the *Roper-clones*.'

'Who the hell are they?'

'Dunno. Bunch of old silverbacks. Old-school, hard-sell types.'

'And where's Tony?'

'Stuck in Melbourne. He even fired the salesperson down there. Now he's running the deal himself.'

'What?' Sue was incredulous. 'But that opportunity was developed by the Melbourne team...'

'I know,' said Coops. 'I reckon he's struggling. And he's giving good people the flick to shift the blame.'

'I'll tell Michelle.'

'You'll have Buckley's getting anyone back though. It's done and dusted.'

Sue's phone rang. She fished it from her bag and snapped into the handset. 'Yes?'

'Sue,' came the uncertain reply, 'it's Robert Meade.'

'Oh, Robert,' said Sue, 'sorry, I was in the middle of something...'

'Should I call back?'

'No, not at all.'

'I just wanted to say thank-you for getting everyone up to Hong Kong. The chance to see a Tesico solution in operation has gone a long way in setting everyone's mind at rest.'

'It has?'

'Yes.' There was a lengthy pause from Meade. 'But there's something more we need...'

'Oh?'

'Peter Ludick has *specific* concerns with the technical deployment of a Tesico solution.'

'Still?' Sue tried to sound surprised but she'd expected this.

'Well, it's good news in a way. These are *new* concerns. The Hong Kong trip gave him a fresh perspective on cloud architecture and I believe he's taking the idea far more seriously.'

'That's good,' said Sue, guarded.

'But taking the solution more seriously has also caused him to think through the deployment in more detail. That's what these issues are about.'

'So,' said Sue, 'can you tell me what they are?'

'I thought it might be best if you hear them from him directly, say tomorrow sometime?'

'Of course,' said Sue.

'Good. I'll be in touch.'

This book comes with free access to an
online reference companion.

By scanning the QR Code or by navigating to
edvance.sale/recap/authenticate/ now, you will gain a deeper
understanding of the EDVANCE process and the methodology
applied by the characters in the preceding four chapters, including:

- Authenticate—the process and methodology
- Validating your proposal
- Validating yourself and your company
- Updated Stakeholder Mapping
- Applying these methods in your own business

NEGOTIATE

NEGOTIATE

45. The Devil in the Details

'But it's all in the technical annexure of their proposal,' said Robert Meade. 'Tesico have already made provision to separate our Security, Network Operations and Customer Experience into dedicated monitoring centres.'

'But that's only part of the issue,' said Peter Ludick.

'Perhaps, but China Prestige have admitted they made a last-minute decision on this and it cost them time. That's not going to happen for Wentworth.'

'Ah, but China Prestige's last-minute changes weren't the entire reason for the delay,' said Ludick, staring across his desk at Sue. 'Were they Miss Novak?'

The three of them sat in Peter Ludick's office. Sue guessed he'd never concede his advantage by visiting Robert's office or the neutral territory of a meeting room. He'd also made a point by not inviting his IT Security Manager, Raf Singh: he wanted to divide Robert and Raf. He wanted no opposed front ranged against him.

Sue tried to soften her disclosure. 'The separation of the monitoring centres caused a great deal of last-minute upheaval for China Prestige, and Tesico. It was the main reason for the delay. But there were other factors. Maybe these contributed, maybe not. We don't know.'

'But isn't it true,' Ludick went on, 'that Tesico had to undertake the emergency build of several APIs outside of the contracted timeframe?'

'Yes,' said Sue. She hoped her face wasn't reddening. 'It's true.'

'And why had Tesico not built these APIs in advance? Why so late?'

'As I understand it,' said Sue, 'this was part-and-parcel of the last-minute deployment changes.'

'Ah, but was it?' Ludick sat forward in his chair. 'Isn't it also true that China Prestige's old security system was an unknown quantity to Tesico?' Wentworth's operational team in Hong Kong had obviously reported back. And they'd dug deep.

'Yes,' said Sue. 'We'd never helped a customer make the switch from a system like theirs before. But as I said, the API builds may have contributed to the delay, they may...'

'And,' interrupted Ludick, 'have Tesico ever helped a customer make the switch from a CBIS firewall before?'

Sue drew a long breath. 'No.'

Ludick sat back. Sue felt like she'd just been slapped in the face.

Robert Meade tried breaking the tension. 'In any case, my understanding is that China Prestige are very happy with their Tesico system now. The deployment issues are ancient history.'

Ludick offered a condescending sigh. 'I hate to remind you Robert, but you weren't here the last time we changed security provisions. No-one in the C-Suite was, apart from Maria and myself.'

Sue was picturing the stakeholder archetype map. Peter Ludick might be edging towards acceptance of a Tesico solution but his pride would never let him admit he'd been wrong, or that he'd changed his mind. He wanted to have the final say; to be the casting vote—because only *he* could understand the implications of the change, only *he* could see the perks and pitfalls. It was a way to explain his former reluctance. *Only I know best.*

'Now I don't want to keep dragging everyone down Memory

NEGOTIATE

Lane,' continued Ludick, 'but you both have to understand that it was a period in the bank's history I do not want to live through again. I will *not* live through again.' He gave a dismissive wave. 'It's very easy for officers in other departments to approve plans like these but it's always down to data security and IT to pick up the pieces when things break.'

'How can I set your mind at rest on this Mister Ludick?' said Sue, looking for a way to move forward.

Peter Ludick eyed Sue for a while. Perhaps it was suspicion, perhaps he was weighing her up.

They will always tear an idea to pieces before acceptance. They want to pressure-test and examine. Sue and Coops had guessed at it before, but now she'd spent time in his presence, Sue was certain: Ludick was every bit the Inquisitor.

The Inquisitor responds to: the truth. Quantifiable evidence.

'I need guarantees,' said Ludick. He seemed less hostile at Sue's question. 'Not just personal guarantees and promises of success. Not that. If this transition goes ahead, I need to be certain it will be seamless. I need to know how you will avoid delays; your fallback options; what are your backup plans? And the last thing I want is another presentation.'

'You want to see proof?' asked Sue.

Ludick nodded, taking her in once more.

'I understand,' said Sue, 'the transition phase is a huge area of concern for your business and your customers.'

'Yes,' said Ludick.

Sue realised this was all a very good sign. She remembered from the archetype cards that hostile questions didn't mean an Inquisitor was being dismissive. It could also mean they were engaged and wanted to learn more.

'Understood,' said Sue.

Ludick almost appeared to smile.

'But I have to ask,' said Sue.

'Yes Miss Novak?'

'Do you have any other concerns? Any areas you foresee problems with taking on a Tesico system?'

Ludick thought for a while. When he spoke his tone was softer. 'Thank you for arranging the trip to Hong Kong Miss Novak. It wasn't completely wasted on me. Seeing Tesico's system at work in China Prestige was, I admit—reassuring.'

'Does that mean you have no remaining concerns?' repeated Sue.

'None that I can think of.'

'So, if I can successfully demonstrate to you that a transition from your current CBIS firewall system to a Tesico cloud-based system will go without a hitch, then you'll be happy to adopt our proposal?'

Ludick blinked. 'Theoretically, yes.'

'Then I'll get you this proof Mister Ludick,' said Sue.

From the corner of her eye, Sue saw Robert Meade smile in her direction.

46. A Rock and a Hard Place

'You promised him *what*?' said Jens.

'Proof. Something he can see with his own eyes,' replied Sue.

'That the deployment will be *seamless*?' Jens was incredulous.

'That the changeover from CBIS to Tesico won't go—*wonky.*' As soon as the word left Sue's mouth she wished she hadn't used it.

'*Wonky?* There's nothing *wonky* about the system or its deployment!' Jens was getting defensive, angry.

'So what kind of proof are we talking about?' asked Jamie DeSouza.

Sue shrugged, lost for an answer.

'Perhaps we get another Tesico client to reassure him the transition won't go pear-shaped?' offered Coops.

Sue gave her a tired half-smile. 'He's been pretty clear Coops. He doesn't want to be told the system won't break. He needs real assurance. He's an Inquisitor,' she explained.

Coops gave a quiet gasp. Apart from Sue, she was the only person in the room who knew what that meant.

The group was gathered around the table in the Tesico sales team meeting room. Sue had called the meeting to find a solution to this latest emergency.

'He won't make a leap of faith,' Sue told the room. 'He needs to see some kind of working model of the deployment. Until then, this deal won't move forward.'

'And how the hell can we do that?' asked Jens. He jumped up from the table and paced the room.

'Well, surely there's some kind of simulation we could run?' offered Sue. 'We rig up a PC with the CBIS firewall on it then we zap it over to the Tesico system in the cloud?'

'*Zap it over?*' said Jens.

'Like a real-time demonstration?' said Coops.

'A proof-of-concept?' suggested Jamie.

'Yes,' said Sue, 'would something like that work—Jens?'

Jens turned. He held his hands out to them, palms upward. 'How?' he implored.

'Surely, a genius like you could knock something up?' said Coops, appealing to his vanity.

'But this is just putting the horse behind the cart!' shouted Jens.

'Cart before the horse,' corrected Coops.

'Yes!' agreed Jens, 'it's all face-about-arse!'

'Arse-about-face, darl,' said Coops.

Jens missed the irony. He blinked, his translator faulty.

'Could you do it though?' asked Coops.

'Of course!' shouted Jens. 'We could find a small department somewhere in Wentworth, or create a test cell with machines from different departments and transition them across to Tesico. Technically it's not difficult, but it's all arse...' He faltered.

'...About face?' finished Coops.

'Yes!' said Jens.

'How?' asked Sue.

Jens began counting off each point on his fingers in turn: 'Because, first we need to understand how decommissioning the CBIS system will affect our system's deployment. Then we need to design workarounds. But we can't do that until we work together with the CBIS engineers, and we can't do that until we are appointed. Until then I can't demonstrate a smooth transition.'

Jamie was drawing a long breath. 'Jens is right. We need Wentworth to sign a contract with us first.'

'But that's not going to happen,' said Sue.

'CBIS will have a clause in their contract,' explained Jamie, 'as outgoing provider, they need to work with us to ensure a smooth transition from their system to ours. Until then, we can't go near the CBIS system. We can't touch their code. It's their IP.'

'So we can't demonstrate a proof-of-concept...' Sue began to postulate.

'Until we get the contract from Wentworth.' said Jamie.

'And we won't get the contract from Wentworth...' continued Coops.

'Until we can demonstrate proof-of-concept to Ludick,' concluded Sue.

'Blimey,' said Coops. 'We're caught between a rock and a hard place.'

'Face-about-arse,' agreed Jens.

* * *

'I understand the problem,' said Meade. 'It's a stalemate.'

'Yes,' agreed Sue over her office phone.

'And there's nothing you can do to set Peter's mind at rest, even without CBIS's involvement?'

'Not really, we can't prove deployment until we get the contract.'

'This is unfortunate but,' said Meade, 'I'll see what I can do.'

Sue felt a flutter of optimism.

'I'll try talking to Peter myself. I'm not sure he's aware of the situation you're in—of the situation we're all in here.'

Sue liked the way he was being inclusive. If this was Wentworth's problem too, that was an encouraging sign. It meant Tesico was on the home stretch and Robert Meade, for one, was cheering them towards the finish line.

'I'll try talking to Maria too, and I'll push it up to Craig Martin. Hopefully they can have a word with Peter.' Meade was in Champion mode once again, Sue's most powerful Change Agent within Wentworth.

'Thanks.'

'He won't walk away from the idea of a proof-of-concept, though,' said Meade.

'No, I don't expect he will.'

'And I'm sure he'll want to retain the option to walk away from Tesico if the proof-of-concept is less than one-hundred percent successful.'

'I understand.'

'Even if a deal with Tesico is struck.'

Sue felt her heart skip a beat. Even with this proviso, were they at that stage already? She guessed they were, but she didn't want to ask outright. She was too frightened, as if, for some superstitious reason, the merest mention of a deal would break the spell and cause it to vanish. 'Of course,' she said.

'Leave it with me.'

'Thank-you Robert.'

47. Defiance

Roper was back in Sydney for *morning prayers* on Monday. He spent the session belittling and criticising the Tesico Sydney employees. Then, once he was on a roll, he summoned Sue and Coops into his office.

'What the hell is this?' he asked, holding up some paperwork.

Sue squinted at the documents in his hand. 'They're my expenses, from the Hong Kong trip.'

Roper tore a collection of receipts away from the form they'd been stapled to and brandished them at Sue. 'You expect me to believe these are legitimate?' Roper thumbed through them. 'Wine? Beer?'

'I was entertaining the prospect. He gave us some useful information,' said Sue.

'And what the hell is *this*?' Roper said, holding up a receipt written entirely in Chinese. 'I can't even read it!'

'Dinner,' said Sue.

'Bullshit more like,' said Roper. 'You're intent on bankrupting this office, aren't you?'

'No,' said Sue. She wanted to *save* this office. But she'd never convince Roper of that.

'You still haven't closed,' railed Roper, 'we still don't have a sale. All you've done is run up a bill you expect the company to pay. This whole thing could've been handled with a few case studies and some recommendations from customers. But *oh no*, instead you want to go piss my budget up against a Hong Kong wall!'

'Tony, the flights and the hotels were paid for by the Singapore office. All those receipts are for meals and for entertaining the prospect. But if it's such a big deal to you then I'll pay for them myself.'

Roper's fist closed around the wad of receipts, his forefinger levelled at Sue's face. 'Bloody right you will!' He waved the receipts in the air. 'I know what this is. It's all part of the plan to spend time with Michelle Yim, isn't it? Well, you can lick her arse as much as you like but you're still on notice. And if you don't land Wentworth you're out on your ear.' Roper paused to catch his breath. 'Now, what about those leads I gave you two, where are we on those?'

Sue frowned in question.

'Well?' pressed Roper.

'Tony,' began Sue, 'they're not leads. They're just a list of businesses...'

'They're leads if I say they're leads.'

'But there's been no trigger, no reason for them to reassess. We don't know if they're dissatisfied with their current arrangement. We have no background on their situation or their needs and we have no idea who the influencers might be.'

'Or who the Change Agents are,' added Coops with a nod, quoting Doug's journal.

Roper frowned in confusion.

'We've got nothing to go on,' said Sue.

Roper shook his head. 'What planet do you two come from? Pick up a phone and call them for an appointment. Then sell them something!'

'So we're a call-centre now? You want us to waste our time cold-calling random companies? Are you serious?' asked Sue.

Roper was nonplussed but was soon back on the attack. 'Do I look anything less than serious to you? Do I? I'm sick of these bloody excuses. I want you two to start developing those leads *immediately*—in case the Wentworth deal falls through—*when* the Wentworth deal falls through!'

Sue got to her feet, resting her weight on her good leg. 'What's the point? If we don't land Wentworth you're going to fire us anyway! So why waste precious time and energy chasing down a few target companies that aren't even real leads? It's just getting in the way of us bringing in Wentworth!'

'You wouldn't know a real lead if it grabbed you on the arse,' said Roper. 'Do you honestly think you get to pick and choose what jobs you get? If you can't handle more than one prospect at time, you don't deserve to work in this office.'

'I don't have to listen to this,' said Sue, turning for the door.

'Don't you turn your back on me,' threatened Roper.

Sue signalled to Coops. 'Neither do you.' Coops stood too and the women left.

'Get back here now!' shouted Roper.

Sue and Coops beat a hasty retreat for the sanctuary of Sue's cubicle, but Roper was already on their heels. He turned and barked at one of his *Roper-clones*. 'Come here!'

The Roper-clone picked his way to stand in front of his boss. His grey hair had a faint nicotine rinse to it. He would have been a redhead once.

'Did you hear me telling these two to get back to my office?' demanded Roper.

The Roper-clone gave Sue and Coops a nervous glance. 'I guess so...'

'And *did* they?'

'Not really...' said the Roper-clone.

Roper rounded on Sue and Coops. 'You two persist in your defiance. Well this time I've had enough. Insubordination is a sackable offence. I don't care if you land Wentworth or not, I don't care if you've stabbed me in the back over a bowl of noodles with Michelle-bloody-Yim. I don't care. Either way, you're both out of here. And soon.'

He stormed back to his office, slamming the door.

'Well,' returned Coops, 'you can stick your job right up your big fat clacker.'

***

The Stockman's Hotel was filled with its usual mix of patrons celebrating the end of the working week.

Sue, Coops and Jens sat on bar-stools around a small, circular table in a quiet corner of the bar. Each was staring at their drink in thought. Compared to the revelry around them, they looked like attendees at a wake.

'I don't know how you put up with him,' offered Jens. 'I've never seen that kind of behaviour in a Tesico office.'

Coops placed a hand on his forearm, grateful for his sympathy.

'He wasn't like that in Singapore,' continued Jens. 'At least, not as far as I know. Michelle wouldn't stand for it. So why now? Why here?'

Sue was prompted to think of Wentworth, of Maria Kutcik, of Robert Meade, and what they'd both said about Wentworth. 'Fear,' she said without looking up. It hadn't occurred to her before but Tesico Sydney was also an organisation in the grip of fear. 'It can bring out the worst in people…'

Sue's phone lay face-down in front of her. It rattled on the table but she was too numb to react. She hoped it wasn't Roper, that it wasn't anything to do with work, but what else could it be? She sighed and flipped the phone over. It was a call from Robert Meade.

'Shit,' said Sue and swept the phone to her ear. 'Hello, hello? Robert?'

Jens and Coops exchanged a look. Eyebrows raised.

'Sorry Sue...' began Meade.

'About what?'

'I couldn't bring Peter Ludick around. I talked with Craig, our CEO, but Craig doesn't want to apply pressure. He wants everyone in the DMU to come to the table of their own accord.'

'So a contract won't be signed?' Sue felt the sickness in her stomach; like she was falling. She glanced at her friends across the table. Jens hung his head.

'No. Peter doesn't think anything should be signed while there are concerns to be addressed. He's right in a way, it's the wrong process,' said Meade.

'So Wentworth will go with another supplier?'

'I didn't say that.'

Sue shook her head. 'Robert, I'm confused.'

There was a long pause before Meade spoke. 'Sue, we all want to proceed with Tesico—with you—and with Onicas. But this is all subject to negotiation now.'

Negotiation?

N is for NEGOTIATE.

Sue was startled. They had entered a new phase of the EDVANCE process, just like Doug said they would. The whole process flowed, it worked. All you had to do was cover off each step in turn and it would flow naturally to the next. Sue began to focus, she was energised now. Both Jens and Coops stared at her, sensing it.

'So, if we can't get a contract just yet,' Sue thought aloud, 'is there another way around this? Would Peter Ludick be happy to ask CBIS to work with us on a deployment model?'

'No. That can't happen.'

'Then how can we satisfy Peter Ludick's concerns without demonstrating a proof-of-concept?'

'He says you need to be creative.'

'Creative?'

'Yes,' said Meade. 'This will be a big part of the negotiation.'

Sue was lost for answers. It had been a tough day, and acting as Roper's punchbag had drained her. Sue knew she had to continue reading Doug's journal. That's where the answers would be. She needed his guidance and, after all the threats and demands, she needed to hear Doug's calming voice in her head.

'Do whatever you can, Sue,' said Meade. 'I urge you to find a solution, a way to get past this.'

'Okay,' said Sue. 'Then we'll be creative.'

NEGOTIATE

48. The Camel's Back

Sue woke early on Saturday morning. She'd been too tired to read Doug's journal after returning home from the Stockman's Hotel. She wanted to be clear-headed.

She made a pot of coffee and took her Android tablet onto her balcony. Then she began to read.

> *N is for NEGOTIATE.*
>
> *All too often, a salesperson can reach the end of a long, hard road and believe the NEGOTIATE step is just last-minute haggling over price.*
>
> *A deal can fall through so easily at this stage. I've seen it happen many times.*
>
> *Usually it occurs because either the salesperson or the prospect didn't realise they were still negotiating; that the concerns of either or both parties still needed to be met.*

Sue looked up. Between the buildings opposite, she saw the first of the sun's rays striking the water in the harbour. She thought of WestInvest and realised the truth of Doug's words.

> *Until then, you have no negotiated outcome; you have no contract; you have no sale, and everything you*

have struggled to achieve up to this point is of no consequence.

The inexperienced salesperson tends to approach negotiation as a process of compromise; as a way both parties can 'meet in the middle'. But compromise means giving up something without getting anything in return.

This is especially true of traditional 'win-lose' negotiating where agreement on each point must be reached before proceeding to the next. Each agreement is then 'locked-in' and cannot be re-negotiated.

The problem with this approach is it assumes that the whole of the negotiation is a series of unrelated issues which must be fought over one-by-one. In this way the negotiation becomes a tally of wins and losses. The inability to re-negotiate contentious issues in the light of other, related issues can create frustration and discord. By its very definition, win-lose negotiation means there will always be a winner. And so there will always be a loser.

There is a better way. I call it 'win-win' negotiating. This is a process where both parties can feel they've reached an acceptable, even beneficial, conclusion. That both vendor and customer have gained something by the experience.

It begins with all parties coming to the table with a clear agreement: nothing is agreed until everything is agreed. Unlike 'win-lose' negotiation it looks at negotiation as a whole; it understands that issues are often interdependent and must be considered in light of each other. For this reason, win-win negotiating allows re-negotiation of each and every point at any time (although all points must be agreed upon before negotiation is concluded). This allows you to give on some issues in return for a gain on others. There is no compromise here, because there are no outright losers. Every party gets something in return for the concessions they trade. I have found it the best way to negotiate for success while preserving trust and goodwill.

It all starts with assessing what you can afford to trade, and what you can't. Which concessions would be low-impact? Which would be high-impact for you? You must also define the point at which the deal will be of no value to you at all. This is the point at which your only option is to walk away. This is your NEGOTIATION CEILING; the straw that will break the camel's back.

You must then go through the same exercise for your customer. What will be their high and low-impact concessions? What will be their negotiation ceiling? Then figure out which of their high-impact needs are low-impact concessions for you, and vice-versa.

The best possible outcome is to arrive at a place where both parties have made low-impact concessions for high-impact rewards. This is win-win negotiating. And it's up to you to steer the negotiation to this conclusion.

At this stage in your relationship it's often the case that both parties need each other more than they admit. Be mindful of this, and don't push your prospect too hard. At all costs you must preserve trust and partnership. Be prepared to make low-impact concessions, but only when pressed. Don't concede too much, or too quickly. And always place a condition on any concession. Always get something in return, but never make the mistake of saying: 'If I... then will you?' The problem with this approach is that you have already demonstrated a willingness to concede. It's always better *to reverse this conditional phrase to: 'If you will... then I might consider...'*

And never say 'no', say 'that depends.'

The most powerful weapon at your disposal during the NEGOTIATE step of the EDVANCE process is knowing the needs of your prospect. Understanding their position will reveal the points they will fight for, and the ones they will concede. It will help you pinpoint areas of dissatisfaction or problems they see with your proposal, both real or imagined.

These are the bargaining chips they will bring to the table.

* * *

Sue's head was a jumble of disconnected thoughts, ideas and questions. Doug's journal had sent her imagination into overdrive. She understood his approach, the big picture, but the implications for Wentworth were like a ball of string. She decided on taking a walk to help her untangle the separate threads. No, better still, she'd go for a walk—*and a swim.*

Sue glanced at her walking cane propped in the corner near the door to her apartment. She hadn't used it in a while and she had no need for it today. Why she kept it was a mystery. Her limp was almost unnoticeable now. It would always be there but it caused her no bother. Like the walking stick, the limp was a memento: a badge of honour that reminded her of all she'd faced and overcome.

With her sunglasses on and her swim-bag over her shoulder Sue walked past the brunch-set seated at their tables on Finger Wharf. She rounded the Art Gallery of New South Wales and headed for the Domain when her phone rang.

'I read your note,' said Michelle Yim. The call from Singapore was scratchy and there was an annoying delay.

'What do you think?' Sue asked, continuing her walk.

NEGOTIATE

'Well, I guess it's good news but I can't see how to solve Ludick's issues.'

'Nor me,' admitted Sue.

'I think we should begin drafting a contract to share with Wentworth. I'll get the legal team onto it.' Michelle sighed. 'This is going to be a long haul, they'll keep negotiating right up until the ink is dry on the contract.'

If we ever get to that, thought Sue.

'Oh, and I'm sending you a negotiation team,' said Michelle. 'They'll help you understand just where you can give and where you should stand your ground.'

'Great. Thanks.'

'And you're going to have to figure out what else Wentworth will bring to the table. Are there any more curve-balls they'll throw at us?'

'Sure,' said Sue.

'The negotiation team can help you with that, too.'

'Okay.'

'And, I hope you don't take this the wrong way...' Michelle sounded hesitant, apologetic.

'Yes?'

'I'd like you to involve Tony in the negotiations.'

Sue halted, mid-stride, on the pathway through the Domain. 'Michelle, do you think that's wise?'

Michelle's reply came slowly. 'I've given this a lot of thought. I know he and I have been in conflict over this whole change management issue and you've been caught in the middle. I'm very sorry about that. He's still recovering from that business in Taipei with Onicas.'

Sue listened.

'But that's all behind us now,' continued Michelle. 'Look Sue, you've got us close to the finish. That's great. Now I know Tony won't want to work with Onicas again but that's okay, I'm sure you'd

313

be happy to. And that's what I've agreed with him. It's just that, when it comes to negotiating, I'm sorry but...'

'Yes?'

'Well, you don't have any experience Sue. And this is a very large deal.'

Sue sighed. Michelle was right.

'You know, sometimes it pays to have a hard head and a thick skin in situations like these,' said Michelle.

At all costs you must preserve trust and partnership. It ran against everything Doug had taught Sue, everything Doug was *still* teaching her.

'I don't know, it worries me Michelle.'

'He's got a lot of experience in negotiation,' said Michelle. 'I'm going to need his help. And so are you.'

'Sure,' said Sue, trying to sound reasonable. But the panic was already rising inside her.

* * *

Sue turned and kicked away, gliding above the lane-line at the bottom of the pool.

How many laps had she done?

She'd forgotten. She'd been thinking.

Breaking the surface of the water, Sue regained the rhythm of her stroke. She could see the clock when she took a breath. She didn't need to count laps. Thirty minutes should do it. That would be a kilometre. Give or take.

In her mind she'd been going over and over the same conundrum: *no proof-of-concept, no contract; no contract, no proof-of-concept.*

Be creative Ludick had said. How the hell would creativity solve this? It was a closed loop, a revolving door with no way out.

Nothing is agreed until everything is agreed.

The thoughts came to Sue one at a time, stroke by stroke.

The win-win sale.

Be prepared to concede but get something in return.

'If you will... then I might consider...'

They were all circular thoughts; all closed loops. Like laps in a pool.

No proof-of-concept, no contract; no contract, no proof-of-concept.

Then Sue heard another voice in her head. It was Doug.

Just break the loop Sue.

Sue surfaced at one end of the pool and clung to the tiled edge, panting. There would be no more laps today. She had to call Michelle.

She knew what had to be done.

# NEGOTIATE

49. Give and Take

It occurred to Sue that the closer you got to finalising a deal, the more people there were in the room.

She was sitting in one of the conference rooms in Wentworth Tower. Beside her, Coops took in the proceedings with fascination. Jens was there too, as was the Tesico negotiation team. Nearby sat Jamie DeSouza and his party from Onicas. Across the table were Peter Ludick, Wentworth's sizeable negotiation team and a few of Ludick's IT security staff. Raf was nowhere to be seen. Robert Meade sat apart, at one end of the long table, his expression weighed with discomfort.

'What is evident from our research at China Prestige is that Tesico missed their delivery deadline.' Wentworth's chief negotiator was a large but athletic-looking man with a confident smile and a nose that had been broken more times than a badly-drafted contract. Sue picked him for a rugby player.

'What your research failed to uncover was that this was due to Prestige's request to separate network, security and customer experience monitoring at the last minute.' Roper was on his feet, acting on behalf of the entire Tesico and Onicas negotiation team who sat idly by.

'This may have accounted for part of the delay,' continued Wentworth's rugby-player chief negotiator, 'but even if this request had not been made, Tesico would still have missed deadline.'

'You don't know that,' said Roper. Sue saw Robert Meade eyeing Roper, the source of his discomfort was now plain.

'But we *do* know that, Mister Roper. The outgoing security system was unfamiliar to Tesico and this caused delays while essential Application Programming Interfaces were built. This alone would have caused you to miss deadline.'

'We were on top of it.'

'The separating of the monitoring functions added a parallel delay. It was a convenient smoke-screen that helped you hide your own deployment mistakes, was it not?'

'Not true!' declared Roper. Meade shifted in his chair.

'Then tell me, is this true,' continued the chief negotiator, 'that Tesico has never engineered a replacement for a CBIS system? That CBIS is also unfamiliar technology to Tesico?'

'It won't be an issue.' Roper wheeled on Jens. 'Will it?'

'Uh, no,' stammered Jens.

'Please answer the question, Mister Roper.'

Roper turned back to the chief negotiator. 'Sure. It's true. But since China Prestige, we've deployed a dozen or so Tesico systems in place of unknown architecture, and not a single hitch. That's the real truth. And we can prove it.'

'How?'

Roper seemed uncertain. 'With testimonials—from the customers.'

Wentworth's chief negotiator placed his pen on the table and sat back with a sigh. 'Unless any of those deployments featured an outgoing CBIS system, Mister Roper, then the point is irrelevant. Besides, testimonials will not provide the assurance we need. Talk is cheap.'

Ludick leaned forward, taking up the cudgels. 'A late deployment

NEGOTIATE

cannot be tolerated for Wentworth,' he said. 'The risks to our business are too great. As I have already stipulated, we want no verbal assurances. We need *something more...*'

Roper began to flounder. 'Like the proof-of-deployment you won't let us demonstrate?'

'We will not sign contract with you just so that can go ahead,' said Ludick. 'It's no basis for a real agreement.'

'Then we're just going round in circles,' said Roper.

Ludick nodded, his tone was grave. 'For once, I agree with you Mister Roper.'

Just break the loop Sue.

Ludick gathered the paperwork on his desk. The negotiation team interpreted the signal and began packing up too.

'What if there was another way?' The words were out of Sue's mouth without her realising.

Ludick stopped his paper-shuffling and looked up. 'Go on,' he urged.

'Well, if you agree to sign a contract with Tesico and Onicas, we might consider inserting a go/no-go clause...'

The room fell silent.

'How would that work, Sue?' It was Meade, his discomfort fading.

'Well, the contract lets us demonstrate deployment, but the go/no-go clause allows you to cancel if the proof-of-concept is unsuccessful.'

'A get-out clause?' asked Ludick, replacing his paperwork on the table.

'Exactly,' said Sue, 'of course, the conditions will need to be ironed out but it gives you the right to veto the contract if deployment isn't proven.'

Roper glowered at Sue. This was noticed by Meade.

'And, is this something you've agreed upon?' asked Meade. 'Something you're happy to table as a company?'

'Yes,' said Sue, staring Roper down. 'It has the approval of our Global Sales Director.'

Ludick stood and gave a short smile before leaving. 'Very well,' he said. 'We'll consider your proposal and get back to you.'

* * *

Jens, Coops and Sue were squashed together in the back of the cab; silent and apprehensive. Roper sat in the front seat, shaking his head. They were less than a minute into the journey back to the Tesico office when Roper spoke.

'Never, ever, contradict me in front of a customer,' said Roper without looking round.

'Tony, I didn't contradict you,' said Sue. 'I just put forward the offer we agreed upon.'

'You gave it all up too early. You caved.'

'They were about to walk out of the room.'

'Who gives a shit?' said Roper turning round. 'This is what happens. Negotiations are a game. You're out of your depth here. You've got to dig your heels in right from the start. It's the only thing they respect.'

'What about trust and partnership?' asked Sue. 'Shouldn't we respect that too?'

'Are you naive enough to believe that bullshit?'

'If it helps us get a signed contract, then yes,' said Sue.

'That's not how negotiations work,' exclaimed Roper. 'It's all about making big demands right from the start, then, bit-by-bit, you gouge the shit out of each other until you reach the middle ground.'

'So it's a compromise?'

'Yes, it's a compromise!'

Compromise means giving up something without getting anything in return.

'Tony, this offer won't affect us. Not really. It's low-impact. But the rewards for us are far greater.'

'You caved.'

'I gave them something we could afford to give, in return for something we really need. We both stand to get something out of that. It's win-win,' said Sue.

'There's no such thing,' scowled Roper. 'Not in my book.'

50. Bolt From the Blue

Sue watched the scenery blur through the window of her Uber as it rounded the northern end of Hyde Park. Sydney was busy starting a new day. The large department stores that bordered the park and lined Market Street were aglow with ornate window displays. A glittering avenue of allure that led straight into the heart of the city.

'So, will you be there?' asked Sue into her phone.

'No, negotiation is not my area,' came the reply from Raf. 'Besides, I don't think Peter wants me around.'

'That's a pity, I could do with a friendly face in the room,' said Sue.

'Well, you've got Robert. You can trust him to do the right thing by all of us.'

'Yes,' mused Sue. It had taken only forty-eight hours for Tesico and Onicas to be invited back to the negotiating table. She was to spend another day locked in negotiation at Wentworth Tower. 'Have you heard anything? About the negotiation?' she asked.

'I've heard Peter Ludick is moving closer to acceptance of Tesico. He's not there yet though,' said Raf.

'Do you know why?'

'Two reasons...'

'Which are?'

'First he needs guarantees.'

'Yes, we know, we're working on that...'

'No,' said Raf, 'he wants more, he wants *additional* guarantees.'

'Beyond the go/no-go clause? Beyond the proof-of-concept?'

'Yes.'

Sue felt a creeping anxiety. As good as it was to hear information like this from her friend and Accomplice, she now felt less prepared for what the day might hold.

'What kind of guarantees?'

'I have no idea.'

'You said there were two reasons Ludick hasn't accepted Tesico yet? What's the second?'

'I think you know.'

'I do?'

'Roper.'

'Oh.'

'Sue, he's bad news for Tesico, bad news for this deal. He's upset Robert and now he's pissing off Ludick. That's not a good scenario. You have to keep him out of that room.'

'Did Robert tell you this?'

'Yes.'

'Raf, it's not my call.'

'Then please get him to listen, instead of just saying *no.*'

'I'll try,' said Sue, knowing that listening was not Tony Roper's strong suit. And if he wasn't prepared to listen to Wentworth, he'd never listen to her.

* * *

'After careful consideration, Wentworth accepts your proposal,' announced the rugby-captain chief negotiator.

Sue maintained her poker face but felt like dancing on the boardroom table. Beside her, Coops let out a squeaky noise. Robert

NEGOTIATE

Meade gave Sue the smallest of nods, the trademark smile evident at the corner of his eyes.

'Please coordinate your legal teams,' continued the negotiator. 'We will begin drafting contracts for all parties so that work may begin on the proof-of-concept. The contract will include a go/no-go clause as you suggest, and...'

And? Here it comes, thought Sue.

'And we propose the inclusion of further provisions.'

Roper was immediately on the defensive. 'That's not the way it works, we've just made a concession and you're already making more demands.'

'Concessions have been made on both sides Mister Roper. These are further provisions for discussion,' the rugby-captain negotiator explained. 'In the contract we propose the inclusion of certain—penalties.'

'Penalties?' said Roper.

'Penalties for late delivery,' explained the negotiator.

'That's what the proof-of-delivery is designed to address,' continued Roper, stabbing a forefinger at the table. 'It'll prove that deployment will go smoothly, and on-time.'

'Then, if late delivery won't be an issue, you should have no objection to the inclusion of penalties?'

'In addition to the proof-of-deployment? You're asking way too much here...' went on Roper. 'If late deployment is your concern, then it's either the go/no-go clause *or* the penalties. You can't have both. It's like using two hammers to crack the same nut.'

Ludick interceded now, his condescension well-oiled. 'Mister Roper, please look at this from our perspective. We agree to the go/no-go clause because it insulates us in case deployment is problematic. It allows us to walk away from any binding agreement, and we appreciate your proposing this...' He smiled at Sue before continuing. 'But let's suppose your proof-of-deployment goes well, and we choose not to invoke the go/no-go clause. Then there is still no guarantee that you will deploy in a timely fashion. The penalties we propose are merely an incentive for Tesico and Onicas to meet the contracted deadline and to share the financial burden if the deadline is missed. Nothing more.'

'We *will* meet deadline,' assured Roper.

'We have no proof of that,' said Ludick. 'The only working example you have shared with us is at China Prestige. And they *missed* deadline.'

'Then we'll show you other examples,' offered Roper.

'They will not provide the assurance we need.'

Sue sensed the negotiation had stalled. 'What kind of penalties?' she asked.

The answer came from the rugby-captain negotiator: 'If you miss the appointed deadline for deployment, then Tesico will provide all Application Programming Interfaces at your own cost.'

Roper directed a huff at the ceiling. Raf had told Sue to expect guarantees, but she wasn't prepared for penalties; not penalties as onerous and punishing as these.

'Build the APIs at our own cost?' said Roper. 'That'll wipe out our entire profit for the first year. You want us to work for free?'

'The penalty only comes into effect if you miss deadline, otherwise, you've nothing to worry about,' added the rugby-captain negotiator. 'And, in any case, you'll still make a fair profit on licensing for the term of the contract.'

'Okay,' said Roper, straightening in his chair. 'Then here's what I propose: that we extend the deployment deadline and increase our costs to cover our bills for the first year. How about that?'

'Unacceptable,' said Ludick. 'The costs and timings in your original proposal still stand. These penalties are *additional*. Besides, we will not wear inflated costs or timings to cover your inability to deploy as proposed.'

'But we're negotiating here, aren't we?' said Roper. 'We're still making proposals, aren't we? Then that's what I propose.' He nodded in a gesture of finality.

'We don't accept,' said Ludick, his frustration clear.

'And we don't accept both a proof-of-concept *and* further penalties. It's one or the other.'

Ludick collected his notepad and stood. Then he walked from the room without a single word. The rugby-captain negotiator let out a lengthy sigh and began packing up. His team did the same.

'What the hell was that?' asked Roper, gesturing to Ludick's empty chair.

'That, Mister Roper,' began Robert Meade, 'is what you call a breakdown in negotiations.'

Sue stared at Roper in alarm. Doug's words rang in her head.

A deal can fall through so easily at this stage. I've seen it happen many times.

Sue ran from the conference room, catching up with Robert Meade in the corridor outside. 'Robert, please...' she begged.

Meade turned to her. 'Sue, this is a deal-breaker for us, and I'm trusting you to understand.' Sue could now see the weariness and disappointment written across his face. 'And your National Sales Manager isn't helping. He's destroying all your hard work, all the consensus you've driven, all the trust you've built. While he's in the room I very much doubt we'll reach any kind of agreement with Tesico.'

Sue could feel his disillusionment. Would he give up the fight for her? Was her Champion in danger of marching away? 'Robert, I'm so sorry...'

'So am I Sue. So am I.'

NEGOTIATE

51. The Back Foot

'Well, Tony's right, building APIs would destroy our margin for the first year, but I wish he hadn't admitted that to Wentworth.' Michelle's frown was evident on Sue's laptop screen. Coops took notes nearby while Jens fidgeted nervously with the stationery on Sue's desk.

'I've gone through the figures in more detail,' said Sue. 'If we miss deadline, it could take years to recoup the loss.'

'In that case we don't miss deadline,' said Michelle.

'But can we take that risk?'

'I don't know,' said Michelle. 'Jens?'

'Maybe, maybe not,' offered Jens.

Michelle looked away from her camera for a moment, gathering her thoughts. 'If there's even the slightest chance we miss deadline, this deal may not be worth pursuing.'

'It *won't* be worth pursuing.' Sue revealed the hard facts. 'We've reached our negotiation ceiling. This is our walk-away point.' She let the thought sink in. 'But, I've made some calculations.'

'And?' Michelle was intrigued.

'As I see it, there are two counter-offers we could table. The first is to reduce the deadline penalty. Instead of Tesico footing the total bill for the API development, we split it fifty-fifty with Wentworth.'

'We go Dutch?' queried Coops.

Jens's eyebrows levitated.

'Would that be enough?' asked Michelle.

'There'd be enough profit to make the first year acceptable,' said Sue. 'And we wouldn't need to chase lost revenue in the subsequent years.'

'That's a plus,' said Michelle. 'Will Wentworth go for it?'

'I think they could be persuaded. I think they'd sympathise with our position that we can't go without profit for twelve months. Sharing the API build is fair also, especially as we could argue that any missed deadline could also be down to *their* involvement. So it's a way for us to keep them honest too, a way we can both share the responsibility.'

'I like it,' said Michelle. 'It demonstrates partnership.'

'It's close to the high point of our negotiation ceiling and low for them, but still within acceptable negotiation range for both parties, so we could agree,' said Sue. 'And it's still a significant penalty, one they'd see as enough of an incentive for us to hit deadline.'

'And what about your second idea?'

'It's not optimal but it could work. We agree to pay for the full API build as a penalty but only under specific circumstances detailed in the contract. They'd have to *prove* that missing the deadline was our fault entirely and not because of their involvement, or any third party, or other external influence.'

'And who would decide this? Not Wentworth?'

'We'd probably need to involve an impartial consulting firm to act as referee,' said Sue. 'And we should push Wentworth to cover this cost on account of the penalty being their initiative.'

'It's less elegant,' said Michelle, 'there would be a lot of negotiation over the conditions.'

'And it doesn't limit our exposure,' said Sue. 'We could still end up footing the entire bill for the API build.'

'Okay, then let's table the first proposal. Your second option will be our final fallback. Let's hope they haven't dug their heels in already.'

'And if they have?' asked Sue.

'Then we walk away,' said Michelle.

Coops wrote on her notepad for Sue to see: *And we walk away from our jobs.* Sue nodded gravely.

'And you'll update Tony?' asked Michelle. 'Where is he by the way?'

'About that...' began Sue. She signalled Coops and Jens to give her some privacy. Sue waited for them to leave before continuing. 'He's flown back down to Melbourne Michelle, but there's a problem.'

'Oh?'

'He's not giving any ground in the negotiations with Wentworth.'

'Well, that sounds like Tony...'

'He's just saying *no* all the time.'

Michelle appeared to toss the thought around in her mind.

'Michelle, he's killing the deal.'

Michelle's eyes bored into Sue, long-distance. 'And how do you know?'

'Just yesterday, Wentworth walked away from the negotiating table. And both Raf and Robert Meade have warned me to keep him away or risk losing the contract.'

'It's gotten that serious?'

'Michelle,' Sue began, 'he doesn't listen. Their concerns are genuine but he won't take them on-board. He just refuses, and frankly, it'll cost us this business. Call Robert yourself if you like. I'm sure he won't mind.'

Michelle's lips pursed. 'Perhaps that's what I should do,' she said. 'Better still, I might fly down to Sydney and talk to him in person. And Sue...'

'Yes?'

'I apologise. I didn't mean to place you in another difficult position.'

'It's alright.'

'No it's not. I'll speak with Robert, and I'll call Tony. And in the meantime...'

'Yes?'

'You make the proposal to Wentworth as outlined.'

'Very well.'

'And Sue...'

'Yes?'

'Save this deal.'

NEGOTIATE

This book comes with free access to an online reference companion.

By scanning the QR code or by navigating to <u>edvance.sale/recap/negotiate</u> now, you will gain a deeper understanding of the EDVANCE process and the methodology applied by the characters in the preceding seven chapters, including:

- Win-Win Negotiating
- The Negotiation Ceiling or BATNA
- Techniques for Negotiating Success
- Applying these methods in your own business

333

COMMIT AND ENACT

COMMIT AND ENACT

52. Grab the Sauce

'It's a bloody institution, that's what it is,' said Coops with her mouth full.

'But it's just a pie,' said Jens.

'It's a handmade Aussie pie, made with Angus beef. The best bloody beef in the world,' said Coops.

'You don't seem that impressed,' said Sue over the crust of her own pie.

Jens gave a non-committal smile across the table.

The three of them were in Tesico's breakout room—it was a working lunch. Dining *al desko* as Coops called it. They'd closed the door to prevent the Roper-clones from eavesdropping. The original Roper was absent today; his jacket hung over the back of his chair but there was no sign of the rest of him.

'You think he's in Melbourne?' asked Coops.

Sue shrugged. 'No idea.'

'As long as he's not *here*, right?' offered Jens.

Coops peeled open a sachet of tomato sauce and squeezed some onto her pie. 'So have we heard anything?'

'About what?' returned Sue.

'You know,' said Coops, 'about Michelle's meeting with Robert Meade.'

'No.' Sue eyed her phone with concern. 'Although we should have by now. She's been here since Monday.'

'What do you reckon's going on?' asked Coops.

'She's trying to get them to accept our counter-offer.'

'The one you made?'

'Yeah.'

'Maybe it's not going so well?' added Jens.

'Oh, she has other business there too. Meade wants to discuss Tesico's commitment to the Wentworth business at a regional level.'

'Meaning?' queried Coops.

'Meaning Robert wants to have a direct line to Michelle in Singapore when the need arises,' said Sue.

'Which is another way of saying he doesn't want to play with Roper,' Coops smiled, 'or us.'

'What's wrong with *us*?' asked Jens.

'Think about it darl,' said Coops. 'If he's dealing with anyone in Sydney, then he's still dealing with Roper. Roper runs the joint, remember?'

Jens chewed, thoughtful. 'Just as well I'm flying out next week,' he admitted.

'You are?' Sue was surprised.

'Michelle wants me to help out with the Dubai deal.'

'Will you be back?' asked Coops.

'If Wentworth signs a contract, then yes, I'll be back to run the proof-of-concept and the final deployment.'

'Well, we'll keep our fingers and toes crossed,' said Coops. 'We'll miss you, you lanky, chisel-arsed clog-maker.'

Jens looked up with a smile. 'I'll miss you guys too,' he said.

'Aw,' said Coops. She gave him a punch in the top of his arm that nearly sent the pie spinning from his hands. Jens tried to grin, despite the pain.

Sue's phone rang. She wasted no time in answering. 'Michelle?'

Jens and Coops were both attentive.

'I'm at the Esperance Hotel,' said Michelle. 'Do you know it?'
'In Circular Quay?'
'Yes, get over here soon as you can.'
'Uh, sure,' said Sue, brushing flakes of pastry from her skirt.
'I'll leave a note at reception. Is there anyone else in the office?'
'Jens and Coops are with me,' muttered Sue.
'Good, bring them along. And be quick.'

* * *

The Esperance Hotel was situated some way back from the buildings that crowded the harbourfront of Circular Quay. What it may have lacked in position, however, it made up for in stature and luxury. It was a work of architectural one-upmanship.

The door to their cab was opened by a sharp-suited concierge and Sue and her team bundled out, making their way in brisk but undignified fashion into the chrome and glass of the lobby. The receptionists were efficient—*yes, a message had been left—yes, they were expected.* A bell-hop whisked them into a lift and pressed the button for the twenty-eighth floor. They emerged into a corridor of function rooms. Straight away, the bell-hop was on the move. He stopped outside a set of tall, panelled doors and with ceremony, opened them.

Stepping inside, Sue's first thought was that there was a mistake; they were in the wrong place. A waitress offered her a glass of sparkling water from a tray. A waiter thrust a platter of canapes at her. Sue waved it away, the pie still sitting heavily in her stomach.

Then, in the centre of the room Sue saw Robert Meade and Maria Kutcik, chatting. Maria turned to Sue, beckoning her over. Now she recognised others too: Jenny Liu, Sally McCrae, and Raf.

'So glad you and your team could make it Sue,' said Robert Meade, greeting her.

'Exactly—what is *this*?' Sue was lost.

Maria Kutcik cocked an eyebrow. 'Can't you guess?'

Robert Meade smiled. 'Your counter-proposal was accepted. We're in agreement.'

Sue was edging her way to understanding. 'You agree to splitting the cost of the APIs as penalty?'

'Yes,' said Meade.

'And there are no other issues in the way?' Sue glanced around the room, still trying to understand.

'None, barring the proof-of-concept, but I'm sure that'll go without a hitch,' he raised his head at Jens, 'right Jens?'

'Right!'

'So negotiations are concluded?' asked Sue.

'Yes.'

'And Wentworth is ready to proceed with our proposal?'

'Yes, we're ready.' He held out a hand. Sue and he shook. 'Take a look,' said Meade, nodding at a point in the room over Sue's shoulder.

Sue turned to see the long table lit with green-glass banker's lamps. She saw the writing-pads and the ink-blotters. Behind the table, leafing through reams of paper, with fountain-pens in hand, sat Michelle Yim and Craig Martin, the Sage and CEO of Wentworth.

Michelle and Craig Martin both put down their pens and turned to each other. As they smiled, a photographer's flash-gun fired.

The room broke into applause and the waiters made a reappearance with their silver trays laden with glasses. This time the glasses were filled with Champagne. Jens reached for one, as did Coops.

'Congratulations,' said a voice at Sue's side. She turned, surprised to find Craig Martin. As they shook hands, Martin leaned close to Sue's ear. 'I don't know how you got everyone on the same page but well done. I hear Hong Kong was a bit of an eye-opener. For some especially...' Then he winked. 'I also hear the technology is inspiring, can't wait, can't wait...' Buttoning his jacket, Martin turned to Robert Meade. 'Sorry Robert but I have to head back to the office.'

COMMIT AND ENACT

'Of course,' said Meade.

Martin turned back to Sue. 'Welcome to the roster of Wentworth's preferred suppliers,' he said. Then he was gone.

'Robert told me the good news this morning,' said Michelle, now joining the group. 'Sorry for the surprise. We wanted to congratulate the team in person.' She handed Sue a glass of Champagne. 'Well done Sue, well done all of you.'

All tilted their glasses in Sue's direction.

Sue had no idea how much stress she'd been carrying around, until now. It had been like a bag of cement on her shoulder: her fears for her career, the Sydney office and the people she cared for. Now the burden of it dropped away and she felt like crying.

Beside her, Coops squealed.

'Excellent, I get to eat meat pies for a while longer,' said Jens with a grin.

Michelle took Sue by the elbow, excusing them both from the group. She guided Sue towards a quiet corner of the room.

'Do I keep my job then?' asked Sue.

'No,' said Michelle, 'you don't.' Sue saw the smile form on Michelle's face. 'Because I'm offering you a new one.'

'A new one?'

'A better one. Something more suited to your talents,' said Michelle. 'Tesico is growing, thanks to you, and I've come to realise our business is spread across three main sectors: corporate, media and finance. I'd like you to run the finance sector.'

Sue's mind was still in pieces. 'So, wait, you want me to go after more financial business, here, in Australia?'

'No,' said Michelle. 'I mean *globally*. Your new title will be Global Sales Manager, Finance Sector.'

Sue was giddy. 'That's huge,' was all she could manage.

Michelle gave a small laugh. 'You'll be travelling a lot. In time you'll train your own team. It'll be hard work, but it'll be rewarding. It'll be *fun*.'

'So, I'll be based in Singapore?'

'Only if you want to,' said Michelle. 'You can be based anywhere you want. Your scope will be global.'

'Can I work from Sydney?'

'Of course,' said Michelle. 'I need you here for the next six months anyway. There's still a lot to be done with Wentworth and they'll need your help—*I'll* need your help.'

Sue looked over at Coops talking with Robert Meade. 'And what about Coops? Will she keep her job?'

'No, I'm offering her a new role too—in sales. Wentworth love her,' said Michelle. 'I think she should take point as sales consultant for their business, don't you? You'll be around long enough to ease her into your shoes.'

'She'll be over the moon,' said Sue. 'But can you keep Roper off her back?'

'You needn't worry about Tony anymore. I've let him go.'

Sue was stunned. 'Let him go?'

'He lost the Melbourne prospect a few days ago, for the same reasons he lost WestInvest and nearly lost Wentworth. I blame myself, I thought he'd begun to move on. But he's so resistant to change, to partnering with other companies who can help us. I couldn't let him jeopardise this deal. Robert told me quite bluntly he didn't want Tony anywhere near his business. And I couldn't let Tony drive away my best salespeople. So yes, I let him go. I suggested that, if he wanted to retire with his pension and a fat bonus, then he should see it as an opportunity.' Michelle's eyes rested on Sue for a moment. 'You know, I miss Doug so much...' she said.

Sue felt the sudden pain of remembering and looked down to the Champagne glass in her hand.

'I miss his counsel,' continued Michelle, 'his professionalism, and his friendship. And I know you do too Sue. But...'

Sue looked up. 'Yes?'

'I see so much of him in you.'

'He taught me a lot,' confessed Sue. She felt the saline sting at the edges of her eyes.

'Well, I'm very grateful to him for all that...'

'Me too.'

They were interrupted by Coops, who was dragging Robert Meade in tow. 'Hey, get this,' she said. 'Robert here is a dead-set jackeroo!'

'Well, not really,' confessed Meade with good humour. 'My family owned a stud in Scone, horse-breeders, so I grew up around the animals.'

Sue was happy to see the two of them forming a relationship. Coops would need that—she'd need a Champion too. For the long haul.

'Well, Robert, you should know that Coops is something of a horsewoman herself.'

'S'right,' said Coops, thumbing her imaginary hat.

'A Cootamundra Rodeo champion, if I'm right?' added Sue.

'S'right,' said Coops. 'First place racing the barrels. Three years in a row!'

Meade smiled. 'I don't doubt it.'

Sue caught sight of Raf stepping onto the balcony alone. Making her apologies, she slipped from the group and followed him. It was a hot, bright day and the heart of the harbour city was spread below them. Raf was leaning against the waist-high safety-railing, glass in hand, gazing at the view. He'd taken off his jacket and looked as cool and collected as ever in a fresh, white shirt. He turned, taking in the whole of her as she approached. Sue hoped her limp wasn't too obvious.

'Hi,' said Raf with a gentle smile, his voice chiming.

'Hi.'

'I only just noticed,' he said. 'You're no longer using a walking-stick.'

'No,' said Sue. 'I'm standing all on my own now.'

Raf smirked. 'You certainly are.' He raised his glass. 'Well done Sue, you nailed it.'

'Not without your help Raf.' She raised her glass in return and propped herself against the balcony rail beside him.

'Oh, I'm only a small cog in a very big machine,' he said.

'But you helped me get to everyone that mattered, you guided me along the way,' said Sue.

Raf shook his head. 'No, you guided us—towards what we needed, not what we thought we wanted.'

'And what about you Raf, did you get what you needed?' In her mind Sue was looking at the blank space next to his name on the stakeholder map: his agenda; his informal criteria. It was still a mystery to her.

'Absolutely,' said Raf.

'And what exactly is that?' asked Sue.

'You.'

'Me?' Sue was shocked.

'Yes,' said Raf. 'I got you.'

Sue fixed him with a puzzled stare.

'Sue, I'm a humble IT security manager. I don't get to make the call on who supplies our security solution. It's my job to work with whatever company the C-Suite decides to appoint. And, very often, that decision isn't the one I would have made. It's tough, but that's my job. So, usually, I end up working with people I'd prefer not to work with. All I've wanted throughout this entire process, all I've hoped and wished for, is finally to work with someone I can talk to; someone who *gets it*; someone I respect...'

Sue felt emotion fizz inside her like the Champagne in her glass. 'A partner?' she asked.

Raf smiled at her. 'Yeah, a partner.'

Sue grinned, offering her hand. 'Then put it there partner...'

They shook.

COMMIT AND ENACT

And there it was.

Sue hadn't felt it when she shook hands with Craig Martin or Robert Meade only minutes before. But she felt it now. She felt it as obviously as she felt the harbour breeze or the warm sunshine on her face. It was the handshake she'd witnessed long ago in a Perth hotel: Doug and the WestInvest client. Only now she understood the handshake for what it truly was. It wasn't the handshake worth millions. It wasn't about the money. It was about something far more valuable; something far more *human*. It was more than just a locking of hands, of eyes. It was a locking of *respect*, of *purpose*, of *understanding*.

It was the handshake of partnership.

* * *

Coops had the window down on her side of the taxi and was shouting at the pedestrians on York Street. 'I'm a sales consultant!'

Sue laughed. Jens sat in the front seat, keen to disassociate himself.

'Hey Sue,' Coops swung round to face her friend.

'Yes?'

'Seeing as I'm now a sales consultant and all, do you think I could get a lend of Doug's journal?'

'I think he'd want you to have your own copy, don't you?'

The splash of freckles creased as Coops smiled. She turned back to the open window and picked on a kerbside businessman. 'Hey you! Guess who's a sales consultant? Yeah *me!*'

Sue laughed again. Her phone rang. Sue didn't recognise the number.

'Hello?'

'Sue Novak?'

'Yes?' said Sue. Coops closed the window so Sue could hear. 'Who is this?'

'Brenda.'

'Brenda Huffington?'

Coops's eyes and mouth formed their characteristic Venn diagram.

'We just heard the news Sue,' said Brenda.

'Oh?'

'I wanted to be the first to congratulate you.'

'Thanks Brenda.'

'You know, not many people go up against CBIS and win—I just wanted you to know, if you ever felt like jumping ship, that there's an office waiting for you here at CBIS.'

'Well,' said Sue, 'that's a very kind offer Brenda, but I won't be leaving Tesico in a hurry.'

'Never say never.'

'I won't.'

'See you around Sue Novak.'

'See you too Brenda. I'll be the one in the opposite corner.'

Sue heard Brenda's laugh in her earpiece.

'I'm counting on it,' said Brenda, 'and I'm looking forward to the competition.'

'Bye.'

'Bye.'

Sue hung up.

'Stone the bloody crows,' said Coops. 'This day just keeps getting better and better!'

* * *

'Aw, crap!' said Coops surveying the mess of half-eaten pies, paper-bags and pastry-crumbs strewn across the breakout room table.

'Well,' said Sue, 'you might be a sales consultant now but you're not above a bit of cleaning. Here, I'll hold the bin...'

Sue held the waste-bin under one edge of the table while Coops attempted to sweep everything into it. Much of the debris missed the bin and made a bigger mess. The two women laughed.

COMMIT AND ENACT

'Happy now are we?' came a voice from nearby.

Sue and Coops looked up to see Tony Roper standing in the doorway. In his arms was a cardboard box filled with the personal effects from his office.

'Without a doubt,' began Roper with quiet vehemence, 'you two are the most shit salespeople I have ever known.'

Sue stood upright. She didn't reply. She knew speaking would only inflame the situation.

'Political, backstabbing bitches…' continued Roper. 'I could've helped you, if you'd let me. I could've trained you properly. I could've turned you into *real* salespeople.'

Sue looked down, shaking her head.

'I gave you my experience, I gave you the leads, I even gave you the freedom to go after Wentworth,' said Roper. 'What the hell did you give me?'

Hearing enough, Sue made to leave. Roper didn't move from the doorway. Sue pushed her way past, then signalled Coops to follow.

'I'll give you something, Tony…' said Coops, approaching Roper. She dropped a leftover sachet of tomato sauce into Roper's cardboard box and slipped past him.

'What the hell is that?' exclaimed Roper, glancing into his cardboard box.

Coops turned and thrust her face into his. All her anger and hurt was out in the open now. 'Just a little something I learned from you…' she said. 'When life hands you a shit sandwich, grab the sauce!'

Then Coops turned her back on him for the last time.

This book comes with free access to an
online reference companion.

By scanning the QR Code or by navigating to
edvance.sale/recap/commit/ now, you will gain a deeper
understanding of the EDVANCE process and the methodology
applied by the characters in the preceding chapter, including:

- Knowing when to Commit
- Asking the Prospect to Commit
- Applying these methods in your own business

53. New Horizons

As the waiter swept their tablecloth clean, Sue allowed Ellen Chadwick to read the contents of the thick, ring-binder file in silence. Sue had chosen Longshore restaurant for a reason. Not just for its airy, open ambience, the wonderfully-prepared seafood or the panoramic views over Darling Harbour towards Cockatoo Island. She had chosen Longshore for this lunch meeting because of the memories it held. It had been their special place—hers and Doug's.

Ellen Chadwick was the publisher behind *Corporation Magazine*. She'd launched many trade magazines and books over the length of her career and had a special interest in the area of business-to-business sales. She looked up from the pages and slid the reading-glasses from her face.

'Well, I see you've taken on most of our editor's suggestions,' said Ellen.

'What do you think?' asked Sue.

'I think there's a market for something like this.'

Sue rotated her glass of Prosecco by the stem.

'If you forgive the pun,' continued Ellen, 'it's quite novel. The idea of bringing a sales manual to life with a fictional case study is a neat idea.'

'It's not entirely fictional though.'

'Oh, I realise that,' said Ellen. '*You* know this is the story behind the Wentworth deal, *I* know it too. But to our readers, it'll be presented as fiction.'

Ellen was correct. Wentworth had stipulated that all names be changed and some of the more sensitive aspects of the deal be omitted.

'And does the story end here?' Ellen tapped the still-open ringbinder file on the table. 'What happened to your IT security contact at Wentworth?'

Sue pictured Raf Singh in his crisp white shirt. She heard the genteel chime of his Oxbridge accent. 'Oh, I still see him from time-to-time. He's a good friend and something of a rising star at Wentworth. He'll make CISO one day, I'm certain.'

'And your other friend, the country girl who made it into sales?'

Sue gave a small laugh. 'She did good. In fact, people can't get enough of her.' As part of her engagement strategy, Coops had indeed set up a YouTube channel called Cybersecurity Round-Up. She wore a white Akubra hat, slim-fitting cowgirl jeans and made a point of conducting her interviews against a rural backdrop. Her good looks, in-depth knowledge, and plucky manner opened the door to captains-of-industry and experts alike. People clamoured to be on her show. She'd become a sought-after commentator in the wider media and there was even talk of a regular slot in a TV business show. Jens was always delighted to appear on her shows, often in person. And when he did, Coops still punched him in the arm.

'And what about the lead character, the heroine?' asked Ellen Chadwick. 'What happened to her?'

'Well,' said Sue, 'she got the keys to the kingdom.'

This much was true. Next week Sue was due to give a keynote address at a cybersecurity conference in Silicon Valley. Then she would board a flight to Santiago to begin a *Journey of Discovery* with a leading Chilean investment bank. She swept her gaze over the lunchtime scene in Longshore. It was where Doug and she had celebrated their successes. It was their special treat: a place of victory, of conclusions.

'And who's Doug?' asked Ellen, as if reading Sue's mind.

Sue was surprised. 'Doug?'

Ellen Chadwick was resting a finger on a page near the beginning of the file. 'Your dedication,' she said. 'It reads: *For Doug.*'

Sue's smile was sad. 'He was my mentor, and...' she began.

Ellen's eyes questioned her over the rim of the reading glasses.

'My friend,' finished Sue. 'In many ways, he wrote much of this book.'

'Of course, Doug Churchill,' said Ellen. 'Such a great loss.'

Sue nodded. 'This book is his legacy. It's what he would have wanted.'

Ellen Chadwick closed the manuscript in the ring-binder file and picked up the receipt for their meal. She stood. 'I'll be in touch Sue,' she said with a final smile. Then she turned and left.

Sue wanted to stay awhile, to be alone with her thoughts. She had no idea when she'd see this place again. Or if she ever would. It was part of a previous life; a memory shared with a friend now gone. And it didn't seem right to hang onto it.

She raised the remains of her glass skyward and watched the sunlight from the tall windows sparkle in the bubbles.

'So long Doug,' she whispered. 'And thanks—for everything.' She drained the glass and set it down.

Through Longshore's windows Sue watched tourists boarding a harbour cruise at Cockle Bay. A green and gold ferry was heading from the Balmain peninsula on its way to Circular Quay, soon it would round Miller's Point, disappearing from sight under the Harbour Bridge. A fishing boat, fresh from deep ocean, laden with catch and harried by gulls, was plying its course toward the Anzac Bridge and the fish markets beyond. Sue saw the sunlight catch the tips of the waves and gleam back at her from apartment windows in Pyrmont. Above, a red-tailed airliner scored a chalk-line across the cloudless cobalt of the sky. It was a skyline she knew and loved. The same skyline she'd marvelled at every day since she'd first started work in this shining city.

Only now, for the first time in a very long while, it looked like a brand-new horizon.

Review

If you have enjoyed *The Wentworth Prospect*, please consider leaving a review where you purchased the book online, or on your favourite online review site such as www.goodreads.com

You'll be helping other readers find our book and learn if it's right for them.

Free Tools

As a reader you can access your free tools at www.edvance.sale/tools

If you are an educator, manager, or in any way responsible for the training of sales staff, you can also find assessment tools to monitor your team's development at: www.edvance.sale/tools

Feel free to contact the authors via LinkedIn if you need more.

About the Authors

John Smibert

John is an Australian who has invested 38 years as a highly successful sales leader in four USA and Japanese multinational IT corporations. For the last 16 years he has assisted B2B selling organisations to transform the way they sell. John is passionate about enhancing the professionalism of salespeople and sales teams. To that end he has founded Sales Leader Forums and Sales Masterminds APAC. John is the creator of the Authentic Selling program and the EDVANCE sales model that underpins The Wentworth Prospect.

Wayne Moloney

Wayne is an Australian business strategist with a passion for sales, marketing and business development. He has spent four decades working in Australia, Asia and Europe, starting out as a door-knocking engineering sales rep and ending up in roles such as Sales and Managing Director. Since leaving his corporate career, Wayne has spent over 15 years helping B2B businesses tackle their business growth challenges by applying LEAN principles for sustainable sales success. Wayne was a co-founder of Sales Leader Forums and a foundation member of Sales Masterminds APAC.

Jeff Clulow

Jeff is a British-Australian writer with over 30 years' experience in the advertising and communications industry. He has worked as both writer, executive creative director and regional creative director with some of the world's largest ad agencies in London, Hong Kong and Sydney. Jeff is also a writer of dark fiction. His stories have been published by Shooting Star Press in Australia and in several anthologies by UK publisher Raven & Drake. He is shortly to be published by Black Ink Fiction in the USA. Today he lives and works as an author and communications specialist in Sydney, Australia. Details of Jeff's fiction can be found at jeffclulow.com

Other Publications

Other books by Wayne Moloney:

Your Roadmap to Sales Management Success

Your Roadmap to Achieving Sales Success

Available from your favourite online retailer or from the author at www.waynemoloney.com

Lightning Source UK Ltd.
Milton Keynes UK
UKHW020748250821
389444UK00014B/820